MICRONATIONS AND THE SEARCH FOR SOVEREIGNTY

Political disagreement is a fact of life. It can prompt people to stand for public office and agitate for political change. Others take a different route; they start their own nation. *Micronations and the Search for Sovereignty* is the first comprehensive examination of the phenomenon of people purporting to secede and create their own country. It analyses why micronations are not states for the purposes of international law, considers the factors that motivate individuals to separate and found their own nation, examines the legal justifications that they offer and explores the responses of recognised sovereign states. In doing so, this book develops a rich body of material through which to reflect on conventional understandings of statehood, sovereignty and legitimate authority. Authored in a lively and accessible style, *Micronations and the Search for Sovereignty* will be valuable reading for scholars and general audiences.

HARRY HOBBS is a Senior Lecturer in the Faculty of Law at the University of Technology Sydney. Dr Hobbs' recent scholarship has explored ideas of sovereignty through the lens of Indigenous peoples' rights, and he is co-Chair of the American Society of International Law Rights of Indigenous Peoples Interest Group.

GEORGE WILLIAMS AO is a Deputy Vice-Chancellor, the Anthony Mason Professor and a Scientia Professor at UNSW Sydney. He has served as Dean of UNSW Law and held an Australian Research Council Laureate Fellowship. He has written widely on constitutional law and has appeared as a barrister in the High Court of Australia on freedom of speech, freedom from racial discrimination and the rule of law.

CAMBRIDGE STUDIES IN CONSTITUTIONAL LAW

The aim of this series is to produce leading monographs in constitutional law. All areas of constitutional law and public law fall within the ambit of the series, including human rights and civil liberties law, administrative law, as well as constitutional theory and the history of constitutional law. A wide variety of scholarly approaches is encouraged, with the governing criterion being simply that the work is of interest to an international audience. Thus, works concerned with only one jurisdiction will be included in the series as appropriate, while, at the same time, the series will include works which are explicitly comparative or theoretical – or both. The series editors likewise welcome proposals that work at the intersection of constitutional and international law, or that seek to bridge the gaps between civil law systems, the US, and the common law jurisdictions of the Commonwealth.

Books in the Series

Fundamental Rights and the Legal Obligations of Business David Bilchitz

Courting Constitutionalism: The Politics of Public Law and Judicial Review in Pakistan Moeen Cheema

Ruling by Cheating: Governance in Illiberal Democracy András Sajó

Local Meanings of Proportionality Afroditi Marketou

Property Rights and Social Justice: Progressive Property in Action Rachael Walsh

Carl Schmitt's Early Legal-Theoretical Writings: Statute and Judgment and the Value of the State and the Significance of the Individual Lars Vinx and Samuel Garrett Zeitlin

Remedies for Human Rights Violations: A Two-Track Approach to Supranational and National Law Kent Roach

Europe's Second Constitution: Crisis, Courts and Community Markus W. Gehring

A.V. Dicey and the Common Law Constitutional Tradition: A Legal Turn of Mind Mark D. Walters

Administrative Competence: Reimagining Administrative Law Elizabeth Fisher and Sidney A. Shapiro

Legal Sabotage: Ernst Fraenkel in Hitler's Germany Douglas Morris

Proportionality in Action: Comparative and Empirical Perspectives on the Judicial Practice Edited by Mordechai Kremnitzer, Tayla Steiner and Andrej Lang

Constitutional Dialogue: Democracy, Rights, Institutions Edited by Geoffrey Sigalet, Grégoire Webber and Rosalind Dixon

The Veiled Sceptre: Reserve Powers of Heads of State in Westminster Systems Anne Twomey

Vigilance and Restraint in the Common Law of Judicial Review Dean Knight

The Alchemists: Questioning Our Faith in Courts as Democracy-Builders Tom Gerald Daly

Australia's Constitution after Whitlam Brendan Lim

Building the Constitution: The Practice of Constitutional Interpretation in Post-Apartheid South Africa James Fowkes

Dimensions of Dignity: The Theory and Practice of Modern Constitutional Law Jacob Weinrib

Reason of State: Law, Prerogative, Empire Thomas Poole

Bills of Rights in the Common Law Robert Leckey

The Guardian of the Constitution: Hans Kelsen and Carl Schmitt on the Limits of Constitutional Law Translated by Lars Vinx, with an introduction and notes by Lars Vinx

Parliamentary Bills of Rights: The Experiences of New Zealand and the United Kingdom Janet L. Hiebert and James B. Kelly

Lawyering for the Rule of Law: Government Lawyers and the Rise of Judicial Power in Israel Yoav Dotan

Balancing Constitutional Rights: The Origins and Meanings of Postwar Legal Discourse Jacco Bomhoff

Judges on Trial: The Independence and Accountability of the English Judiciary Shimon Shetreet and Sophie Turenne

Proportionality and Constitutional Culture Moshe Cohen-Eliya and Iddo Porat

The Politics of Principle: The First South African Constitutional Court, 1995–2005 Theunis Roux

The New Commonwealth Model of Constitutionalism: Theory and Practice Stephen Gardbaum

Searching for the State in British Legal Thought: Competing Conceptions of the Public Sphere Janet McLean

Judging Social Rights Jeff King

Proportionality: Constitutional Rights and Their Limitations Aharon Barak

Parliamentary Sovereignty: Contemporary Debates Jeffrey Goldsworthy

MICRONATIONS AND THE SEARCH FOR SOVEREIGNTY

HARRY HOBBS
University of Technology Sydney
GEORGE WILLIAMS
University of New South Wales

CAMBRIDGE
UNIVERSITY PRESS

CAMBRIDGE
UNIVERSITY PRESS

University Printing House, Cambridge CB2 8BS, United Kingdom

One Liberty Plaza, 20th Floor, New York, NY 10006, USA

477 Williamstown Road, Port Melbourne, VIC 3207, Australia

314–321, 3rd Floor, Plot 3, Splendor Forum, Jasola District Centre, New Delhi – 110025, India

103 Penang Road, #05–06/07, Visioncrest Commercial, Singapore 238467

Cambridge University Press is part of the University of Cambridge.

It furthers the University's mission by disseminating knowledge in the pursuit of education, learning, and research at the highest international levels of excellence.

www.cambridge.org
Information on this title: www.cambridge.org/9781009150125
DOI: 10.1017/9781009150132

First published 2022

A catalogue record for this publication is available from the British Library.

ISBN 978-1-009-15012-5 Hardback

CONTENTS

PREFACE

People across the world have sought to secede and establish their own independent micronation. Their motivations for doing so can reflect their personal commitments and eccentricities and are as diverse as the nations they seek to create. Secession might be seen as the only possible course of action to resolve a long-running dispute with the local council or as a final act of defiance after decades of frustration with regulation and government bureaucracy. Establishing a new country might also be designed to promote tourism to a region, to create an art project, to parody the workings of the state or even to defraud unsuspecting people.

Micronations have been founded around the globe for these and other reasons. Once established, they seek to assert their claims to sovereignty in a myriad of ways. They issue coins, print stamps, compose national anthems, invest themselves with royal titles and sometimes even declare war on recognised states. Roy Bates – or to use his full title, Prince Roy of Sealand – who graces our cover from his Principality in the North Sea, is just one of the many micronationalists who has taken such steps.

Micronations are a subject of fascination for many people, and regularly attract worldwide attention. There is something inherently interesting about the idea that any one of us could break away to form our own nation, complete with royal titles and the trappings of a real state. Despite this, the phenomenon has been almost completely ignored by legal scholars and political scientists. This reflects a view that micronations are more suited to humour than serious study. After all, the prospect that an individual or small band of people could separate from a recognised state and establish their own legally recognised nation is fanciful.

We have written this book because there is more to this story. By dressing in the language of sovereignty, micronations challenge understandings of and approaches to international legal personality. They also catalyse larger questions about the nature of statehood, sovereignty and legitimate authority. The creativity and persistent attempts of micronations to find cracks in the law to justify their existence also raise important legal and political questions. Can the proponents of sea steading create a viable state by constructing floating structures on the high seas outside of national jurisdiction? How do states respond to these potential challengers? Does state acquiescence to the continued existence of a micronation have any legal effect? Could a micronation ever become a state? If not, what value do micronationalists see in statehood? These are some of the questions that micronations pose. They are the sorts of issue that motivated us to write this book to provide the first comprehensive treatment of micronations from a legal and political vantage point.

Many people have helped to shape this book. We thank colleagues at the Faculty of Law at the University of Technology Sydney and the Faculty of Law and Justice at the University of New South Wales, who offered helpful comments on draft papers. In particular, we thank Katherine Biber, Sara Dehm, Rosalind Dixon, Kun Fan, Fleur Johns, Zsofia Korosy, David Leary, Lucas Lixinski, Jane McAdam, Nicola McGarrity, Brian Opeskin, Prue Vines, Genevieve Wilkinson and Stephen Young. We also thank Tom Randall from Cambridge University Press for his enthusiasm for this project and Priyanka Durai for her excellent work on the manuscript.

Harry also thanks Annabel Johnson for her patience as he excitedly recounted the exploits of micronationalists on long walks together, as well as his parents, Karina and Neil, and sister, Georgia, who encouraged his love of world maps and flags. George thanks Emma Armson, and their children Edward and Eleanor, whose attempts at independence and rule of their household augurs well for their future as micronationalists.

Finally, this book could not have been written without the drive and energy of those many people – some of whom we discuss – who made the decision to throw off the shackles of the old and create their own country.

1

Prince Leonard Prepares for War

On a rainy and gloomy 2 September 1967, Roy Bates, a World War II veteran and former major in the British Army, declared himself the ruler of the new Principality of Sealand. Like many political entities seeking statehood, several challenges immediately confronted the apparent nation. The difficulties facing Sealand appeared particularly grave. To begin with, the entirety of the Principality's territorial claim consisted of a 4,100-tonne decommissioned artificial naval installation located off the coast of Essex in the River Thames estuary. Initially built in 1942 to guard the United Kingdom (UK) port of Harwich from invasion, the until recently abandoned naval fort possessed no arable land. In fact, it possessed very little habitable land at all. The purportedly independent state resembled an abandoned oil rig in being comprised of a 51-by-27-metre pontoon supported by two 18-metre hollow reinforced concrete towers of around 7.3 metres in diameter.

To make matters worse, the UK government was listening.[1] Thankfully for Bates, the United Kingdom was unsure how to respond. Bates, his family, and a small band of supporters had occupied the fort since late 1966, initially intending to operate a pirate radio station from the platform, and the government had spent much of the time since considering what it should do. While some officials demanded the fort's immediate destruction, the Navy were reluctant to intervene, wary of the formidable, improvised arsenal Bates had apparently stocked. Other officials were not entirely sure what to make of the situation. The

[1] Unless otherwise cited, material in this section is drawn from Adrian Johns, *Death of a Pirate: British Radio and the Making of the Information Age* (W.W. Norton & Co, 2011) 249–53; James Grimmelmann, 'Sealand, Havenco, and the Rule of Law' (2012) 2 *University of Illinois Law Review* 405, 412–24; Dylan Taylor-Lehman, *Sealand: The True Story of the World's Most Stubborn Micronation* (Icon Books, 2020). The Principality of Sealand is explored in more detail in Chapter 3.

Ministry of Defence, for instance, considered his actions bizarre rather than threatening, remarking that his behaviour was 'ludicrous. Mr. Bates is trespassing and it now looks as if he is being very foolish.'[2] Complicating matters further were difficult questions of jurisdiction. As the fort was located outside the United Kingdom's three-mile territorial waters and the government had abandoned the site some years previously, it was not clear whether Bates' occupation violated any law.[3] Certainly, it was beyond doubt that Bates himself was causing trouble; reports suggest that he was repelling attempted intruders with home-made petrol bombs and air rifles.[4] In light of this development, the Cabinet ultimately determined to 'dislodge' Bates and his supporters, apparently 'to prevent it falling into the hands of foreign interests'.[5]

'Operation Callow' was relatively straightforward. Officials would remind Bates that the installation belonged to the Ministry of Defence and demand that he leave. If necessary, they would offer him an ex-gratia payment of £5,000 and assist in the removal of his property. Once the Bates family had been safely escorted off the site, the fort would be demolished to prevent them or anyone else from attempting reoccupation. However, Bates refused to cooperate. Baulking at the government's offer, he instead demanded £90,000. When this was not forthcoming, he refused to entertain any suggestions that he relinquish possession. In the meantime, journalists discovered that a detachment of Royal Marine commandos were preparing to seize the fort. Anxious to avoid negative publicity, the government felt that it had no option but to stand down.[6]

Other strategies were actively considered. David Belasco, a disaffected Bates supporter, approached the government proposing to betray his former leader and allow the military safe entry. While the Ministry of Defence considered the plan 'implausible', it did let Belasco know that it was 'prepared to take the Fort over' if he was able to obtain possession without force.[7] Ultimately this too did not eventuate. The Ministry backed out when it became clear that Belasco wanted the Navy to blow

[2] 'Independent Isle "Ludicrous"', *The Times* (London, 4 September 1967) 3.

[3] Grant Hibberd, 'The Last Great Adventure of the Twentieth Century: The Sealand Affair in British Diplomacy' (2011) 4(2) *Britain and the World* 269, 271.

[4] 'Struggle for Sea Fort', *The Times* (London, 28 June 1967) 1; 'Sea Fort Repels Boarders: Raiders Faced Flamethrower', *The Times* (London, 30 June 1967) 2.

[5] Grimmelmann (n 1) 420; 'Commandos Set to Seize Fort', *The Times* (London, 8 August 1967) 1.

[6] 'Commandos Set to Seize Fort' (n 5); 'Ministry Says Talks Over Fort Broke Down', *The Times* (9 August 1967) 2.

[7] Grimmelmann (n 1) 422; Taylor-Lehman (n 1) 57–8.

the fort up to provide a stunning finale to a book he was writing. In any event, the abortive plan quickly got out of hand when Belasco swore an affidavit claiming that the Ministry had asked him to capture the tower by force. This accusation was taken up by Bates and became the subject of a story in the *Daily Telegraph* and, much to the government's embarrassment, was raised in Parliament.[8]

Still other approaches were considered. In order to maintain provisions, Bates regularly sailed between the fort and his home on the UK mainland. To delay and frustrate Bates, Customs sometimes refused to clear his boat for departure, arguing that it lacked a load line certificate. Resourcefully, Bates again approached the papers, alleging that the government had 'marooned' his children who were living on the fort by dredging up 'some obscure bit of marine law'.[9] Although Customs maintained that Bates had merely to 'hire another boat if his own does not conform to the regulations',[10] they eventually relented. Another plan to prosecute Bates for failing to ensure that his 14-year-old son Michael attended school was similarly dismissed.[11] So too was the suggestion that the UK government pass legislation to expand Britain's territorial waters to encompass the fort. As one official noted, such a 'huge undertaking for a relatively small purpose would be "a ponderous move, inviting ridicule"'.[12]

The United Kingdom had not yet given up. After several months, legal advice was finally delivered concluding that although a civil action for possession of the fort 'would be likely to fail for lack of jurisdiction',[13] criminal jurisdiction over offences committed by British citizens might well extend to the site. In November 1967, Michael Bates fired several shots from the fort towards HMS *Egeria*, a Royal Navy survey minesweeper. However, no damage was recorded, and the evidence was uncertain, so the incident was ignored. The Director of Public Prosecutions did not have to wait long for a clearer case. In May 1968, Michael Bates fired a pistol in the direction of lighthouse staff working on

[8] Kenneth Clarke and James Allan, 'Ministry Planned to Seize Sea Fort', *The Daily Telegraph* (30 May 1968); United Kingdom, *Parliamentary Debates*, House of Commons, 18 December 1968, vol 775 col 377W.

[9] 'Radio Man's Children "Marooned"', *The Times* (London, 7 March 1968) 3.

[10] 'Children "Not Marooned"', *The Times* (London, 8 March 1968) 3.

[11] Taylor-Lehman (n 1) 39.

[12] Ibid 40.

[13] Elwyn Jones and Dingle Foot, 'Continental Shelf Roughs Tower Fort' (21 August 1967). See further Letter from Basil Hall to Sir William Dale (8 August 1967). Sources cited in Grimmelmann (n 1) 421.

a buoy near the tower. When Roy and Michael were next ashore, they were both indicted for violations of the 1937 Firearms Act. And yet, at the moment of its triumph the government vacillated; 'It was decided not to take advantage of Mr. Bates' attendance in Court to try and occupy the Fort, as this smacked of sharp practice.'[14]

Unfortunately for the government, the case was ultimately dismissed for want of jurisdiction. Justice Chapman of the Essex Assizes held that although Parliament possessed 'the power to make it an offense for a British subject to have a firearm with intent to endanger life in Istanbul or Buenos Aires, or where have you', it had not done so in this case as the Firearms Act was held to 'operate only within the ordinary territorial limits'.[15] While the court did not hold that Sealand was independent – and in fact concluded that Parliament could extend its jurisdiction to encompass the offshore platform – Bates nonetheless saw the decision as providing de facto recognition of his Principality.[16]

Some journalists and lower level officials were also uncertain of this distinction. In a feature on 'the beautiful Princess Joan of Sealand'[17] published in the aftermath of the decision, the *Sunday Mirror* reported: 'Last week a British judge ruled that the tower was outside British legal jurisdiction, which means that Mr and Mrs Bates have sovereignty over their island fort.'[18] Customs officials in Essex also apparently began 'treating Sealand ... as a foreign country' informing journalists that they were 'awaiting directives about the necessity of passports'.[19] Amidst the confusion, the Foreign Office remained firm: 'Of course we don't recognise it as a foreign state. It's a fort in the North Sea, that's all. It's not a state ... it's a building.'[20]

Following Justice Chapman's ruling, the issue was returned to Cabinet, which eventually reached a practical resolution. Bates' continued occupation may have been undesirable, but as he was 'doing no actual

14 Grimmelmann (n 1) 423.

15 *R v Bates*, The Shire Hall, Chelmsford (25 October 1968) 8 (Chapman J); 'Sea Tower Outside Court Limit', *The Times* (London, 22 October 1968) 3. The United Kingdom extended its territorial jurisdiction to 12 miles, encompassing Rough Towers, in 1987: *Territorial Sea Act 1987* c 49, s 1(a) (UK).

16 Sealand, *About the Principality of Sealand* (2019) www.sealandgov.org/about/.

17 As befitting a Principality, Sealand enjoys its own system of royal titles. Princess Joan was the wife of Roy Bates (otherwise known as Prince Roy).

18 Gordon McGill, 'The Princess on Sentry Go', *The Sunday Mirror* (London, 27 October 1968) 11.

19 Ibid.

20 Ibid.

harm . . . and the Ministry of Defence had not need of the Fort themselves', 'there were no pressing reasons for evicting Mr Bates, certainly none that would justify the use of force or the passage of special legislation'.[21] It was also agreed that in any case, 'there was some advantage in refraining from prosecutions which would enhance Mr Bates's local reputation as a colourful adventurer prosecuted by authority'.[22]

The decision set in place the United Kingdom's approach to the Principality over the following decades. The United Kingdom generally ignores Sealand on the basis it is a non-state actor with no legitimate claim to jurisdictional authority – provided that it does not cause too much trouble. This approach has much wisdom to commend it, but it has allowed Sealand space to attempt to develop into a fully fledged entity. In 1975, Bates introduced a constitution for his Principality. Consisting of twenty-three articles and purportedly based on the common law, its preamble reads:

> In consciousness of his responsibility before God and before man, and inspired by the will to serve the cause of Peace for his People and for all peoples in the world, the sovereign ruler of the PRINCIPALITY OF SEALAND, His Majesty Prince Roy of SEALAND, for himself and for his successors to the throne, by virtue of his constitutional authority resolves, swears and proclaims:[23]

Bates has adopted further state symbols. The Principality has its own flag, coat of arms, national anthem (in 2005, the anthem was recorded by the Slovak Symphony Orchestra as part of its series on national anthems of the world)[24] and motto – E Mare, Libertas (From the Sea, Freedom). It also mints its own currency, commissions postage stamps, issues its own national passport and sells noble titles. The Principality has also often pursued diplomatic relations with other sovereign states.

* * *

On the other side of the world, a former UK colony soon found itself tangling with a similarly stubborn and eccentric individual, though it adopted a different approach. At 5.10 p.m. on Friday 2 December 1977,

[21] *Minutes of Meeting Re: Roughs Tower* (5 November 1968) cited in Grimmelmann (n 1) 423.

[22] Taylor-Lehman (n 1) 61.

[23] Wikisource, 'Principality of Sealand: *Constitution of 1975*' https://en.wikisource.org/wiki/Constitutions_of_1975 and of 1989/Constitution of 1975.

[24] Slovak Symphony Orchestra, 'Sealand' www.youtube.com/watch?reload=9&v=ENwjBz3m5Y8.

Prince Leonard Casley of the Hutt River Province cabled a telegram to Sir John Kerr, the Governor-General of Australia. The telegram's contents were ominous:

> Confirming my letter of 28th November re your Governments [sic] lack of respect of the laws not only on my people but also on people of your own country and Mr. Keatings [sic] further disrespect to the courts. Previous acknowledgement of duress having been applicable it is my official responsibility to declare that a state of war now exists between our respective countries and diplomatic relations are at this time now severed.[25]

With a permanent population of fewer than twenty residents, no standing army, and the Province's 75-square-kilometre territory entirely enclosed by the state of Western Australia, Prince Leonard was unprepared for war. Two days later, at 3.30 p.m. on Sunday 4 December 1977, he cabled a second telegram announcing, 'that the state of war between our countries has now ceased'.[26] The Australian government responded to neither correspondence, but Prince Leonard nonetheless claimed victory. According to his reading of the Geneva Conventions of 1949, a state should show full respect to a nation undefeated in war. As the Hutt River Province was undefeated, Australia must recognise its sovereignty.

Australia has never recognised the sovereignty of the Hutt River Province, but its founding reveals how a combination of frustration with government regulation and anxiety over the ability to secure a safe and prosperous life for one's family can set people on a curious path. Australia's response, or lack thereof, also illustrates the diversity of approaches that can be adopted when dealing with self-declared states.

In the 1960s, Leonard Casley bought a property in the Australian state of Western Australia. Situated at Hutt River in the district of Yallabatharra, about 500 kilometres north of the state capital, Perth, Casley intended to establish a wheat farm. The Australian wheat industry had undergone a significant transition over the previous decades that had generated long-term resentment amongst many farmers. The Great Depression led to the failure of countless small farms across the country. Seeking to counteract the nation's adverse trade balance and restore economic prosperity, the Australian government initiated a campaign

[25] 'Telegram from Prince Leonard Casley to Sir John Kerr (Governor General of Australia)' (2 December 1977).

[26] 'Telegram from Prince Leonard Casley to Sir John Kerr (Governor General of Australia)' (4 December 1977).

to 'Grow More Wheat'. Although leading to a 30 per cent increase in production, the program quickly turned into 'one of the greatest disasters in Australian economic history'.[27] Political bickering meant that the government could only pay 40 per cent of what it had initially promised, leaving up to 20,000 small farmers who had borrowed heavily to plant larger acreage bankrupt.[28] A subsequent 'Eat More Bread' campaign, launched in an effort to absorb 1 million bushels of wheat unsold from the previous harvest,[29] did little to rectify these issues.

Industry consolidation and rising production levels through the 1930s began to challenge the capacity of smaller, independent farmers to compete in a global market. Large-scale grain producers were able to leverage their size to better negotiate with domestic and international wheat buyers and drive down prices. Emerging state intervention aimed at standardising prices was fast-tracked by the outbreak of World War II. In 1939, the government established the Australian Wheat Board (AWB) to oversee the marketing, storage, shipping, pooling and payment of the country's wheat output. Throughout the war, the AWB implemented price stabilisation measures, including by guaranteeing prices, creating a stabilisation fund and regulating the issuing of new growing licences. By the end of the war, both industry and government accepted the necessity and desirability of maintaining a policy of stabilisation during peacetime.

When Casley bought his property, the AWB still regulated and managed the industry. National and State Boards sought to shelter growers from volatility by stabilising prices and incomes. The Board compulsorily acquired and pooled all wheat produced in Australia, established a home consumption price, and had the sole authority to market wheat domestically and internationally. Following a bumper harvest in 1968, industry sought the introduction of production quotas to reduce stock build-up and maintain pricing levels. The Western Australian government agreed, imposing quotas for the summer harvest.

The quotas had a deleterious effect on many farmers, including Casley. In November 1969, while preparing to harvest around 6,000 acres of wheat, Casley received a letter notifying him that he would be permitted

27 Edgars Dunsdorfs, *The Australian Wheat Growing Industry 1788–1948* (Melbourne University Press, 1956) 270–5.

28 Wendy Way, *A New Idea Each Morning: How Food and Agriculture Came Together in One International Organisation* (Australian National University Press, 2013) 140.

29 'Endorsement by Minister; Whole Community Will Benefit', *Evening News* (Sydney, 26 May 1930) 10; '"Eat More Bread" Campaign in NSW', *Barrier Miner* (Broken Hill, 15 August 1930) 1.

to sell only 100 acres. As Casley explained in a letter to the Governor of Western Australia,

> Under this new quota, it would have taken five hundred years to crop the same average amount of wheat that had been harvested in the previous twenty years. The gross proceeds would not have even paid the interest on the hire purchase on two four-wheel drive tractors that were in use. This did not allow any return for maintenance of their homes and families, no income on which to survive let alone profit.[30]

Considering the quotas illegal, Casley called for compensation in the form of 1.8 million acres of land, 'whose rentals will thus be a fair settlement of our losses thus being brought about by the Wheat Quota'. He also sought that the Governor 'grant us our independence, under the Queen and a part of the British Commonwealth'.

Casley's call fell on deaf ears. Despite filing complaints with the Wheat Quota Board, as well as the Premier and Governor of Western Australia, he was informed that there would be no change to the quota. Concerned that the state might resume or forcibly acquire his property, he served a formal notice of secession to the Commonwealth and State governments on 21 April 1970. After observing what he considered a legally required two-year notice period, Casley officially declared the formation of a new state on 21 April 1972.

Casley purported to establish his nation based upon 'the rights of the Magna Carta and the rights of the Atlantic Treaty and the International rights to' create 'Self Preservation Governments'.[31] However, neither document supports the assertion of independence, meaning that there is no sound legal basis for Prince Leonard's action. For this reason, neither the Australian nor the Western Australian government responded.

Nonetheless, Casley continued to act as though his claim was lawful. Consistent with the British diplomatic laws of recognition, following independence a flag was chosen and correspondence delivered to the Governor-General of neighbouring Australia. In March 1971, a Bill of Rights was adopted promising all persons the full protection of the law. Hutt River coins were minted, postage stamps and passports issued and

[30] 'Letter from Leonard Casley to Sir Douglas Kendrew, Governor of Western Australia', 3 November 1969.

[31] 'Fate Accompli: Declaration from Leonard Casley to Sir David Brand, Western Australia Premier', 21 April 1970.

a national anthem recorded. Casley also sent numerous letters to representatives of various states seeking diplomatic recognition.

In the months following his purported declaration of independence, Casley was anxious that the Australian government might act to dissolve his aspirant state. Casting around for a more secure legal basis for its existence, Casley identified a law passed during King Henry VII's reign as critical to shoring up the independence of Hutt River. The Treason Act 1495 was passed to heal lingering resentment following the War of the Roses. Aiming to encourage former advocates of Richard III to support Henry VII against any potential attempt by the House of York to retake the throne, it provided that anyone serving or fighting for the king de facto (Henry) against the king de jure (potentially those with a rival claim through Richard) would not be guilty of any offence. Drawing on this provision, Casley invested himself as His Royal Highness Prince Casley and transformed the Hutt River Province into the Principality of Hutt River. As he (wrongly) understood it, because he was a de facto prince, the law would preclude Australia prosecuting him or his family for any offences they committed while he attained his throne and would prevent the Australian government from interfering with him 'in the discharge of his Princely duties'.[32] Prince Leonard need not have worried. Australia largely ignored the Principality over the fifty years following its founding, save only to ensure that it complied with taxation laws.

* * *

Prince Leonard's declaration of war indicates that self-declared states can be particularly inventive in seeking to have their sovereignty recognised. But not all attempts to ground international recognition need be so hostile. In 1992, Dean Kamen, the inventor of the Segway and mobile insulin pump, as well as self-appointed ruler of the Kingdom of North Dumpling, convinced his friend, President George HW Bush, to sign a non-aggression pact between their two countries – though the United States does not formally recognise the Kingdom.[33]

The Kingdom of North Dumpling is also known as North Dumpling Island. It is a privately owned, three-acre island in Fishers Island Sound, around one mile off the coast of Connecticut. Originally within the traditional lands of the Pequot Indians, the island was acquired by John Winthrop, son of the governor of the Massachusetts Bay Colony, in 1639. The island was owned by the Winthrop family until 1847, when it was

32 Hutt River Province, 'Formation of the Hutt River Province'.

33 Clarice Butkus, 'North Dumpling Island: Micronationality, the Media and the American Dream' (2014) 8 *Shima: The International Journal of Research into Island Cultures* 84.

sold to the federal government to construct a lighthouse. In 1959, the lighthouse beacon was automated, and the island sold to a private party. In 1986, Kamen bought it for USD 2.5 million.

The following year, Kamen sought permission from authorities in New York State's Suffolk County to construct a 100-foot wind turbine on his property. Permission was denied, as regulations restricted structures more than 40 feet tall in residential areas. Rather than amend his plans, Kamen purported to secede from the United States. As *The New York Times* reported at the time:

> Although owning an island in the Sound and considering it to be a land apart is not an unheard of notion, few people have gone to such theatrical lengths to establish a semblance of sovereignty.[34]

Theatrical is the correct word. Styling himself as Lord Dumpling II, Kamen has staged 'various tongue-in-cheek performances of sovereignty'.[35] He drafted, or rather claims to have unearthed, a constitution that bears striking resemblance to the US Constitution, 'which is why the Dumplonians and Americans have gotten along for so many years'.[36] He also composed a national anthem, designed a flag and created a currency 'which features a 250,000 Dumpling note bearing a portrait of Kamen in bowtie and propeller-donned cap'.[37] Kamen also named a Cabinet, appointing several of his friends to important positions, including the founders of Ben and Jerry's ice cream, Ben Cohen and Jerry Greenfield, as Ministers of Ice Cream.[38]

The Kingdom of North Dumpling clearly differs from both the Principalities of Sealand and Hutt River. While all three self-declared states trade on a currency of popular fasciation or bemusement, Kamen has used his personal fiefdom to garner media exposure and attention for his various endeavours and scientific activities. In hundreds of interviews with national and international media, Kamen has characterised the Kingdom as 'a proof of concept center' for his inventions,[39] or a 'working model for how the

[34] Nick Ravo, 'From L.I. Sound, A New Nation Asserts Itself', *The New York Times* (22 April 1988).

[35] Butkus (n 33) 87.

[36] *How to Start Your Own Country* (Everyday Pictures, 2010).

[37] Butkus (n 33) 87.

[38] Michael Inbar, 'Welcome to Secret Island of an Eccentric Genius', *Today* (22 October 2010) www.today.com/news/welcome-secret-island-eccentric-genius-wbna39775733.

[39] John Richardson, 'How Dean Kamen's Magical Water Machine Could Save the World', *Esquire* (24 November 2008) www.esquire.com/news-politics/a5319/dean-kamen-1208/.

United States should handle many of its energy issues'.[40] As he told the *Guardian* newspaper in 2009:

> 'Dumpling is completely carbon neutral,' he says. 'We have solar panels on every building, a 10kW wind turbine, our own little Stirling engine for backup power, burning only local fuel. We're making our own water out of the ocean with Slingshot [a water purification invention].'[41]

That was not all; 'we are now developing a foreign aid program to help the US',[42] Kamen added mischievously.

* * *

The Principality of Sealand, the Principality of Hutt River and the Kingdom of North Dumpling are not independent sovereign states. Instead, they are examples of the many people around the world who have claimed to secede and create their own country. A new state is, of course, the goal of secessionist movements across the globe, including in South Sudan, Kosovo, Scotland, Catalonia, Quebec and elsewhere. As should be clear by now, however, the purported attempts at secession of Roy Bates, Leonard Casley and Dean Kamen differ fundamentally from these efforts. Built around a committed and eccentric individual, possessing only a very small resident population and unrecognised by sovereign states, these would-be countries are 'aspirant' or 'wannabe' states.[43] More commonly, they are known as micronations.

In contrast to true secessionist movements, micronations are generally considered trivial and are often – though not always – ignored by the state. This may be because a micronation does not pose a security threat and lacks a foundation in domestic and international law for its claim to independence. It may also be because, like the Kingdom of North Dumpling, it is not clear that statehood is genuinely prized. In all cases, however, micronations distinguish themselves by dressing in the language of statehood and performing acts of sovereignty; they draft constitutions, issue coins, print stamps, compose national anthems and seek to engage in diplomatic relations with recognised states. In doing so,

[40] Butkus (n 33) 91.

[41] Mark Harris, 'Segway Inventor on Future Technology – and Why Videogames Aren't It', *Guardian* (23 July 2009) www.theguardian.com/technology/2009/jul/22/dean-kamen-interview.

[42] Ibid,

[43] Philip Streich, 'To the Sea! Sealand and Other Wannabe States' in David Bell Mislan and Philip Streich (eds), *Weird IR: Deviant Cases in International Relations* (Palgrave Macmillan, 2019) 15, 17; Adam Grydehøj, 'Captain Calamity's Sovereign State of Forvik' (2014) 8 *Shima: The International Journal of Research into Island Cultures* 34, 34.

micronations critique and challenge understandings of and approaches to international legal personality. They also catalyse larger questions over the nature of statehood, sovereignty, security and legitimate authority. Put simply, micronations are an oddity that sits outside conventional understandings that help us to challenge and better understand the law.

The vignettes that we have chosen to introduce our study highlight several key themes of micronationalism. In each case, an entity led by a dedicated and unconventional character sought to engineer international recognition of its statehood. Although none of these micronations has ever achieved actual legal recognition, they nonetheless consider their efforts a success. This is because performative assertions, or mimetic reproductions, of sovereignty have value and an effect regardless of how a state responds.[44] If, like Australia and the Principality of Hutt River, the state refrains from action, the micronation may regard that non-response as an implicit acceptance of its sovereignty. Likewise, if the state reacts by simply acknowledging receipt, suggesting an alternative department to contact, or even signing a faux non-aggression pact, the micronation may assert that its sovereignty has been recognised. Finally, if, as in the case of the Principality of Sealand, the state responds by implying that the micronation has engaged in some form of criminality, it opens up space for political and legal debate for the micronation to contest its claim. As Stuart Hill, the leader of the Sovereign State of Forvik – a micronation claiming sovereignty over an uninhabited 2.5-acre island in the Shetland Islands, 170 kilometres north of mainland Scotland – has remarked, 'it's a win-win situation'.[45]

The nature of micronations and the ease with which they can be established (and abandoned) make it difficult to assess the total number of such entities across the globe. The growth of the Internet and web-based micronational communities make accurate assessment even more challenging. A brief survey reveals that thousands of micronations exist entirely on social media platforms, like Facebook,[46] Reddit[47] and MicroWiki.[48]

[44] Fiona McConnell, Terri Moreau and Jason Dittmer , 'Mimicking State Diplomacy: The Legitimizing Strategies of Unofficial Diplomacies' (2013) 43 *Geoform* 804, 810.

[45] Cited in Ibid.

[46] Facebook, 'Micronations and Alternative Polities' www.facebook.com/groups/micronations andalternativepolities/.

[47] Reddit, 'Micronations – Small Nations, New Country Projects, Seasteading' www.reddit.com/r/micronations.

[48] Microwiki https://micronations.wiki/Main_Page.

Several lists of micronations have been developed. The interdisciplinary academic journal *Shima*, which serves as a forum for research into island cultures, insular communities and imaginations of autonomy, has published an anthology on micronationality that stretches to twenty papers and fifteen micronations.[49] Atlas Obscura, an online magazine and travel company that specialises in providing guides to strange and odd places around the world, has written forty-four articles on around thirty micronations.[50] The *Lonely Planet Guide to Home-Made Nations*, published in 2006, features detailed discussion on fifty micronations.[51] A 'Micronations World Map', a user-edited online map that allows people to tag micronations on parts of the globe, catalogues sixty-seven different micronations.[52] A list on Wikipedia stretches to eighty-nine distinct entries.[53] Another user-edited online map created by Matthew Hubbard (formerly the ruler of the now defunct Republic of Matthewopia) identifies over 100 micronations and other like entities.[54] Complicating matters, however, is the fact that each list includes several micronations that others do not. Adding these up to produce an estimated total number of micronations suggests a figure of at least 135 micronations, though many of these entities are no longer active and it is unlikely that even this tally is comprehensive.[55] In an appendix, we list the micronations that we discuss in this book.

The entities catalogued in these lists are limited to micronations that physically claim territory in some manner. In most cases, this means that the micronation extends so far as the real property owned or occupied by

49 Shima, 'Micronationality Anthology' https://shimajournal.org/anthologies/micronationality.php.

50 Atlas Obscura, 'Micro-nations' www.atlasobscura.com/categories/micro-nations.

51 John Ryan, George Dunford and Simon Sellars, *Micronations: The Lonely Planet Guide to Home-Made Nations* (Lonely Planet, 2006).

52 Micronations World Map www.google.com/maps/d/viewer?msa=0&mid=1VzMWnhHJbOWfCFkaEt TSw_3cNO4&ll=-10.102620343996707%2C-100.46428450000002&z=2.

53 Wikipedia, 'List of Micronations' https://en.wikipedia.org/wiki/List_of_micronations.

54 Matthew Hubbard, 'Micronations World Map' https://earth.google.com/web/@-1.99921679,0.00000001,63.91320881a,14045213.08685379d,30y,0h,0.00000106t,0r.

55 It does not, for instance, include any of the entities that emerged during the Japanese micronational boom in the 1980s. See, for example, Adam Pasion, 'The Will to Secede: Japan's Micro-Nation Boom', *Japan Daily* (9 February 2016) https://japandaily.jp/will-secede-japans-micro-nation-boom-2573/. Information on this phenomenon is difficult to gather, suggesting that our tally may overlook micronations in non-English speaking countries.

its founder. With this relatively secure land base, these founders institute the trappings of statehood; seek to regulate citizenship, issue passports, grant visas, draft constitutions and compose national anthems. While they may be distinguished according to how 'serious' their claims for secession appear to be – compare the Principality of Sealand with the Kingdom of North Dumpling – all make a formal and persistent claim to sovereignty in the real world.

Not all micronations are territorial or 'secessionist' in the same way. Spurred by the rise of internet access, many thousands of micronations are entirely 'virtual' or 'simulationist'. Existing almost wholly online, these imaginary countries often function more as a political or cultural simulation than an inchoate or emerging state. Their terrain is message boards and online forums; it is here where government business is simulated, non-aggression pacts signed and tips for nation-building shared. In some cases, these virtual nations maintain physical embassies and attend micronational conferences or summits, but the physical territory they claim is fictional or impossible to reach. In other cases, simulationist micronations may be expressly described as conceptual or non-territorial. One may not be able to visit these nations, but because they claim sovereignty, establish governments and generally act like a nation, they are also properly characterised as micronations.

One early micronation declared its independence in 1811. The previous year, Massachusetts whaler Jonathan Lambert landed on a remote volcanic island group around 2,800 kilometres from Cape Town and more than 4,000 kilometres from the Falkland Islands in the South Atlantic Ocean. Although first sighted in 1506 by Portuguese explorer Tristão da Cunha, who named the largest of the four uninhabited islands after himself, Lambert and his three-man party were the first ever to settle permanently. On 4 February 1811, Lambert declared himself sovereign and sole possessor of the group of islands:

> As no European powers whatever had hitherto publicly claimed the said Islands, by right of discovery, or of possession: Therefore be it known to all nations, tongues, and languages, that from and ever after the date of this public instrument, I constitute my individual self the sole proprietor of the above-mentioned islands, grounding my right and claim on the rational and sure ground of absolute occupancy.[56]

[56] A Watson, 'Tristan d'Acunha, &c; Jonathan Lambert, late Sovereign thereof' (1818) 4(21) *Blackwood's Edinburgh Magazine* 280, 282.

Lambert adopted a flag, renamed the anglicised Tristan da Cunha, the 'Island of Refreshment', and sent his declaration of sovereignty to the United States and governments in Europe.[57] Copies and summaries appeared in scores of newspapers, but Lambert's claims were dismissed. Charles Dickens later derided him as 'Prince Jonathan',[58] while a more recent account belittled the 'toy king on his desert island'.[59]

The Island of Refreshment did not survive for long. Lambert and two other men were presumed drowned while fishing the following year. Larger geopolitical concerns soon intervened. In 1816, the islands were annexed by the British to prevent the French from using them as a base for a rescue operation to free the exiled Napoleon I from his prison on Saint Helena, some 2,400 kilometres away, as well as to stop the Americans from using it as a staging ground for naval cruisers, as they had during the war of 1812. Two men, including one who had initially arrived with Lambert, were found living on the island; both were 'glad to place themselves under the protection of the British flag'.[60]

More than 200 years later, micronationalism is alive and well, but developments in technology continue to affect and influence the phenomenon. In October 2016, Russian-Azerbaijani scientist Igor Ashurbeyli announced the establishment of Asgardia. Asgardia's territory is small and remote; also called the Space Kingdom of Asgardia, its territory is putatively based on a 10 cm x 10 cm x 20 cm satellite Ashurbeyli had launched into low-earth orbit.[61] Somehow, he hopes that this satellite will augur the creation of a space colony. For Ashurbeyli, Asgardia was established with four overarching goals: 'to ensure the peaceful use of space, to protect the Earth from space hazards, . . . to create a demilitarized and free scientific base of knowledge in space . . . [and] set[] up habitable platforms in space and build[]

[57] James Fichter, 'The British Empire and the American Atlantic on Tristan da Cunha, 1811–1816' (2008) 36(4) *Journal of Imperial and Commonwealth History* 567, 570.

[58] Charles Dickens, 'The Diminutive Dependency' in *All the Year Round* (Volume XVIII, 31 March 1877) 111, 112.

[59] Margaret Mackay, *Angry Island: The Story of Tristan da Cunha (1506–1963)* (Rand, McNally & Company, 1963) 31.

[60] Fichter (n 56) 582; Watson (n 55) 282; Stephen Royle, 'Perilous Shipwreck, Misery and Unhappiness: The British Military at Trista da Cunha, 1816–1817' (2003) 29(4) *Journal of Historical Geography* 516, 517.

[61] *Constitution of the Space Kingdom of Asgardia*, art 5 (9 September 2017); Leah Crane, 'The "Space Nation" Asgardia Just Launched Its First Satellite', *New Scientist* (13 November 2017) www.newscientist.com/article/2153196-the-space-nation-asgardia-just-launched-its-first-satellite/.

settlements on the Moon'.[62] Assuming that the (significant) technological challenges can be overcome, Ashurbeyli is hopeful that his 'nation above the clouds'[63] can take shape. Perhaps small steps are encouraging. Over 1,200 people have paid a residency fee as a first step to obtaining citizenship, with more than a million more people registering as followers on the Kingdom's website.[64]

Inchoate efforts at international recognition have followed. Drawing on a personal friendship, Ashurbeyli has met with Prince Michael of Kent – cousin to Queen Elizabeth II of the United Kingdom – to discuss Asgardia.[65] Ashurbeyli has also written to at least thirty-two recognised states, declared that he intends to apply for membership of the United Nations[66] and has sought to promote Asgardia as a home for peoples without states:

> Asgardia will unite the representatives of all nations who aspire to self-determination in the narrow boundaries of earthly states. It is in Asgardia where they will get their freedom.[67]

Asgardia remains experimental and unrealised, but the growth of the Internet has allowed Ashurbeyli to market his project, attract supporters and raise funds.

The story of the short-lived Island of Refreshment and the avant-garde Space Kingdom of Asgardia illustrate how micronations challenge conventional understandings of statehood. Indeed, Jonathan Lambert's claim of sovereignty appears to have been established consistently with the law at the time. Tristan da Cunha was uninhabited and unsettled. According to the prevailing theories of international law, discovery of such lands, accompanied by symbolic acts such as raising a flag, provided

[62] Asgardia, 'Concept: Asgardia – the Space Nation, https://asgardia.space/en/word.

[63] Humaid Alshamsi, Roy Balleste and Michelle Hanlon , 'Space Station Asgardia 2117: From Theoretical Science to a New Nation in Outer Space' (2018) 16(1) *Santa Clara Journal of International Law* 36, 55.

[64] Asgardia, 'Take Your Steps Toward Becoming a Resident' https://asgardia.space/en/page/resident-card.

[65] Ivan Cherbeko, 'Head of Nation Talks of Asgardia to Queen Elizabeth II's Cousin', *Asgardia* (8 March 2019) https://asgardia.space/en/news/Head of-Nation-talks-of-Asgardia-to-Queen-Elizabeths-II-Cousin.

[66] Imogen Saunders, 'The "Space Kingdom" Asgardia Has Its Own Flag and Anthem, but a State It Is Not', *The Conversation* (15 August 2018) https://theconversation.com/the-space-kingdom-asgardia-has-its-own-flag-and-anthem-but-a-state-it-is-not-101250.

[67] Cited in Sergey Krichevsky and Sergey Udartsev, 'Space State on Earth and Beyond: Philosophy, Models, Experience and Prospects' (2019) 23 *Philosophy and Cosmology* 30, 45.

an inchoate title against other states. That inchoate title could then be perfected by taking actual possession and forming settlements.[68] This is precisely what Lambert did. On what basis then was his sovereignty denied? Asgardia may currently possess and occupy no territory, but if technology develops to allow permanent habitation in space, how should international law and recognised sovereign states assess the status of those communities?

Micronations are diverse in form and function. Some are established on uninhabited islands or abandoned manmade structures. Others are in remote locations within the territory of existing sovereign states, or even in outer space. Still others are dreamed up entirely within college dorm rooms and built on message boards. In light of this heterogeneity is it even possible to speak of a single phenomenon?

This book contends that it is. We argue that, despite their broad variety, micronations are a particular and peculiar type of political entity. In exploring that diversity, the book examines the legal questions that are catalysed by micronationalism. It analyses whether micronations are or could be states for the purposes of international law. It considers the factors that motivate countless individuals all over the world to secede and create their own country as well as the numerous quasi or faux legal justifications that they offer. It also explores how recognised sovereign states respond to the challenge posed by micronations.

We begin in Chapter 2 by developing a conceptual framework and definition of micronations. As we have seen, micronations are an incredibly diverse phenomenon, but all micronations share central features. Each makes a claim for statehood despite having no legal basis for doing so. Drawing on this insight, we compare and contrast micronations with other entities that purport to exercise political and legal authority. As we outline, a wide variety of entities with more or less effective government, more or less legitimate claims to statehood, and more or less recognition and acceptance by individual states and the international community, exist around the world. By developing a 'statehood spectrum' along which a range of state and state-like entities may be placed, these complexities can be unravelled and a clearer picture of what makes micronations distinct emerges. We find that micronations are self-declared nations that perform and mimic acts of sovereignty, and adopt many of the protocols of nations, but lack a foundation in domestic and

[68] Emer de Vattel, *The Law of Nations* (1797) §208.

international law for their existence and are not recognised as nations in domestic or international forums.

Drawing on our conceptual framework, Chapter 3 surveys a wide cross-section of micronations, focusing on the varied motivations for their creation, as often expressed by their founders. Such stories are part of a micronation's self-created history and narrative. While they may be aggrandising or performative, they are nonetheless valuable in understanding the reasons why a person chooses to found their own country. Our survey reveals that some are established as conceptual art projects designed to critique understandings of statehood and sovereignty. Others are founded in a combination of frustration with regulation and a burning sense of a political injustice. Still others owe their formation to their creators' sense of personal expression and desire for attention. In many cases a combination of these and other impetuses motivates secession. In all cases, however, although micronations may purport to assert sovereignty in any number of ways, they remain conceptually distinct from recognised sovereign states.

The varied motivations behind the establishment of micronations has consequences for the political and legal issues they provoke. For instance, micronations that purport to claim authority over specified territory give rise to questions over the recognition and regulation of acts of secession and state creation, while micronations that reclaim land, develop floating structures on the sea, or seek to build habitable structures in space, elicit enquiries into the conditions for statehood under international law. In contrast, micronations established as a humorous endeavour or a conceptual art project may not intend to seriously engage in these debates, but they too still face questions over the enforcement of domestic laws. These questions are explored in Chapters 4 and 5.

In Chapter 4, we examine how micronations seek to legitimate their sovereignty. Founders and proponents of micronations may be eccentric or unconventional but they can be careful in their attempts to validate their actions. Mimicking recognised states, they adopt statehood protocols, including designing and developing national symbols and pursuing diplomatic relations. Furthermore, although they may have little legal training, they use a wide variety of materials to find a lawful basis for their claims. Micronations search for a foothold in international legal instruments as if finding a gap or inconsistency in, for example, the law of the sea, can ground a claim for sovereignty.

In declaring independence, drafting a constitution, regulating citizenship and issuing passports, micronations position themselves as rival sites of authority. In Chapter 5, we explore the different ways that internationally recognised states respond to micronations' claims to sovereignty. This chapter reveals that even though micronations are largely ignored in the international relations, political science and legal literature, in practice states must take notice and consider appropriate ways to engage. In some cases, states perceive their existence as a provocation or threat to their own claims of authority and to jurisdiction and can act in swift and decisive ways to foreclose micronations' scope of action. In other cases, states ignore micronations, considering them to be trivial or unthreatening. In all circumstances, however, states deny the international legal personality of micronations and ensure that any encounter occurs entirely within and according to domestic law.

In the final chapter we consider the future of micronationalism. We outline the five major themes that emerge from our larger study, exploring in more detail the relationship between micronations and recognised states, as well as the creativity, diversity, temporality and gendered nature of micronationalism. Having drawn out these points we reflect more broadly on the key characteristic shared by all wannabe states: despite having no legal basis for their assertions, all micronations make a claim for statehood. Why? What value do founders and proponents see in the language of statehood? Are their claims intended to be taken seriously or are they simply a cry for relevance? Finally, we contemplate the success or failure of micronations. In circumstances where no micronation has ever become a sovereign state, is the future of micronationalism still bright?

2

Statehood and Micronations

Micronations have received little attention in the academic literature. When it comes to legal scholarship, there is no account that outlines the common features and outer bounds of what it means to be a micronation. In fact, very few efforts offer an explanatory account of micronationalism at all. In this chapter, we develop a detailed conceptual framework for micronations to better understand and interrogate their common features and considerable diversity. We begin from a simple starting point. Entities like the Kingdom of North Dumpling and the Principality of Sealand have pretensions to statehood, but they are clearly not states. Notwithstanding their forceful or eccentric assertions to the contrary, their claims to statehood have no legitimate foundation in domestic or international law.

Our starting point frames micronations in opposition to states. Understanding what a micronation is therefore requires attention to statehood. Unfortunately, this task is complicated by the fact that while states are the primary subjects of the international legal system, no universally accepted legal account of what is and what is not a state exists. In this chapter we examine these complexities by developing a 'statehood spectrum' along which a range of state and state-like entities may be placed. At one end sit internationally recognised sovereign political communities like the United States of America, Portugal and South Africa. At the other end sit entities with a more tenuous grasp of statehood, perhaps because of some legal flaw in their purported creation or political impediment to their capacity to exercise authority and jurisdiction.

Not all entities can be placed on the statehood spectrum. At a minimum, a political community must make and purport to perfect a claim of and for statehood. For many reasons, a variety of entities exercising political authority over a territorially bounded community do not make such a claim. Moving beyond the statehood spectrum enriches our understanding of both statehood and micronations. It reveals that micronations can be distinguished from similar entities on the basis of two key elements: the absence of any legitimate foundation in domestic or international law for their existence, and, nonetheless, a claim for statehood and international legal personality, whether earnest, plaintive, delusional, satirical or otherwise. By probing these features, we can more clearly identify what makes micronations distinctive.

Clearing the field of similar but distinct entities allows us to focus on developing a legal definition of micronations to guide our discussion throughout this book. After exploring several classificatory accounts that identify commonalities and distinctions among and between different types of micronation, we outline our definition. We find that micronations are self-declared nations that perform and mimic acts of sovereignty, and adopt many of the protocols of nations, but lack a foundation in domestic and international law for their existence and are not recognised as states in domestic or international forums.

2.1 What Is a State?

When the United Nations officially came into existence in October 1945, it consisted of fifty-one member states. Seventy-six years later, membership has swelled to 193 states.[1] This substantial growth reflects several major trends, the most prominent of which has been the development and articulation of self-determination as a foundational principle of international law.[2] First expressed in the nineteenth century, the principle of self-determination played a key role in the development of the modern state system.[3] Fuelling two waves of state formation in the period after World War II, it sparked the dismantling of European colonial

1 United Nations, 'Growth in United Nations Membership, 1945–Present', www.un.org/en/sections/member-states/growth-united-nations-membership-1945-present/index.html.

2 See, generally, Antonio Cassese, *Self-Determination of Peoples: A Legal Reappraisal* (Cambridge University Press, 1995). James Anaya, *Indigenous Peoples in International Law* (Oxford University Press, 2nd ed, 2004), Pt 2.

3 *Declaration on the Granting of Independence to Colonial Countries and Peoples*, UNGA Res 1514 (14 December 1960); *Declaration on Principles of International Law Concerning Friendly Relations and Co-operation Among States in Accordance with the Charter of the United Nations*, UNGA Res 2625 (24 October 1970) ('*Friendly Relations Declaration*'); *Legal Consequences for States of the Continued Presence of South Africa in Namibia (South-West Africa) Notwithstanding Security Council Resolution 276 (1970) (Advisory Opinion)* [1970] ICJ Rep 16, 31 [52]; *Western Sahara (Advisory Opinion)* [1975] 12, 31–3 [54]–[58].

empires in Africa and Asia in the 1950s and 1960s and underlay the restoration of sovereign republics in Eastern Europe and Asia as part of the dissolution of the Soviet Union.

Self-determination holds that all people have the right to freely choose their political status.[4] As this principle took hold across the globe and the number of sovereign states increased, the term 'state' increasingly became synonymous with the concept of a 'nation'. In some cases, the words were hyphenated as scholars described the division of the world into a community of 'nation-states'.[5] The terms can also be treated as identifying distinct concepts. While a state exercises jurisdiction over particular territory irrespective of the population who inhabit that territory, a nation is an 'imagined community',[6] comprising a people that share a 'psychological bond'.[7] That bond is formed on the basis of a mix of collective cultural, linguistic, religious or ethnic identities, as well as shared 'symbols, memories, myths, values and traditions'.[8] A nation-state is thus a sovereign political entity whose territorial borders are coterminous with the boundaries of a nation.[9]

States can have a real and direct impact on the lives of citizens and residents. And yet, however innate or logical they may appear to be, states are not natural entities.[10] As James Crawford has explained, '[a] state is not a fact in the sense that a chair is a fact'.[11] What then is a state?

[4] See *International Covenant on Civil and Political Rights*, opened for signature 16 December 1966, 999 UNTS 171 (entered into force 23 March 1976) art 1; *International Covenant on Economic, Social and Cultural Rights*, opened for signature 19 December 1966, 993 UNTS 3 (entered into force 3 January 1976) art 1.

[5] Ernest Gellner, *Nations and Nationalism* (Cornell University Press, 2nd ed, 2006) ch 1.

[6] Benedict Anderson, *Imagined Communities: Reflections on the Origin and Spread of Nationalism* (Verso, 3rd ed, 2006).

[7] Walker Connor, 'A Nation Is a Nation, Is a State, Is an Ethnic Group Is a . . .' (1978) 1(4) *Ethnic and Racial Studies* 377, 382.

[8] Anthony Smith, 'When Is a Nation' (2002) 7(2) *Geopolitics* 5, 14–15. See also, Anthony Smith, 'The Origins of Nations' (1989) 12(3) *Ethnic and Racial Studies* 340.

[9] Note that given the distinction between 'nation' and 'state', the terminology 'micronations' is a little awkward. However, it is the accepted naming for these entities, and we adopt it for that reason. If nothing else, it also helpfully distinguishes micronations from microstates. As we explore later, microstates may be very small, but they are states at international law.

[10] Robert Jackson, *Quasi-States: Sovereignty, International Relations, and the Third World* (Cambridge University Press, 1990) 7.

[11] James Crawford, *The Creation of States in International Law* (Oxford University Press, 2nd ed, 2007) 5.

2.1.1 Statehood and International Law

One way to answer this question is by turning to international law. Historically, states were considered the sole subjects of the international legal system. As the Permanent Court of International Justice noted in 1927, '[i]nternational law governs relations between independent states'.[12] International legal scholars have questioned whether this position was ever entirely true, but in any case, political developments have since complicated the picture. Today, a range of inter-state political entities, international organisations, transnational social movements, corporations and even rivers possess varying degrees of international personality.[13] And yet, 'in spite of the complexities', states remain the primary subjects of international law.[14] The state 'continues to be the only actor in international law that really matters, that is, the actor that plays the decisive role in making, interpreting, and enforcing international law'.[15]

To be a state is to enjoy a suite of legal privileges and competencies in the international sphere. At least five principles that 'constitute the core of the concept of statehood' can be identified.[16] First, formally, if not in practice, all states have equal status and standing.[17] While the United States dwarfs Nauru in economic, political and military might, both states have one vote in the United Nations General Assembly. Second, all states possess plenary competence to make treaties and perform other international acts.[18] Third, subject to any international legal obligations, all states enjoy exclusive competence with respect to their internal affairs.[19] In other words, the United Kingdom is not permitted to intervene or

[12] *SS 'Lotus' (France v Turkey) (Judgment)* [1927] PCIJ (ser A) No 10, 18.

[13] See, for example, Hersch Lauterpacht, 'The Subjects of the Law of Nations' (1947) 63 *Law Quarterly Review* 438; *Reparation for Injuries Suffered in the Service of the United Nations (Advisory Opinion)* [1949] ICJ Rep 174, 178; Gabriel Eckstein et al, 'Conferring Legal Personality on the World's Rivers: A Brief Intellectual Assessment' (2019) 44(6–7) *Water International* 804.

[14] Thomas Grant, 'Defining Statehood: The Montevideo Convention and Its Discontents' (1999) 37 *Columbia Journal of Transnational Law* 403, 407; James Crawford, *Brownlie's Principles of Public International Law* (Oxford University Press, 9th ed, 2018) 106.

[15] Karen Knop, 'Re/Statements: Feminism and State Sovereignty in International Law' (1993) 3 *Transnational and Contemporary Problems* 293, 297.

[16] Crawford (n 11) 42. See also International Law Commission, *Draft Declaration on the Rights and Duties of States* (1949) arts 1–3, 5, 12.

[17] *Charter of the United Nations* art 2(1).

[18] *Case Concerning Military and Paramilitary Activities in and Against Nicaragua (Nicaragua v United States of America) (Merits)* [1986] ICJ Rep 14, 133 [265].

[19] *Charter of the United Nations* art 2(7); *Friendly Relations Declaration* (n 3).

intrude on French domestic or foreign policy. Fourth, states are not subject to compulsory international process, jurisdiction or settlement without their consent.[20] If Australia does not agree to be bound by the International Court of Justice, for example, it cannot be forced to comply with any judgment of that Court. Finally, derogations from these principles are not lightly assumed. In case of doubt, 'an international court or tribunal will tend to decide in favour of the freedom of action of states, whether with respect to external or internal affairs, or as not having consented to a specific exercise of international jurisdiction, or to a particular derogation from equality'.[21]

These legal privileges and competencies mean that states are powerful actors in the international sphere. However, while these principles illuminate the core of statehood, they do not help us identify whether an entity is or is not a state; they are 'consequences of statehood rather than constitutive elements of it'.[22] A definition is still required.

2.1.2 Definition and Criteria

Despite their centrality in the international legal system, no unanimously accepted legal definition of what it means to be a state exists.[23] Perhaps more perplexing is the fact that international legal scholars have argued against the utility or even possibility of establishing a clear definition.

One of the early attempts at forming a definition occurred in the late 1940s. In 1949, the International Law Commission – a body of experts elected by the United Nations General Assembly and responsible for helping to develop and codify international law – examined this issue when considering the proposed *Declaration on the Rights and Duties of States*. While many members of the Commission suggested that a definition of the word 'state' would be essential for the Declaration, others demurred. British international lawyer James Brierly, for instance, noted that a definition 'would be difficult to establish and highly controversial',[24] arguing instead that the word 'state' 'was commonly

[20] *Case of the Monetary Gold Removed from Rome in 1943 (Preliminary Question) (Italy v France, United Kingdom and United States of America)* [1954] ICJ Rep 19.

[21] Crawford (n 11) 41. References removed.

[22] David Raič, *Statehood and the Law of Self-Determination* (Kluwer Law International, 2002) 24.

[23] Crawford (n 11) 37, 198; Grant (n 14) 408.

[24] United Nations, *International Law Commission Yearbook* (1949), 1st sess, 8th mtg, 22 April 1949, 65 [21] ('*Yearbook of the ILC*').

used in documents and speech, and its meaning had been understood without definition'.[25] French international jurist Georges Scelle agreed, considering 'that it would be almost impossible to arrive at a universally satisfactory definition of the term'.[26] The following year, Scelle expanded on this, explaining that:

> He himself had been active in international law for more than fifty years, and still did not know what a state was; and he felt sure that he would not find out before he died. He was convinced that the Commission could not tell him.[27]

The Commission resolved its work by avoiding the problem. It concluded that 'no useful purpose would be served by an effort to define the term "state"', and it refrained from outlining the conditions necessary for an entity to become a state.[28]

The difficulty in attaining a clear definition has not prevented legal scholars from seeking this goal. For many years, this task was complicated by the connection between statehood and 'recognition'. In the nineteenth century, statehood became entwined with the notion that recognition played a formal role in the creation of states. The constitutive theory of statehood, as it is known, holds that a sovereign state is 'constituted' or brought into existence by an act of recognition. In the words of Lassa Oppenheim, 'a state is, and becomes, an International Person through recognition only and exclusively'.[29] The account begins from the position that the subjects of any legal system must be identifiable with certainty. A particular community cannot automatically be considered a subject of the international legal system without some entity making that determination. As Hersch Lauterpacht explained, in the absence of a properly constituted 'impartial international organ to perform that function ... [it] must be fulfilled by states'.[30]

The constitutive theory focuses attention on the 'juristic baptism'; that is, the idea that recognition is 'the agency of admission into "civilized society"'.[31] As existing sovereign states were deemed the proper gatekeepers

25 Ibid.

26 Ibid 68 [67].

27 United Nations, *International Law Commission Yearbook* (1950), 2nd sess, 52nd mtg, 22 June 1950, 84 [22].

28 *Yearbook of the ILC* (n 24) 289 [49].

29 Lassa Oppenheim, *International Law: A Treatise* (Longman, Green and Company, 1st ed, 1905) vol 1, 108 [71].

30 Hersch Lauterpacht, *Recognition in International Law* (Cambridge University Press, 1947) 5.

31 Crawford (n 11) 16.

to the international community, it endowed them with considerable authority. While a particular community may govern itself according to its own law and custom, it would not be considered a member of the 'society of nations' unless and until it was implicitly or expressly recognised by other (primarily European) states. Absent that recognition, international law would take no notice of the entity; it would not be bound by nor gain the protections of the law. Unsurprisingly, the constitutive theory played a significant role in facilitating colonisation and imperialism. Recognised states drew on discriminatory notions of 'civilisation' to deny Indigenous peoples and communities in the Americas, Africa, Oceania and elsewhere the right to govern themselves.[32] The constitutive theory was also used within Europe. The 1815 Congress of Vienna sought to settle disputes arising from the French Revolutionary Wars and the Napoleonic Wars. While the Congress admitted the representatives of more than 200 European polities, it recognised only thirty-nine states in the Final Act.[33]

The constitutive theory of statehood produces serious complications. Putting to one side its historical role in denying international legal status to Indigenous and other political communities, it seems to suggest that statehood is relative and contingent on universal recognition.[34] If this is the case then it may have significant consequences for international peace and security. For example, North Korea and South Korea do not formally recognise each other as states, but this does not mean that North Korea is free to invade and forcibly acquire Seoul, nor South Korea, Pyongyang. Any armed conflict between these two entities will be regulated by international law.[35] Furthermore, as Stefan Talmon has noted, 'the idea of one state deciding upon another state's personality in international law is at odds with the fundamental principle of the sovereign equality of states'.[36] These obvious shortcomings in the constitutive account have

[32] Antony Anghie, *Imperialism, Sovereignty and the Making of International Law* (Cambridge University Press, 2012); Ntina Tzouvala, *Capitalism as Civilisation: A History of International Law* (Cambridge University Press, 2020).

[33] Kalevi Jaakko Holsti, *Taming the Sovereigns: Institutional Change in International Politics* (Cambridge University Press, 2004) 128–9; Randall Lesaffer, 'The Congress of Vienna (1814–1815)', *Oxford Public International Law*, https://opil.ouplaw.com/page/congress-vienna-1814-1815.

[34] Hans Kelsen, 'Recognition in International Law' (1941) 35(4) *American Journal of International Law* 605, 609.

[35] Crawford (n 11) 21.

[36] Stefan Talmon, 'The Constitutive Versus the Declaratory Theory of Recognition: *Tertium Non Datur*?' (2004) 75(1) *British Yearbook of International Law* 101, 102. See also *Charter of the United Nations* art 2(1).

prompted creative attempts to codify rules governing recognition, including by imposing an obligation on states to recognise other states.[37] None of these efforts has been successful.[38]

In view of these and other challenges, the declaratory theory of statehood is generally accepted today.[39] This account views recognition as a political act, separate from legal questions over the existence of a state. In the words of a 1929 German-Polish Mixed Arbitration Tribunal, '[t]he state exists by itself . . . recognition is nothing else than a declaration of this existence, recognised by the states from which it emanates'.[40] The Arbitration Commission of the Hague Conference on Yugoslavia (also known as the Badinter Commission), established by the European Economic Community to consider legal questions arising from the dissolution of the Socialist Federal Republic of Yugoslavia, reached the same conclusion. In its Opinion No 1, issued in 1991, the Commission held that 'the existence . . . of the state is a question of fact; . . . the effects of recognition by other states are purely declaratory'.[41] On this account, North and South Korea's mutual non-recognition has no legal consequence for their status; both are states, and both are bound by international law.

Nonetheless, problems also persist under the declaratory account. For one, without widespread recognition it is difficult in practice for a state to actually engage in diplomatic relations or exercise its rights and obligations under international law.[42] Recognition may be status-confirming rather than status-creating, but it is still necessary for an entity to operate as a state. Indeed, as Crawford has noted, in some cases, general recognition 'may be practically conclusive' as to whether an entity is a state or not.[43]

The declaratory theory shifts attention away from subjective recognition to objective criteria. After all, if the effect of recognition by other states is purely declaratory of a pre-existing fact, it becomes necessary to identify some content or standard for statehood. While the International

37 Lauterpacht (n 30) 32–3, 73–5.
38 Crawford (n 11) 38.
39 Ibid 25; Talmon (n 36) 106.
40 *Deutsche Continental Gas Gesellschaft v Polish State* (1929) 5 ILR 11, 13.
41 Arbitration Commission of the Hague Conference on Yugoslavia ('Badinter Commission'), *Opinion No 1* (1993) 92 ILR 162, 165. Affirmed in *Opinion No 8* (1993) 92 ILR 199, 201.
42 Jessica Almqvist, 'The Politics of Recognition: Kosovo's Final Status' in Duncan French (ed), *Statehood and Self-Determination* (Cambridge University Press, 2013) 165, 170.
43 Crawford (n 11) 27.

Law Commission may have refrained from adopting any criteria, a relatively stable list exists. The 'best known formulation of the basic criteria for statehood'[44] is found in the 1934 Convention on the Rights and Duties of States (the Montevideo Convention).[45] The Montevideo Convention outlines four criteria an entity must meet to be regarded as a state: (1) a defined territory, (2) a permanent population, (3) a government, and (4) a capacity to enter into relations with other states.[46]

The list seems clear on its face but there are complications. First, many scholars consider the Montevideo Convention criteria under- and over-inclusive,[47] both enumerating elements not essential to statehood and failing to provide a complete definition. The fourth condition has come under the most scrutiny, with scholars remarking that capacity to enter into diplomatic relations is 'a consequence rather than a condition of statehood',[48] and one that varies with 'the status and situation of particular states'.[49] Others have noted that the competence to enter treaties is also not reserved only to states; international organisations can negotiate and sign treaties.

Second, the criteria themselves are malleable. As we explore in greater detail in the next section, a wide 'variety of entities with differing circumstances' fall within the definition.[50] For example, entities with a very small territorial footprint, like the Vatican City (0.49 square kilometres), Monaco (2.1 square kilometres) and Nauru (21 square kilometres) continue to be considered and treated as states. The same is true for some entities that possess no territory. Poland and Czechoslovakia, for instance, were both recognised by France in World War I despite not possessing any land.[51] Countries with miniscule resident populations are also internationally recognised. The Vatican City lays claim to 618

[44] Ibid 45.

[45] *Convention on the Rights and Duties of States*, 165 L.N.T.S. 19, art 1 (signed 26 December 1933 and entered into force 26 December 1934) ('*Montevideo Convention*').

[46] These criteria were adopted by the Badinter Commission, *Opinion No 1* (1993) 92 ILR 165.

[47] See, for example, Grant (n 14); Alison Eggers, 'When Is a State a State? The Case for Recognition of Somaliland' (2007) 30 *Boston College International and Comparative Law Review* 211; Bruno Coppieters, '"Statehood", "de facto Authorities", and "Occupation": Contested Concepts and the EU's Engagement in Its European Neighbourhood' (2018) 17 *Ethnopolitics* 343, 345.

[48] Ingrid Detter, *The International Legal Order* (Aldershot, 1994) 43.

[49] Crawford (n 11) 61.

[50] Ibid 197.

[51] Grant (n 14) 436.

citizens, of which only 246 live within its boundaries,[52] while Tuvalu and Nauru both possess fewer than 11,000 people.

The government criterion is also elastic. There is a strong presumption of state continuity in international law. This presumption operates to avoid the premature recognition of another state, which would be considered 'an unlawful interference in its domestic affairs'.[53] For this reason, the Badinter Commission explained that finding that a state has lost its international personality must be approached with the 'greatest caution'.[54] In practice, this means that a new state attempting to secede will need to demonstrate 'substantial independence, both formal and real' before it will be regarded as 'definitively created'.[55] Conversely, a state that no longer possesses an effective government is unlikely to immediately lose its status.[56] Indeed, the absence of any effective or even existent government for many years did not derail Somalia's status as a state for the purposes of international law.[57] At the same time, for more complicated geopolitical reasons some entities that easily satisfy the Montevideo Convention requirements, such as Taiwan,[58] are not considered to be states. There is simply no rule prescribing a minimum area of territory, size of population or effectiveness of government.[59] Statehood appears to be 'ultimately contingent upon claim and response'.[60]

Third, the criteria are passive rather than active. They set out elements that a state must possess, but 'do not prescribe specific rights, powers or

[52] Stato Della Città del Vaticano, 'Popolazione' (3 July 2018) www.vaticanstate.va/it/stato-governo/note-generali/popolazione.html.

[53] Jane McAdam, *Climate Change, Forced Migration, and International Law* (Oxford University Press, 2012) 134.

[54] Badinter Commission, *Opinion No 8* (1993) 92 ILR 199, 201.

[55] Crawford (n 11) 63.

[56] Guglielmo Verdirame, 'Sovereignty' in Jean D'Aspremont and Sahib Singh (eds), *Concepts for International Law: Contributions to Disciplinary Thought* (Edward Elgar, 2019) 827, 837.

[57] Dimitrios Lalos, 'Between Statehood and Somalia: Reflections of Somaliland Statehood' (2011) 10 *Washington University Global Studies Law Review* 789; Ken Menkhaus, 'Governance without Government in Somalia: Spoilers, State Building, and the Politics of Coping' (2007) 31(3) *International Security* 74.

[58] Nii Lante Wallace-Bruce, 'Taiwan and Somalia: International Legal Curiosities' (1997) 22 *Queen's Law Journal* 453.

[59] Crawford (n 11) 46, 52. See further Jorri Duursma, *Fragmentation and the International Relations of Micro-States: Self-Determination and Statehood* (Cambridge University Press, 1996); Jackson (n 10) 24.

[60] Duncan French, 'Introduction' in Duncan French (ed), *Statehood and Self-Determination: Reconciling Tradition and Modernity in International Law* (Cambridge University Press, 2013) 1, 2.

capacities'[61] that a state must be able to exercise in order to qualify as a state. This framing is intentional, as substantial variety in practice precludes definition along capability lines. After all, even if independence – what Crawford describes as 'the central criterion for statehood'[62] – is added, significant peculiarities must be countenanced. The rise of regional and global international organisations, for example, has limited the capacity of states to act in certain ways, while many microstates delegate powers to neighbours without risking loss of their status.[63]

Finally, although the criteria for statehood set out in the Montevideo Convention are 'essentially based on the principle of effectiveness',[64] statehood is more than merely effective governance. An entity must meet certain conditions of legality before it will be considered a state. In its *Advisory Opinion on Kosovo's Declaration of Independence*, for instance, the International Court of Justice confirmed that an entity will not be regarded as a state when its establishment is 'connected with the unlawful use of force or other egregious violations of norms of general international law, in particular those of a peremptory character (*jus cogens*)'.[65] Hence, despite the Turkish Republic of Northern Cyprus meeting the Montevideo Convention definition, it is not a state because it was formed as a result of the illegal use of force. Similarly, Southern Rhodesia's unilateral declaration of independence was never recognised as lawful because the territorial entity was established in violation of the right of self-determination.

These considerations remove the possibility of a straightforward definition of statehood. In fact, it is likely that no definitive account can be devised. For one, the centrality of states in the formation of rules of international law creates 'something of a logical impasse for international lawyers when they attempt to conceptualise how that same law might

[61] Crawford (n 11) 44–5.
[62] Ibid 62.
[63] Ibid 70; Zbigniew Dumienski, *Microstates as Modern Protected States: Towards a New Definition of Micro-Statehood* (The Centre for Small State Studies, 2014).
[64] Crawford (n 11) 97.
[65] *Accordance with International Law of the Unilateral Declaration of Independence in Respect of Kosovo (Advisory Opinion)* [2010] ICJ Rep 403, 437 [81]. See further *Legal Consequences of the Construction of a Wall in the Occupied Palestinian Territory (Advisory Opinion)* [2004] ICJ Rep 136, 171 [87]; International Law Commission, Draft Articles on the Responsibility of States for Internationally Wrongful Acts, UN Doc A/56/2001 (November 2001) art 41(2); Roland Portman, *International Legal Personality in International Law* (Cambridge University Press, 2010) 252.

regulate states' existence or demise'.[66] Second, in practice, the question only arises in 'borderline cases, where a new entity has emerged bearing some but not all characteristics of statehood'.[67] For this reason, it may be better to conceive of statehood as a spectrum, consisting of a variety of entities with more or less legitimate claims. In the following part, we explore the statehood spectrum with the aim of understanding where and how micronations may be placed.

2.2 The Statehood Spectrum

The Montevideo Convention reflects an understandable attempt to regulate the criteria of statehood and identify the primary subjects of international law with as much certainty as possible. As we have noted, however, notwithstanding the existence of a relatively clear set of conditions, determining whether an entity is or is not a state can be more difficult in practice. Statehood is not a binary yes or no; there are many shades of grey.

For our purposes, we can usefully conceive of statehood as a spectrum of entities with a strong claim to statehood through to those with only a weak claim. This is not to suggest that every territorial entity purporting to exercise political authority falls somewhere along this range. Some degree of effective governance, political, legal or historical legitimacy, and a claim for statehood is a prerequisite. In this part, we develop the statehood spectrum by examining the status of several state and state-like entities that satisfy this minimum condition.

2.2.1 Microstates

One entity firmly on the strong claim to statehood end of the spectrum is the microstate. The Montevideo Convention does not prescribe a minimum requirement as to territory or population, and a diverse cast of entities, 'exceptionally small in area, population and human and economic resources'[68] assert their status as states. In the nineteenth and twentieth centuries, many political scientists and international relations

[66] Matthew Craven and Rose Parfitt, 'Statehood, Self-Determination and Recognition' in Malcolm Evans (ed), *International Law* (Oxford University Press, 5th ed, 2018).

[67] Crawford (n 11) 40.

[68] United Nations Secretary-General, *Introduction to the Annual Report of the Secretary-General on the Work of the Organization, 16 June 1966–15 June 1967*, UN Doc A/6701/Add.1 (1967) 20 [163].

scholars considered that the very existence of extremely small states was precarious,[69] predicting that they 'will fade from international life', either swallowed whole by larger powers or compelled to integrate by virtue of their material handicaps.[70] Others considered these entities more akin to 'pseudo-states'[71] with 'pretensions that far outreached the capacities normally understood to be those of sovereign statehood'.[72]

The development of the international principle of self-determination as well as norms against violating the territorial integrity of states altered that expected landscape. In fact, in several (though certainly not all) cases, microstates have prospered and overcome their material disadvantages. Many microstates 'profit by selling or renting out their sovereign prerogatives',[73] including by selling stamps, souvenirs and memorabilia, and even citizenship,[74] diplomatic recognition[75] and positions in international organisations.[76] Some, like Luxembourg, Liechtenstein, Malta and the Bahamas, also 'serve as off-shore financial centres and tax havens, free ports, and flags-of-convenience'.[77] These nations may be small relative to their neighbours, but provided they possess formal and actual independence and exercise political authority over defined territory not lawfully claimed by another state, they meet international conditions for statehood.

Echoing earlier debates over the appropriate definition of a 'state', ascertaining precisely what a microstate is has proven challenging. 'Presumably', Zbigniew Dumieński notes, 'microstates are polities distinctive enough to merit being treated in separation from both "normal" and "small" states', but while everyone agrees that a microstate is a 'very

69 Niels Amstrup, 'The Perennial Problem of Small States: A Survey of Research Efforts' (1976) 11 *Cooperation and Conflict* 163, 163.

70 See, Thomas Grant, 'Between Diversity and Disorder: A Review of Jorri C. Duursma, Fragmentation and the International Relations of Micro-States: Self-Determination and Statehood' (1997) 12(4) *American University Journal of International Law and Policy* 629, 630.

71 David Vital, *The Inequality of States* (Clarendon Press, 1967) 7.

72 John Bartmann, 'Micro-States in the International System: The Challenge of Sovereignty' (PhD Thesis, The London School of Economics, 1997) 15.

73 JC Sharman, 'Sovereignty at the Extremes: Micro-States in World Polities' (2017) 65(3) *Political Studies* 559, 561.

74 Vikram Mansharamani, 'The $2 Billion Market for Passports', *Fortune Magazine* (2 April 2016) http://fortune.com/2016/04/02/passports-citizenship-investment/.

75 Kevin Stringer, 'Pacific Island Microstates: Pawns or Players in Pacific Rim Diplomacy?' (2006) 17(3) *Diplomacy and Statecraft* 547.

76 Abram Chayes and Antonia Handler Chayes, *The New Sovereignty: Compliance with International Regulatory Agreements* (Harvard University Press, 1995) 266.

77 Bartmann (n 72) 303.

small state', 'there is little consensus' over what constitutes 'small size and which states should be labelled as "small"'.[78] The problem is that there are many ways to measure size, including both quantitative measures such as 'population, geographical area, economic activity',[79] and military might,[80] and qualitative indicators such as relative power in international affairs.[81] While some scholars have proposed creating a composite index of these factors and identifying those on the lowest position of the scale as microstates,[82] others have criticised such an approach as 'too cumbersome and arbitrary'.[83] For this reason, a single variable is more commonly adopted, generally either territory or population.

Even this remains problematic. First, there is no agreement on territory or population thresholds beyond which a state is properly classified as a microstate. Although a population of 'one million inhabitants seems to be the most widely used cut-off point, the literature presents many alternative propositions ranging from 100,000 to 10 million'.[84] The World Bank's Small State Forum, for example, has adopted a population figure of 1.5 million for small states, and 200,000 for microstates.[85] Proposed thresholds can be incredibly specific: one scholar has nominated a limit of 2,928,000 inhabitants.[86] In view of such disagreement, any attempt to draw a clear line or threshold on territory or population is arbitrary. Second, the difficulty is amplified by the fact that states with similar territory or populations may otherwise differ radically. Both Singapore and Tonga, for example, possess around 730 square kilometres of territory, yet 'it is difficult to imagine more contrasting states when it comes to such matters as economic performance, military

[78] Dumieński (n 63) 3–4, 8.

[79] Edward Warrington, 'Lilliput Revisited' (1994) 16(1) *Asian Journal of Public Administration* 3, 4.

[80] Maurice East, 'Size and Foreign Policy Behavior: A Test of Two Models' (1973) 25 *World Politics* 556, 557.

[81] Matthias Maass, 'The Elusive Definition of the Small State' (2009) 46(1) *International Politics* 65, 72–3.

[82] See, for example, George Reid, *Impact of Very Small Size on the International Behaviour of Microstates* (Sage, 1975).

[83] Ueantabo Neemia, 'Smallness, Islandness and Foreign Policy Behaviour: Aspects of Island Microstates Foreign Policy Behaviour with Special Reference to Cook Islands and Kiribati' (PhD Thesis, University of Wollongong, 1995) 14.

[84] Dumieński (n 63) 11.

[85] The World Bank, 'The World Bank in Small States: Overview' www.worldbank.org/en/country/smallstates/overview.

[86] Charles Taylor, 'Statistical Typology of Micro-States and Territories' (1969) 8(3) *Social Science Information* 101, 109.

strength and international standing'.[87] Similarly, Qatar and Namibia have a similar population, but Namibia is seventy-one times the size of the Gulf State.

Reflecting on these challenges, Dumieński proposes a definition of microstates that focuses on 'their qualitative political uniqueness'.[88] He defines microstates as 'modern protected states', that is, 'sovereign states that have been able to unilaterally depute certain attributes of sovereignty to larger powers in exchange for benign protection of their political and economic viability against their geographic or demographic constraints'.[89] This definition accords with Jorri Duursma's study on small European states, and is valuable as it emphasizes microstates' independence and sovereign status – a key condition of statehood – as well as their relations with larger neighbours. Critical to this definition is the fact that, by virtue of their small size, microstates delegate some areas of governmental competence, often in the areas of defence and international relations, to larger states. Significantly, such delegation is not inconsistent with formal and actual independence. Otherwise, the status of microstates as 'states' would be at risk.

Several examples help elucidate this condition. The Principality of Andorra is a 468-square-kilometre landlocked state situated in the eastern Pyrenees between France and Spain.[90] Believed to have been established by King Charlemagne in 795 CE as a buffer region to protect against a Moorish invasion of France, Andorra was initially ruled by the Count of Urgell. Over the following several centuries, ownership of the valleys was passed between various hands, including the Roman Catholic Bishop of Urgell, the Lord of Caboet and the Count of Foix. In 1278, following a dispute between the Count of Foix and the Bishop of Urgell, the two parties agreed to govern the territory jointly. The practice of shared sovereignty has continued since, despite dramatic changes in personal rule. In 1590, the then Count of Foix acceded to the French throne as Henry IV, and in 1607 the King incorporated his personal domain in the French Crown. From then, the head of the French state (along with the Bishop of Urgell) has simultaneously served in his or her personal capacity as co-Prince of Andorra.

For much of the twentieth century, this peculiar arrangement was at the centre of debate over whether Andorra was a state. Doubts were

[87] Dumieński (n 63) 10.
[88] Ibid 22.
[89] Ibid.
[90] Duursma (n 59) 317–20.

finally displaced in 1993 when Andorra approved a new constitution that clarified its legal and political structure and signed the *Treaty of Vicinage* with France and Spain, which narrowed and defined the scope and extent of external interference.[91] Some complications persist. The Treaty requires that Andorra act consistently with the 'fundamental interests' of France and Spain,[92] while those two states and the Holy See maintain some degree of influence in Andorra through the office of the co-Princes. Nonetheless, putting any doubt to rest, Andorra was admitted to the United Nations as a full member in 1993.[93]

Not all microstates are members of the United Nations. The Cook Islands is a self-governing entity in the South Pacific Ocean with an unusual political status. Initially settled by Polynesian societies around 1000 CE, the fifteen islands comprising about 236 square kilometres became a British protectorate in 1888, were annexed by the United Kingdom in 1900 and administratively passed to New Zealand (then a British colony) in 1901.[94] The Cook Islands remained a New Zealand dependency until 1965, when it became a self-governing territory in 'free association' with New Zealand.[95] This means that while the Cook Islands has full autonomy over its internal affairs, New Zealand is responsible for its defence and may support and assist the Cook Islands to engage in external affairs.[96] Unusually, there is no Cook Island citizenship – all inhabitants are New Zealand citizens.[97]

This legal relationship has left the Cook Islands' international legal status somewhat unclear. In 2005, for instance, the New Zealand Ministry of Foreign Affairs and Trade issued a memo declaring that 'the Cook

[91] Crawford (n 11) 76 n 182; Duursma (n 59) 338–48.

[92] *Treaty of Vicinage*, 1993, art 4. Republished in (1994) 98 *Revue Générale de Droit International Public* 525.

[93] United Nations General Assembly, *Admission of the Principality of Andorra to Membership of the United Nations*, UN Doc A/RES/47/232 (28 July 1993).

[94] *New Zealand Gazette* (13 June 1901) 1307.

[95] *Cook Islands Constitution Act 1964* (NZ); *Cook Islands Constitution Amendment Act 1965* (NZ). For discussion see Caroline McDonald, 'An Exemplary Leader?: New Zealand and Decolonization of the Cook Islands and Niue' (2020) 55(3) *The Journal of Pacific History* 394; Alison Quentin-Baxter, 'The New Zealand Model of Free Association: What Does It Mean for New Zealand?' (2008) 38 *Victoria University of Wellington Law Review* 607.

[96] *Cook Islands Constitution Act 1964* (NZ) s 5. For the evolution of these arrangements see Alison Quentin-Baxter, 'Pacific States and Territories: Cook Islands' in Robert Smellie (ed), *The Laws of New Zealand* (LexisNexis, 2016) [29].

[97] For some of the complications that can arise see discussion in Elisabeth Perham, 'Citizenship Laws in the Realm of New Zealand' (2011) 9 *New Zealand Yearbook of International Law* 219.

Islands has developed a separate international identity from that of New Zealand' but cautioning that it did not consider that 'the Cook Islands is, in constitutional terms, an independent sovereign state'.[98] Crawford has also noted in passing that the Cook Islands is not a state but has some degree of 'separate international status'.[99] On the other hand, New Zealand courts have found that 'the Cook Islands is a fully sovereign independent state and that the special relationship between the Cook Islands and New Zealand does not affect this issue'.[100] The Cook Islands has been admitted to a range of United Nations agencies, including the World Health Organization; membership of which is open to 'all States'.[101] It also maintains diplomatic relations with fifty-two states, and the European Union, and is a party to several international treaties. Although not a United Nations member – New Zealand does not support membership – the Cook Islands is characterised as a 'non-member state',[102] and for all intents and purposes appears to be a state.[103]

Microstates, like Andorra and the Cook Islands, are members of many international organisations, but they have not always been welcomed by larger states. In 1920, San Marino, Monaco and Liechtenstein were all denied membership in the League of Nations,[104] though only Liechtenstein's request was considered in detail. The sub-committee charged with examining the request recommended against membership, concluding that the Principality 'could not discharge all the international obligations which would be imposed on her by the Covenant'.[105] Officially this was because Liechtenstein had 'chosen to depute to others

[98] New Zealand Ministry of Foreign Affairs and Trade, Legal Division, 'Cook Islands: Constitutional Status and International Personality' (May 2005).

[99] Crawford (n 11) 492. Cf. Stephen Eliot Smith, 'Uncharted Waters: Has the Cook Islands Become Eligible for Membership in the United Nations?' (2010) 8 *New Zealand Journal of Public and International Law* 169.

[100] *Controller and Auditor-General v Sir Ronald Davison* [1996] 2 NZLR 278, 288 (CA); Affirmed by the Judicial Committee of the Privy Council in *Brannigan v Sir Ronald Davison* [1997] 1 NZLR 140, 144 (PC); [1997] AC 238, 247.

[101] *Constitution of the World Health Organization* (opened for signature 22 July 1946, entered into force 7April 1948) art 3.

[102] United Nations, *Repertory of Practice of United Nations Organs* (Supplement No 8, Volume VI, 1989–1994) 10 [10]–[11].

[103] See further Quentin-Baxter (n 96); Alison Quentin-Baxter and Janet McLean, *This Realm of New Zealand: The Sovereign, the Governor-General, the Crown* (Auckland University Press, 2017) 111.

[104] Duursma (n 59) 133; Crawford (n 11) 184.

[105] Cited in Duursma (n 59) 171; Michael Gunter, 'Liechtenstein and the League of Nations: A Precedent for the United Nation's Ministate Problem?' (1974) 68 *American Journal of International Law* 496, 498.

some of the attributes of sovereignty' and had no army.[106] However, Duursma and Michael Gunter argue that the 'real reason[]' was 'its smallness'; the League believed it 'unacceptable to grant Liechtenstein, or any other Micro-State, the same right to vote, including a veto right when unanimity was required, as larger states'.[107] Instead, suggestions were raised that the Charter of the League of Nations should be amended to provide for a second tier of membership, with limited or no voting rights. No microstate announced their intention to apply for such an alternative membership and no amendment to the Charter was forthcoming.

The same concern reappeared in the United Nations during the era of decolonisation in the late 1960s and early 1970s. In 1964, David Wainhouse argued that 'to admit all the bits and pieces of former empires as independent states would not only debase the coinage of membership, but would surely be more than the UN structure could bear'.[108] Calculations at the time suggested that if every potential microstate of fewer than 300,000 inhabitants were admitted, they would constitute a two-thirds majority in the General Assembly, cover 10 per cent of the budget and represent 4 per cent of the world's total population.[109] For this reason, initially there was wide consensus against admitting such states as full members. United Nations Secretary-General U Thant proposed providing microstates with observer status,[110] while the United States and the United Kingdom offered alternative options that would also deny voting rights.[111] Only Nepal spoke in favour of full membership, emphasising 'the principle of universality' of the United Nations and 'the principle of the sovereign equality of states'.[112] Ultimately, the

[106] Cited in Duursma (n 59) 171; Gunter (n 105) 498.

[107] Duursma (n 59) 173–174; Gunter (n 105) 499.

[108] David Wainhouse, *Remnants of Empire: The United Nations and the End of Colonialism* (Council of Foreign Relations, 1964) 134.

[109] Dieter Ehrhardt, 'Mikrostaaten als UN-Mitglieder? Zum Strukturproblem der Weltorganisation' (1970) 4(70) *Vereinte Nationen* 111; William Harris, 'Microstates in the United Nations: A Broader Purpose' (1970) 9(1) *Columbia Journal of Transnational Law* 23, 25; Duursma (n 59) 135.

[110] United Nations Secretary-General (n 68) 20 [164].

[111] United Nations Security Council, 'Interim Report to the Security Council of the Committee of Experts Established by the Security Council at Its 1506th Meeting', UN Doc S/9836 (15 June 1970) Annex I and Annex II. See further a range of options discussed in: United Nations Institute for Training and Research, *Status and Problems of Very Small States and Territories* (1969) 155–6; Harris (n 109) 41–50.

[112] United Nations Security Council Official Records, 1506th meeting, UN Doc S/PV.1506 (29 August 1969) 2 [15]–[16].

various proposals foundered on the inability to develop a simple definition of a microstate.[113] The issue itself eventually dissipated when it became clear that the expected explosion in United Nations membership would not occur; many potential microstates opted instead to integrate with their larger neighbours.

Today, many – though not all – microstates are members of the United Nations. In the 1990s, Liechtenstein, Micronesia, the Marshall Islands, San Marino, Monaco, Andorra, Palau, Kiribati, Nauru and Tonga obtained full membership. In 2000, they were joined by Tuvalu. United Nations membership is significant. It not only provides formal recognition of a microstate's status as a sovereign state, but also strengthens their sovereignty by offering enhanced judicial and political protection against external interference in their domestic affairs.[114] Membership also allows microstates to trade on their sovereign prerogatives. JC Sharman notes that Nauru received USD 50 million in development aid and soft loans from Russia after formally recognising the breakaway Caucasus states of Abkhazia and South Ossetia,[115] while many Pacific microstates have sold passports and other forms of economic citizenship to wealthy individuals.[116] These examples show how microstates can commodify their sovereign privileges to compensate for their limited economic and human resources. Provided they maintain formal and actual independence, they are free to do so.

2.2.2 'Disappearing' States

The existence of microstates demonstrates that 'infinitesimal smallness' is not a reason to deny self-determination to a population.[117] Despite their very small size, all microstates exercise political authority over a defined portion of territory and a resident population; but must a state possess these two features? Can a state exist without territory or without a population? Although this question may appear fantastical, the effects of climate change force a closer consideration.

[113] Duursma (n 59) 138.

[114] Ibid 142.

[115] Sharman (n 73) 571.

[116] Anthony van Fossen, 'Citizenship for Sale: Passports of Convenience from Pacific Island Tax Havens' (2007) 45(2) *Commonwealth & Comparative Politics* 138.

[117] Thomas Franck and Paul Hoffman, 'The Right of Self-Determination in Very Small Places' (1976) 8 *New York University Journal of International Law and Politics* 331, 383.

Climate change is expected to challenge the viability, and perhaps even existence, of many states. Low-lying islands are at particular risk. The Intergovernmental Panel on Climate Change predicts that global mean sea levels will likely rise between 29 and 110 centimetres by the end of the century, while increasing ocean acidification will affect fisheries, aquaculture and tourism, placing further pressure on the continuing habitability of such islands.[118] For many years, leaders of island nations have sought to raise international awareness of these challenges. In 2009, Pacific Island states sponsored a United Nations General Assembly Resolution on 'Climate Change and its Possible Security Implications',[119] and drew attention to the possibility that without concerted climate action, some nations 'will be submerged'.[120] The 'image of an island disappearing beneath the rising sea' is 'frightening', but, as Jane McAdam has noted, these islands are more likely to become uninhabitable due to 'diminished water supplies long before they physically disappear'.[121] In other words, they are more likely to lose their population before their territory.

The prospect of a state becoming uninhabitable raises difficult political and legal questions over state continuity and succession.[122] Can relocated communities be legally and politically reconstituted as self-governing entities?[123] Understandably, potentially affected states have raised concerns that 'cross-border relocation may negatively impact on nationhood, control over land and sea territory, sovereignty, culture and livelihoods'.[124] Apprehension does not stop planning. In 2009, the Maldives raised the possibility of buying land in Sri Lanka or India in anticipation of future need, while in 2014, Kiribati purchased around 20 square kilometres of land on a Fijian island about 2,000 kilometres away as a food security measure.[125]

118 See Intergovernmental Panel on Climate Change, *Special Report on the Ocean and Cryosphere in a Changing Environment: Summary for Policymakers* (2019).

119 United Nations General Assembly Resolution 63/281, UN Doc A/RES/63/281 (11 June 2009).

120 United Nations General Assembly, 63rd Sess, 11th pln mtg, UN Doc A/63/PV.11 (26 September 2009) 6 (Republic of Vanuatu).

121 McAdam (n 53) 123–4.

122 Jenny Grote Stoutenberg, *Disappearing Island States in International Law* (Brill Nijhoff, 2015) ch 4.

123 See, for example, John Campbell, 'Climate Change Migration in the Pacific' (2014) 26(1) *The Contemporary Pacific* 1; McAdam (n 53).

124 Nansen Initiative, Human Mobility, Natural Disasters and Climate Change in the Pacific (Outcome Report, 21–24 May 2013) 7.

125 Laurence Caramel, 'Besieged by the Rising Tides of Climate Change, Kiribati Buys Land in Fiji', *The Guardian* (1 July 2014) www.theguardian.com/environment/2014/jul/01/kiribati-climate-change-fiji-vanua-levu.

Relocation has also been considered at the international level. The Cancun Adaptation Framework, adopted as part of the 2010 United Nations Climate Change Conference, invites states to improve action on adaptation by undertaking 'measures to enhance understanding, coordination and cooperation with regard to climate change induced displacement migration and planned relocation, where appropriate, at national, regional and international levels'.[126]

Territory is essential for state creation, but it does not appear to be necessary for the continued existence of a state. Reflecting the strong presumption of state continuity, a state may persist even though it does not exercise any control over its de jure territory, perhaps as a result of belligerent occupation or the illegal use of force. Hence, Poland and Czechoslovakia were both recognised by France in World War I despite not holding any land.[127] Similarly, the Baltic states of Estonia, Latvia and Lithuania maintained a government-in-exile or diplomatic legation that was formally recognised as a legal subject under international law during German and Soviet occupation.[128] Although a government-in-exile must follow the law of the host state, it continues to maintain and exercise state functions (to the extent permitted by the host). Such functions have included 'treaty-making, diplomatic relations, immunity, privileges, and jurisdiction over nationals'.[129]

The existence of governments-in-exile suggests that there are no legal impediments to a host state inviting the people of another state to exercise state-like functions on its territory. Whether the concept is feasible in the case of climate change induced displacement is another question. Governments-in-exile are generally considered to be both 'temporary and exceptional',[130] while the prospect of permanently relocating entire communities is neither. Close attention will also need

126 United Nations Framework Convention on Climate Change, *Conference of the Parties: Decisions Adopted by the Conference of Parties*, 'Decision 1/CP.16 – The Cancun Agreements: Outcome of the Work of the Ad Hoc Working Group on Long-Term Cooperative Action under the Convention', UN Doc FCCC/CP/2010/7/Add.1 (15 March 2011) 14(f).

127 Grant (n 14) 436.

128 Peter van Elsuwege, 'State Continuity and Its Consequences: The Case of the Baltic States' (2003) 16 *Leiden Journal of International Law* 377.

129 Stefan Talmon, *Recognition of Governments in International Law: With Particular Reference to Governments in Exile* (Oxford University Press, 1998) 15. In the context of climate change induced displacement see: Susin Park, 'Climate Change and the Risk of Statelessness: The Situation of Low-Lying Island States' (UNHCR Legal and Protection Policy Research Series, PPLA/2011/04, May 2011) 7.

130 McAdam (n 53) 130.

to be paid to the precise legal agreement reached between the two states. The key to statehood is not territory per se but the 'ability to rightfully claim the territory as a domain of exclusive authority'.[131] It is not sufficient that a community exercises political authority over lands legally belonging to another state; sovereignty over those lands must be transferred.

Climate change has raised the potential for significant international relocation, but these issues are not novel. The history of cross-border relocations is much longer. As McAdam notes:

> In the 1930s and 40s, there were three cross-border relocations in the Pacific. Each occurred for a different reason – to facilitate phosphate mining (Banaba/Rabi), to safeguard against future overcrowding on the home island (Vaitupu/Kioa) and to overcome resource scarcity on account of poor environmental conditions (Phoenix Islands/British Solomon Islands Protectorate).[132]

Consider the Banaban relocation. In 1945, almost the entire Banaban community of Ocean Island, in present-day Kiribati, was relocated to Rabi Island in Fiji – over 2,000 kilometres away. Rabi Island was uninhabited, offering both advantages and disadvantages for the Banabans. No proper housing or bustling towns existed (as the Banabans had been led to believe), leaving them to shelter in temporary canvas tents and causing immediate privation. However, without the need to integrate within a pre-existing community, innovative institutional arrangements to encourage their permanent resettlement could be developed. Indeed, the Banabans on Rabi Island were granted considerable local self-rule within Fiji and have retained distinctive rights of 'entry, residence, and parliamentary representation in Kiribati, even if they were not citizens of that country'.[133]

131 Craven and Parfitt (n 66). Crawford (n 11) 56, 254. See also Vaughan Lowe, *International Law* (Oxford University Press, 2007) 138.

132 Jane McAdam, 'Relocation and Resettlement from Colonisation to Climate Change: The Perennial Solution to "Danger Zones"' (2015) 3(1) *London Review of International Law* 93, 97.

133 Jane McAdam, '"Under Two Jurisdictions": Immigration, Citizenship, and Self-Governance in Cross-Border Community Relocations' (2016) 34(2) *Law and History Review* 281. See also Jane McAdam, 'Self-Determination and Self-Governance for Communities Relocated across International Borders: The Quest for Banaban Independence' (2017) 24 *International Journal on Minority and Group Rights* 428; Jane McAdam, 'Historical Cross-Border Relocations in the Pacific: Lessons for Planned Relocations in the Context of Climate Change' (2014) 49(3) *The Journal of Pacific History* 301.

Other proposals to relocate or resettle entire communities have not been carried out. In the 1950s and 1960s, several efforts to relocate the Nauruan community to an island off the coast of Australia were unsuccessful.[134] Years of phosphate mining had caused significant environmental degradation to the 21-square-kilometre island – then designated a United Nations Trust Territory administered by Australia. The damage was so severe that successive visiting UN Missions to Nauru had regarded the island as likely to become uninhabitable in the near future. As the costs of rehabilitation were considered prohibitive, resettlement was deemed the best option. Ultimately, despite the identification of several promising sites off the coast of Queensland, resettlement did not occur. While the Nauruans proposed 'the creation of a sovereign Nauruan nation governed by Nauruans in their own interest but related to Australia by a treaty of friendship' and would accept Australian authority in the areas of external affairs, defence, civil aviation and quarantine,[135] Australia was never willing to transfer sovereignty to a 'new Nauru'. Instead, Australia suggested conferring the community with powers akin to local government and envisaged the eventual assimilation of the Nauruans into Australian society. Nauruan agitation for greater autonomy finally culminated in their independence in 1968.[136]

These cases were contemplated, and in the case of the Banabans, completed, during the colonial period. Resettlement was simpler in this era because international borders had not calcified; colonial authorities could relocate entire communities within their colonial possessions without needing to deal with significant legal constraints nor genuinely consider the wishes of the affected people.[137] As the Nauruan example demonstrates, potential host states may today be unwilling to consider ceding sovereign authority over defined portions of their territory to

[134] See Jane McAdam, 'The High Price of Resettlement: The Proposed Environmental Relocation of Nauru to Australia' (2017) 48(1) *Australian Geographer* 7; Gil Marvel Tabucanon and Brian Opeskin, 'The Resettlement of Nauruans in Australia: An Early Case of Failed Environmental Migration' (2011) 46(3) *The Journal of Pacific History* 337; Merze Tate, 'Nauru, Phosphate, and the Nauruans' (1968) 14(2) *Australian Journal of Politics and History* 177.

[135] United Nations General Assembly, *Report of the Trusteeship Council*, UN GAOR, 17th sess, 20 July 1961 – 20 July 1962, UN Doc. A/5204 (Supp) 35.

[136] See, generally, Cait Storr, *International Status in the Shadow of Empire: Nauru and the Histories of International Law* (Cambridge University Press, 2020) ch 5.

[137] John Campbell, 'Climate-Induced Community Relocation in the Pacific: The Meaning and Importance of Land' in Jane McAdam (ed), *Climate Change and Displacement: Multidisciplinary Perspectives* (Hart, 2010) 57, 77.

accommodate affected island nations – if relocation is even what the affected community desires.[138]

Alternative options exist. Drawing on her fieldwork in Kiribati and Tuvalu, McAdam suggests that island states may be more interested in maintaining their community, identity, and cultural and social traditions than the European construct of statehood.[139] If this is the case, creative institutional solutions can be considered, including the prospect of 'self-governance in free association with another state',[140] like the Cook Islands discussed earlier in the chapter. The island nation of Niue is also a self-governing community in free association with New Zealand. Unlike the Cook Islands, it 'has resisted being treated like an independent state',[141] suggesting that a degree of flexibility is available for affected communities and potential host states to develop models that meet the desires of both parties. These entities would no longer be states for the purposes of international law, but they could still possess some degree of international personality.

2.2.3 Entities with Limited or No Recognition

International law does not impose a duty on states to recognise other entities as states.[142] In practice, recognition is often withheld for a variety of reasons, including political protest and/or concerns over the legality of an entity's creation. In either case, non-recognition has no legal consequences. A state does not become a non-state purely because it is not recognised as such by another country, and a non-state does not become a state simply because it is recognised as such by a few or more nations. Nevertheless, in the absence of widespread or general recognition, questions may be raised over both the capacity of an entity to exercise state functions, and even its status as a state.

In many cases, a state will not recognise another country if both entities claim the same territory. For instance, the Democratic People's Republic of Korea (North Korea) and the Republic of Korea (South Korea) consider themselves to be the sole legitimate sovereign of the entire Korean landmass. Although both are members of the United

138 McAdam (n 53) 143–60.
139 Ibid 154.
140 Ibid.
141 Ibid. See also Alison Quentin-Baxter, 'Niue's Relationship of Free Association with New Zealand' (1999) 30 *Victoria University of Wellington Law Review* 583, 593.
142 Badinter Commission, *Opinion No 10* (1993) 92 ILR 206, 208.

Nations and maintain irregular informal diplomatic relations with each other, neither formally recognises the other as a state. Nonetheless, notwithstanding mutual non-recognition the legal status of North and South Korea as states is clear; membership of the United Nations is open only to states.

The situation is more complex for entities with limited or no recognition that are also not members of the United Nations. These political communities are sometimes described as proto or 'de facto' states, because although they may control territory and undertake substantial governance functions, they are not recognised as a legitimate member of the international community. As Scott Pegg explains, these entities

> feature long-term, effective, and popularly-supported organized political leaderships that provide governmental services to a given population in a defined territorial area. They seek international recognition and view themselves as capable of meeting the obligations of sovereign statehood. They are, however, unable to secure widespread juridical recognition and therefore function outside the boundaries of international legitimacy.[143]

Consider the Sahrawi Arab Democratic Republic (SADR).[144] The SADR has claimed sovereignty over the former Spanish colony of Western Sahara since its 1976 declaration of independence, but it controls only around 20–25 per cent of the territory. The remainder of its claimed territory is administered by the neighbouring Kingdom of Morocco, which it considers its Southern Provinces. The political status of the territory is complicated. In its 1975 Advisory Opinion, the International Court of Justice held that decolonisation of Western Sahara should follow the 'free and genuine expression of the will of the peoples of the Territory'.[145] Reflecting this judgment, the United Nations General Assembly issued a resolution in 1979 deploring Moroccan occupation and recognising the political movement behind the SADR as the lawful representatives of Western Sahara.[146]

143 Scott Pegg, *International Society and the De Facto State* (Routledge, 1998) 4.

144 See generally Anthony Pazzanita, 'Legal Aspects of Membership in the Organization of African Unity: The Case of Western Sahara' (1985) 17(1) *Case Western Reserve Journal of International Law* 123; Sidi Omar, 'The Right to Self-Determination and the Indigenous People of Western Sahara' (2008) 21(1) *Cambridge Review of International Affairs* 41.

145 *Western Sahara* (n 3) 68 [162].

146 United Nations General Assembly Resolution 34/37, UN Doc A/RES/34/37 (21 November 1979) [5].

Yet international recognition is mixed. The SADR is a full member of the African Union and has been recognised by at least eighty-five states – though forty-four of these have since withdrawn or frozen their recognition for various reasons (a mechanism of no legal force but nonetheless politically significant). In contrast, while Morocco's claim is supported by the Arab League, only one United Nations member state has ever officially recognised Moroccan sovereignty over the territory. That one country is the United States. In December 2020, during the lame duck period following Donald Trump's electoral loss but before Joe Biden's inauguration, Trump announced that the United States would recognise Morocco's claim 'over the entire Western Sahara territory'.[147] At the time of writing, political pressure is building on the Biden administration to reverse this move.[148] In view of these complexities, the SADR might be best described as a partially recognised state with de facto control of only a small portion of its claimed territory.

The status of the Republic of Somaliland also raises difficult questions. The Republic is a semi-autonomous region of Somalia that declared its independence in 1991, claiming to be the successor of the State of Somaliland.[149] The State of Somaliland was the name assumed by the former British protectorate upon independence from the United Kingdom on 26 June 1960. It lasted only five days, joining with the Italian-administered Trust Territory of Somaliland to form the Federal Republic of Somalia on 1 July 1960. Despite arguably meeting the international law conditions for statehood, the Republic of Somaliland is not recognised by any other state because recognition would violate the territorial integrity of the Federal Republic of Somalia – a state that has operated without a functional government for many years.[150]

[147] United States Executive Office of the President, *Recognizing the Sovereignty of the Kingdom of Morocco Over the Western Sahara* (15 December 2020) www.federalregister.gov/documents/2020/12/15/2020-27738/recognizing-the-sovereignty-of-the-kingdom-of-morocco-over-the-western-sahara.

[148] Barak Ravid, 'Biden in No Rush to Reverse Trump's Move on Western Sahara', *Axios* (24 February 2021) www.axios.com/biden-western-sahara-morocco-sovereignty-trump-43dfdc5d-863a-49a2-83f1-600ac927c134.html.

[149] Alison Eggers, 'When Is a State a State? The Case for Recognition of Somaliland' (2007) 30 *Boston College International and Comparative Law Review* 211, 213.

[150] Lalos (n 57); Benjamin Farley, 'Calling a State a State: Somaliland and International Recognition' (2010) 24 *Emory International Law Review* 777. Interestingly, Somaliland established formal diplomatic relations with the Republic of Liberland, a micronation located on the Danube River: 'Somaliland: Liberland States Mutual Recognition Process with Government in Hargeisa', *Somaliland Sun* (12 October 2017) https://web

The Republic of China (commonly known as Taiwan) also occupies the liminal space between state and non-state. As Crawford has explained, the ROC 'appears to comply in all respects with the criteria for statehood ... but is universally agreed not to be a separate state'.[151] This is a consequence of the complex political relationship between the ROC and the People's Republic of China (PRC). The ROC is the de facto government of Taiwan, but the PRC asserts that it is the sole legitimate government of all China – including Taiwan. In 1971, the United Nations General Assembly appeared to have accepted this position, voting to eject representatives of Taiwan from the United Nations and admitting the PRC as 'the only legitimate representative of China to the United Nations'.[152] However, complications remain. Under its 'One-China' policy, the PRC refuses to maintain diplomatic relations with any state that formally recognises Taiwan. Owing to the PRC's political, economic and military strength, many states have broken off formal diplomatic relations with Taiwan over the years – in September 2019, for instance, the Solomon Islands and Kiribati cut ties with the ROC in favour of the PRC.[153] Today, only fourteen states and the Holy See recognise Taiwan. Nonetheless, many states that formally recognise the PRC maintain unofficial consular links with Taiwan.

Questions exist over the international legal status of the entities discussed earlier largely because of political factors. In other cases, non-recognition may be a consequence of the illegal creation of a territorial entity. Under customary international law, an entity established in violation of general principles of international law is not considered a state, irrespective of its capacity to meet the Montevideo Convention criteria or its political independence.[154] In the words of Christian Hillgruber, these entities' claim to statehood are defeated by an 'error at birth'.[155]

This was the situation that faced the white minority government of Rhodesia from the mid-1960s. In 1960, amidst mounting nationalistic

.archive.org/web/20180308232441/http://www.somalilandsun.com/2017/10/12/somaliland-liberland-starts-mutual-recognition-process-with-government-in-hargeisa/.

151 Crawford (n 11) 198. See further Wallace-Bruce (n 58).

152 United Nations General Assembly Resolution 2758, UN Doc A/RES/2758 (25 October 1971).

153 Kate Lyons, 'Taiwan Loses Second Ally in a Week as Kiribati Switches to China', *The Guardian* (20 September 2019) www.theguardian.com/world/2019/sep/20/taiwan-loses-second-ally-in-a-week-as-kiribati-switches-to-china.

154 See above (n 65).

155 Christian Hilgruber, *Die Aufnahme neuer Staaten in die Völkerrechtsgemeinschaft* (Peter Lang GmbH, 1998) 601. Cited in Crawford (n 11) 130.

and democratic pressure for decolonisation across the continent, the United Kingdom announced that it would no longer prevent its African colonies from transitioning to independence – provided that the colony implemented majority rule. The Rhodesian government rejected this condition, and in 1965 issued a unilateral declaration of independence, seeking to form an Apartheid state.[156] Denounced by the United Nations Security Council as an 'illegal racist minority regime',[157] no state formally recognised Rhodesia during its existence, though South Africa and Portugal maintained consular relations.[158] Following democratic elections, the new Republic of Zimbabwe was granted independence from the United Kingdom in 1980 and recognition quickly ensued.

Rhodesia was never a state. Many other entities with de facto control of territory are also not considered states because of concerns over the legality of their creation. The Republics of South Ossetia and Abkhazia, for instance, declared their independence from Georgia in 1991 and 1999. Since then neither has gained widespread international recognition; both are recognised only by Russia, Venezuela, Nicaragua, Nauru and Syria. For its part, Georgia considers both entities to be integral parts of its own territory, albeit currently under Russian military occupation. The United Nations Security Council agrees, having called on all member states to commit to the 'sovereignty, independence and territorial integrity of Georgia within its internationally recognised borders'.[159]

These two Caucasus republics are often characterised as proto-states. While they exercise de facto control over a specific region, they lack institutional cohesion and are not recognised as states by the international community because of concerns over the legality of their creation and the fact that recognition would violate the territorial sovereignty of another state, in this case Georgia. Despite limited recognition, proto-states can engage in considerable state-like activity; they may conduct diplomatic relations with allied regimes, provide limited

[156] See Robert Good, *U.D.I: The International Politics of the Rhodesian Rebellion* (Princeton University Press, 1973). Jackson (n 10) 107–8. See also Isaak Dore, 'Recognition of Rhodesia and Traditional International Law: Some Conceptual Problems' (1980) 13 *Vanderbilt Journal of Transnational Law* 25, 31.

[157] United Nations Security Council Resolution 216, UN Doc S/RES/216 (12 November 1965) [2].

[158] Portugal withdrew its consulate following its 1974 Carnation revolution which overthrew the authoritarian government.

[159] United Nations Security Council Resolution 1808, UN Doc S/RES/1808 (15 April 2008) [1].

social services and engage in external trade.[160] Many such proto-states exist across the globe. Some emerge in the aftermath of internecine conflict, as ethnic or culturally distinct groups seize territory and assume the role of a de facto government. Secessionist or insurgent proto-states of varying legality include the Donetsk People's Republic in Ukraine, Dar al-Kuti in the Central African Republic and perhaps even the Islamic State of Iraq and the Levant.[161]

Other proto-states are administrative regions within a sovereign state that comprise distinct social, ethnic or cultural groups. Examples of this class of proto-states include Scotland and Wales in the United Kingdom, Quebec in Canada, Bougainville in Papua New Guinea and Guam in the United States. As this collection suggests, proto-states generally share a collective sense of national identity and have established some institutional state apparatus. Provided that they follow the proper legal path, they can make the transition to full statehood. This was the story of Singapore, which was a constituent state of Malaysia between 1963 and 1965. Following the successful 2019 referendum on independence,[162] it may also be Bougainville's path. Whether Catalonia or Iraqi Kurdistan will ever be able to make this transition is unclear.

Many other state-like entities have been established with questionable legality. Another example is the Turkish Republic of Northern Cyprus.[163] In 1960, Cyprus attained its independence from the United Kingdom. Ethnic divisions between Greek Cypriots and Turkish Cypriots led to a complex constitutional arrangement whereby public offices and government positions were allocated by ethnic quotas. Among other elements, the President was elected by Greek Cypriots, while the Vice-President was elected separately by Turkish Cypriots, though he or she enjoyed a veto

160 On how Abkhazians respond to the complicated status of their homeland see: Kieran Pender, 'Letter from Abkhazia: A Former Jewel in the Soviet Crown Hoping to Sparkle Once More', *The Calvert Journal* (12 October 2017) www.calvertjournal.com/features/show/9055/letter-from-abkhazia-former-jewel-soviet-crown-tourism-stalin.

161 See Anicée Van Engeland, 'Statehood, Proto States and International Law: New Challenges, Looking at the Case of ISIS' in James Crawford, Abdul Koroma, Said Mahmoudi and Alain Pellet (eds), *The International Legal Order: Current Needs and Possible Responses – Essays in Honour of Djamchid Momatz* (Brill, 2017) 75.

162 Kate Lyons, 'Bougainville Referendum: Region Votes Overwhelmingly for Independence from Papua New Guinea', *The Guardian* (11 December 2019) www.theguardian.com/world/2019/dec/11/bougainville-referendum-region-votes-overwhelmingly-for-independence-from-papua-new-guinea.

163 Tozun Bahcheli, 'Under Turkey's Wings: The Turkish Republic of Northern Cyprus, the Struggle for International Acceptance' in Tozun Bahcheli, Barry Bartmann and Henry Srebnik (eds), *De Facto States: The Quest for Sovereignty* (Routledge, 2004) 164.

power over legislation and policy passed by the legislature and executive. Unsurprisingly this model caused extreme difficulties and provoked inter-communal tensions and violence. Pressure soon increased. In 1967, the democratically elected Greek government was overthrown by a military junta intent on unifying Cyprus and Greece. In 1974, the junta launched a coup d'état in Cyprus, replacing Cypriot President Makarios III with pro-union nationalist Nikos Sampson. Five days later Turkey invaded.

Turkey sought to justify its actions under international law.[164] The 1960 Treaty of Guarantee, signed by Cyprus, the United Kingdom, Greece and Turkey, secured the independence of the new country. Article II required all parties to guarantee the independence, territorial integrity and security of Cyprus, while Article IV provided that:

> In the event of a breach of the provisions of the present Treaty, Greece, Turkey and the United Kingdom undertake to consult together with respect to the representations or measures necessary to ensure observance of those provisions.
>
> In so far as common or concerted action may not prove possible, each of the three guaranteeing Powers reserves the right to take action with the sole aim of re-establishing the state of affairs created by the present Treaty.

Within days the Sampson government and the Greek military junta collapsed. However, when Makarios resumed power and called for a ceasefire, Turkey continued its offensive. By the time the second invasion concluded, around 36 per cent of the island was under Turkish control. In 1983, after several years of stalemate, the Turkish Cypriot Assembly declared the independence of the Turkish Republic of Northern Cyprus. The United Nations Security Council immediately issued a resolution deploring 'the purported secession' and called upon 'all states not to recognise any Cypriot State other than the Republic of Cyprus'.[165] That resolution has been reaffirmed every subsequent year,[166] but Cyprus remains divided. The Turkish Republic of Northern Cyprus

[164] On the legality of the invasion and subsequent declaration of independence, see, R. St. J. McDonald, 'International Law and the Conflict in Cyprus' (1981) 19 *Canadian Yearbook of International Law* 3; Zaim M. Necatigil, *The Cyprus Question and the Turkish Position in International Law* (Oxford University Press, 2nd ed, 1993). *Cyprus v Turkey* [GC] no 2571/94, ECHR 2001-IV, 120 ILR 10.

[165] United Nations Security Council Resolution 541, UN Doc S/RES/541 (18 November 1983) [1], [7]; United Nations Security Council Resolution 550, UN Doc S/RES/550 (11 May 1984).

[166] Permanent Mission of the Republic of Cyprus to the United Nations, 'Resolutions Adopted by the Security Council' (27 January 2012) www.cyprusun.org/?cat=52.

maintains effective de facto control of the north of the island and delivers services to its population but is recognised as a legitimate state only by Turkey. In contrast, the Republic of Cyprus is recognised by the rest of the international community as the legitimate government of both Greek and Turkish Cypriots, whose jurisdiction encompasses the entire island. Nonetheless, the Turkish Republic of Northern Cyprus has gained some forms of international recognition, having been granted observer status in several intergovernmental organisations.

The white-minority Rhodesian government, the Turkish Republic of Northern Cyprus and the two putative Caucasus republics had and have de facto control over territory but were and are not widely regarded as de jure states. Some entities by contrast are considered de jure states in the absence of any actual control over territory. This includes governments-in-exile. It also includes Palestine.[167] The entirety of Palestinian territory is under the de facto control of Israel, but Palestine is recognised as a state by over 130 United Nations members. While its membership of the United Nations has been stalled for many years on the objections of Israel and the United States, in 2012 the General Assembly voted to upgrade Palestine's status to a non-member observer state.[168]

2.2.4 *Internationally Recognised Sovereign Non-State Entities*

Statehood brings considerable rights and privileges in international law. It is for this reason that many political communities make a claim for statehood, whether or not their claim has any grounding in law. But as we have seen, states are not the only subjects of the international legal system, and a range of other entities possess varying degrees of international legal personality.[169] This includes international organisations like the United Nations, as well as private, non-government associations such as the International Committee of the Red Cross.[170] It also includes a peculiar sovereign non-state entity: The Sovereign Military Order of Malta (SMOM).[171]

[167] Jure Vidmar, 'Palestine and the Conceptual Problem of Implicit Statehood' (2013) 12 *Chinese Journal of International Law* 19.

[168] United Nations General Assembly Resolution 67/19, UN Doc A/RES/67/19 (4 December 2012).

[169] *Reparation for Injuries Suffered* (n 13) 178.

[170] *Prosecutor v Simic et al (Decision on the Prosecution Motion under Rule 73 for a Ruling concerning the Testimony of a Witness)* (ICTY Trial Chamber 27 July 1999) [46]. See further Portman (n 65) 110–14.

[171] The status of the Holy See is more complex. While James Crawford argues that the Holy See is a state: (n 11) 221–33, Jorri Duursma contends that it is a sovereign non-state

The SMOM – officially, the Sovereign Military Hospitaller Order of Saint John of Jerusalem, of Rhodes and of Malta – emerged as a result of friendly commercial relations between merchants from the Duchy of Amalfi and the Fatimid Caliph, Al-Mustansir Billah.[172] In 1048, the Caliph permitted the merchants to build a hospital in Jerusalem to care for Christian pilgrims visiting the Holy Lands. In 1100, following the capture of Jerusalem in the First Crusade the previous year, the rector of the hospital established the monastic Order of St John of Jerusalem. In 1113, Pope Paschal II issued a Papal bull formally recognising the Order and confirming its sovereignty and independence.[173] Over the following centuries the Order was forced to relocate several times. After the fall of Jerusalem to Saladin of the Ayyubid dynasty in 1187, it moved to Acre, before it too fell in 1291, this time to the Mamluks, and the Order settled in Cyprus. In 1310, it moved to the island of Rhodes, before withdrawing to Sicily following the Ottoman conquest of Rhodes in 1522. Finally, in 1530, the Holy Roman Emperor Charles V granted the Order the island of Malta, where it operated as an international person by sending diplomatic representatives, signing treaties, and the like, until expelled by French Emperor Napoleon I in 1798.

The status of the SMOM became complicated thereafter. Under Article 10 of the 1802 Treaty of Amiens, which temporarily ended hostilities between France and Great Britain during the French Revolutionary Wars, Malta was to be restored to the Order of St John and their sovereignty over the island would be guaranteed. However, the Treaty was never implemented, leaving the Order without territory. The 1815 Congress of Vienna confirmed the loss of Malta, gifting the island to Great Britain. The SMOM has not exercised jurisdiction over any territory since 1798 and is not strictly a state. Nonetheless, the Order retains a 'certain international personality'.[174] Based in two buildings in Rome that enjoy diplomatic immunity, it maintains diplomatic relations with 107 states, has UN permanent observer status, and issues its own passports, stamps and coins. Italian courts have repeatedly upheld its

entity: (n 59) 386–8. In any event, there is no doubt that the Holy See is an international legal person. See also Portman (n 65) 115–18.

[172] See, generally, C. D'Olivier Ferran, 'The Sovereign Order of Malta in International Law' (1954) 3 *International and Comparative Law Quarterly* 217; Karol Karski, 'The International Legal Status of the Sovereign Military Hospitaller Order of St. John of Jerusalem of Rhodes and of Malta' (2012) 14 *International Community Law Review* 19.

[173] *Pie postulatio voluntatis* (15 February 1113).

[174] Crawford (n 11) 232.

sovereign status, confirming that the Order 'is a sovereign subject of international law, recognised as such by the other subjects of the international community'.[175] The SMOM is a curious entity, but as the Italian Court of Cassation remarked in 1935, 'sovereignty is a complex notion'.[176] It may no longer exercise political authority over territory, but the SMOM can be placed on the statehood spectrum, because it retains a degree of legitimate sovereign authority.

2.2.5 *Indigenous Nations*

The existence of the Sovereign Military Order of Malta illustrates the diversity of the statehood spectrum. A wide range of entities may exercise forms of sovereignty and enjoy a degree of international legal personality irrespective of whether they are characterised as a state for the purposes of international law. What is important is that an entity possesses some degree of effective governance and legitimacy for its claim. This is particularly relevant for another form of political community that asserts a right to sovereignty and self-government: Indigenous nations.

From time immemorial, Indigenous peoples across the globe have exercised political authority over their lands and communities. Self-government was practised and applied in different ways according to the cultural and political traditions of each people. For example, on the Australian continent and surrounding islands, the body of norms, values and traditions that Aboriginal and Torres Strait Islander communities developed and applied over thousands of generations is intimately connected to the particular country that each nation is connected to and is responsible for; as Kombumerri and Munaljahlai legal scholar Christine Black has explained, 'the Land is the source of Law'.[177]

European colonisation displaced Indigenous communities in Australia, North America, Aotearoa (New Zealand) and elsewhere, challenging and contesting their ability to exercise political authority. Indeed, the states that emerged and consolidated their positions on the lands of Indigenous nations sought to extinguish and deny those communities' inherent rights to sovereignty. These efforts did not succeed. Indigenous communities continue to exercise their own forms of political authority

[175] *Ministry of Finance v Association of Italian Knights of the Order of Malta* (1978) 65 ILR 320, 323.

[176] *Nanni v Pace and the Sovereign Order of Malta* (1935) 8 ILR 2, 4.

[177] Christine Black, *The Land Is the Source of Law: A Dialogic Encounter with Indigenous Jurisprudence* (Routledge, 2010).

in myriad ways. In upholding their responsibilities to country and meeting their obligations under their law, Indigenous communities continue to exercise their right to self-government.

Indigenous nations may still exercise self-government according to their own laws and traditions, but are they states? Indigenous nations appear to meet the Montevideo Convention criteria for statehood – many even have larger populations and territory than recognised states. Consider the Navajo Nation as an example. The Navajo (Diné in the Navajo language) are a Native American people of the Southwestern United States.[178] In the mid-nineteenth century, many Navajo were forcibly marched from their traditional lands and imprisoned in Bosque Redondo (a military fort) by the US government. In 1868, a treaty was negotiated between the Navajo and the United States that established the Navajo Indian Reservation.[179] Although the Navajo were initially provided with a little more than half the land designated under the treaty, the reservation has expanded over the years. Today, the Navajo Nation stretches across north-eastern Arizona, south-eastern Utah and north-western New Mexico and consists of over 71,000 square kilometres – a land area greater than Israel. Over 332,000 people are enrolled members of the Navajo Nation, with about 156,000 Navajo members living on Navajo land. This number compares favourably with the approximately 336,000 Icelanders, and far exceeds the 38,000 people who live in Liechtenstein.

The Navajo Nation also possesses an effective government. Since 1989, government has comprised an executive branch headed by a President and Vice-President who serve four-year terms, a popularly elected twenty-four -member Council (legislature), and a judiciary that consists of seven District Courts, seven Family Courts, seven Peacemaker Courts and a Supreme Court. As this structure suggests, Navajo government has been influenced by the United States in many ways, but its practice and operation remain underscored by 'Diné values, principles, laws, tradition and culture'.[180] As Raymond Austin, a former justice of the Navajo Nation Supreme Court, has documented, Navajo courts continue to apply fundamental Navajo doctrines and principles to contemporary legal disputes.[181]

[178] See David Wilkins, *The Navajo Political Experience* (Rowman & Littlefield, 4th ed, 2013).

[179] *Treaty of Bosque Redondo* (signed and entered into force 1 June 1868) (In Navajo: Naal Tsoos Sani).

[180] *Office of the Navajo Nation President v Navajo Nation Council (Shirley v Morgan)*, SC-CV-02-10 (28 May 2010) 17.

[181] Raymond Austin, *Navajo Courts and Navajo Common Law: A Tradition of Tribal Self-Government* (University of Minnesota Press, 2009).

Drawing on their inherent sovereignty and exercise of self-government, the Navajo also meet the fourth condition of the Montevideo Convention by entering into relations with other Indigenous communities and recognised states.[182]

Despite this, the Navajo Nation is not a state. Although it exercises self-government over discrete (and considerable) territory, that land is regarded ultimately as under the jurisdiction of the United States and the Navajo are not considered to be international legal persons.[183] The same is true of other Indigenous nations. This has not always been the case, however. When European powers and Indigenous nations met, they often negotiated treaties to regulate and structure their interactions. Over many centuries, hundreds of treaties were negotiated between Indigenous peoples and colonial powers in North America alone. In 1997, Miguel Alfonso Martinez, the Special Rapporteur on the Sub-Commission on Prevention of Discrimination and Protection of Minorities, considered the legal consequences flowing from these negotiations:

> [I]n establishing formal legal relationships with peoples overseas, the European parties were clearly aware that they were negotiating and entering into contractual relations with sovereign nations, with all the international legal implications of that term during the period under consideration.[184]

By entering into formal agreements with the Indigenous peoples they met, the European powers acknowledged the legal capacity of those peoples to make such treaties.

As the colonial powers strengthened their position, they began to disregard the commitments that they had made. Nation-to-nation agreements were 'domesticated' within the colonial power's own legal system.[185] As Martinez explained, the process of domestication allowed the state to remove 'the Indigenous question' 'from the sphere of international law' and place it within its own exclusive competence.[186] In

182 See, for example, United States Bureau of the Interior, 'Contract between the United States and the Navajo Nation' Contract No 10-WC-40-384 (17 December 2010).

183 *Johnson v M'Intosh*, 21 US (8 Wheat) 543 (1823).

184 Miguel Alfonso Martinez, Special Rapporteur, *Studies on Treaties, Agreements and Other Constructive Arrangements between States and Indigenous Populations*, UN Doc E/CN.4/Sub.2/1999/20 (22 June 1999) 18 [110].

185 Harry Hobbs and Stephen Young, 'Modern Treaty Making and the Limits of the Law' (2021) 71(2) *University of Toronto Law Journal* 234.

186 Martinez (n 184) 24 [192].

doing so, colonial powers stripped Indigenous nations of most of their attributes of sovereignty, including the control of land, the operation of their governing structures and their status under international law.[187]

Today, Indigenous nations are not regarded as states, but their inherent right to self-government (within the state) is recognised in the domestic law of many states and protected under international law.[188] In the United States, the Supreme Court recognised the inherent sovereignty of Native American tribes as early as 1823.[189] While tribal sovereignty is limited and defeasible by Congressional action,[190] it persists. Across the country, Native American Nations possess inherent power over their internal and local affairs, including the authority to exercise criminal jurisdiction over Native Americans and regulate the activities of non-Native Americans in certain cases.[191]

Indigenous sovereignty and self-government are also recognised in Canada. Since 1973, Canada has negotiated twenty-six comprehensive agreements with First Nations, eighteen of which include provisions related to self-government. While each is specific to the particular First Nation, as well as place, history and circumstance, all modern-day treaties protect and promote culturally appropriate forms of decision-making, amounting to a degree of self-government in internal and local affairs, and provide recurrent financing as a means to ensure their autonomous functioning.[192] Likewise, in Aotearoa New Zealand, the Treaty of Waitangi regulates the relationship between Māori and Pākehā (non-Indigenous New Zealanders). The Treaty promises Māori that their *tino rangatiratanga* (full authority) over their land, people and treasure will not be disturbed. As the Waitangi Tribunal has explained, *tino rangatiratanga* relates to self-governance. It is

> the ability of tribal communities to govern themselves as they had for centuries, to determine their own internal political, economic, and social

[187] Ibid 18 [110].

[188] For discussion see George Williams and Harry Hobbs, *Treaty* (Federation Press, 2nd ed, 2020) ch 6.

[189] *Johnson v M'Intosh* (n 183).

[190] *United States v Wheeler*, 435 US 313, 323 (Stewart J) (1978).

[191] 25 USC § 1301 (2018); *United States v Lara*, 541 US 193 (2004); *Duro v Reina*, 495 US 676, 696 (Kennedy J) (1990).

[192] Christina Godlewska and Jeremy Webber, 'The Calder Decision, Aboriginal Title, and the Nisga'a' in Hamar Foster, Heather Raven and Jeremy Webber (eds), *Let Right Be Done: Aboriginal Title, the Calder Case, and the Future of Indigenous Rights* (UBC Press, 2007) 1, 17–18.

> rights and objectives, and to act collectively in accordance with those determinants.[193]

Indigenous nations have also been able to attain standing in international forums.[194] The Saramaka peoples have sought to protect and promote their rights before the Inter-American Commission on Human Rights, the Western Shoshone Tribe have appeared before the Committee on the Elimination of Racial Discrimination, and over decades of political negotiation Indigenous leaders from all over the world secured General Assembly endorsement of the United Nations Declaration on the Rights of Indigenous Peoples. Although not legally binding, many of the Declaration's articles reflect customary international law. The most significant international instrument on the rights of Indigenous peoples, the Declaration guarantees Indigenous peoples the right to self-determination, the right to self-government or autonomy in matters relating to internal or local affairs, and the right to maintain their distinct political, legal, economic, social and cultural institutions.[195] It also protects Indigenous peoples' right to maintain and develop contacts across international borders.[196]

Indigenous nations are not states and their independent capacity to exercise sovereignty and self-government has been qualified by colonisation. Nonetheless, they sit on the statehood spectrum because their claim to sovereignty is deeply rooted. Indigenous nations are distinct political communities composed of individuals united by identity that have a long history of operating as a distinct society, with a unique economic, religious and spiritual relationship to their land.[197] This historical foundation grounds their claim for sovereignty and their possession of distinct legal rights.

2.3 Beyond the Statehood Spectrum

A wide spectrum of state and state-like entities exist. However, not all entities that purport to exercise political authority over a defined territory

[193] Waitangi Tribunal, *Turanga Tangata Turanga Whenua* (Wai 814, 2004) 113.

[194] Lillian Aponte Miranda, 'Indigenous Peoples as International Lawmakers' (2010) 32(1) *University of Pennsylvania Journal of International Law* 203; Sheryl Lightfoot, *Global Indigenous Politics: A Subtle Revolution* (Routledge, 2016).

[195] GA Res 61/295, UN GAOR, 61st sess, 107th plen mtg, Supp No 49, UN Doc A/RES/61/295 (13 September 2007) arts 3–5.

[196] Ibid art 36.

[197] Erica-Irene Daes, 'An Overview of the History of Indigenous Peoples: Self-determination and the United Nations' (2008) 21(1) *Cambridge Review of International Affairs* 7, 13.

and population sit within this range. Many entities simply do not belong on the spectrum at all. In this part, we explore three such entities with the goal of reaching a more holistic understanding of states and non-states.

2.3.1 *Intentional Communities*

An intentional community is a collection of people who 'consciously and purposefully' live together in common to realise or attain a certain set of goals.[198] These goals may be religious, spiritual, ideological, social or something else. The particular values that are fostered are myriad, but common to all such communities is the fact that the group perceives itself as different from the wider society because of those values. To protect and promote its unique vision, the group actively chooses to withdraw from society at large and purports to operate independently according to its own internal rules and principles.

Intentional communities are prevalent around the world. Many of the more prominent are built around shared religious belief. Some of the best-known are Anabaptist groups, such as the Amish, Hutterites, Mennonites and Bruderhof. Anabaptism first emerged in parts of modern-day Switzerland, Germany and the Netherlands in the 1520s. Under its interpretation of scripture, baptism into the Christian faith was only valid when made by an adult making an informed decision to confess; for adherents, the wide practice of infant baptism was invalid because a child could not make that decision. Anabaptists were also generally pacifistic and refused to participate in civil government.[199] Owing to the intertwinement of church and state, these positions threatened civil order and over many centuries Anabaptists were persecuted by both Roman Catholics and Protestants.[200] Seeking to avoid religious discrimination and harassment, many Anabaptist groups emigrated. Amish

[198] Barry Shenker, *Intentional Communities: Ideology and Alienation in Communal Societies* (Routledge, 1986) 6. See further Ayala Cnaan and Steve Breyman, 'Alternative or Intentional? Towards a Definition of "Unusual" Communities' in Ram Cnaan and Carl Milofsky (eds), *Handbook of Community Movements and Local Organisations* (Springer, 2007) 246. Lyman Tower Sargent, 'Theorizing Intentional Community in the Twenty-First Century' in Eliezer Ben-Rafael, Yaacov Oved and Menachem Topel (eds), *The Communal Idea in the 21st Century* (Brill, 2012) 53.

[199] Harold Bender, 'The Pacifism of the Sixteenth Century Anabaptists' (1955) 24(2) *Church History* 119.

[200] Gary Waite, *Eradicating the Devil's Minions: Anabaptists and Witches in Reformation Europe, 1525–1600* (University of Toronto Press, 2007).

communities left Switzerland and settled in Pennsylvania in the early eighteenth century, while Hutterite families who had migrated to Russia, left for the Dakotas and Montana in the 1870s. Facing persecution for their pacifism during World War I, many Hutterites subsequently moved north to Alberta and Saskatchewan. Upon arriving in the United States and Canada, these groups re-established their traditional communal lifestyle and refrained from engaging with wider society.[201] Despite many challenges in maintaining their traditions and way of life, hundreds of Anabaptist intentional communities continue to exist in North America alone.

Not all intentional communities are religious. In the mid-nineteenth century, French politician, journalist and author Étienne Cabet established a utopian socialist movement called the Icarians. In 1848, Cabet led his followers to the United States where they built egalitarian communes in Texas, Illinois, Iowa, Missouri and California. Colonisation proved challenging and political revolution in France encouraged many to return home. In 1898, the last group of Icarians, located near Corning, Iowa, unanimously voted to dissolve their community and rejoin the wider society.[202] Other intentional communities have proved more resilient. In Israel, collective communities traditionally based on agriculture and built on socialist and Zionist beliefs were established as early as 1910.[203] Known as kibbutzim (literally: 'gathering, clustering'), the nature of these intentional communities has changed over time in response to larger financial pressures.[204] Nonetheless, around 127,000 kibbutzniks live and work in some 260 kibbutzim today.[205]

Intentional communities withdraw from the state and assert the authority to manage their internal affairs according to their own legal,

[201] Douglas Sanders, 'The Hutterites: A Case Study in Minority Rights' (1964) 42 *The Canadian Bar Review* 225.

[202] Ruth Gallagher, 'Icaria and the Icarians' (1921) 2(4) *The Palimpsest* 97. Mark Holloway, *Heaven on Earth: Utopian Communities in America, 1680–1880* (Dover Publications, 1966) 198–212.

[203] Henry Near, *The Kibbutz Movement: A History, Origins and Growth, 1909–1939* (Liverpool University Press, 2007).

[204] Alon Gan, 'From "We" to "Me": The Ideological Roots of the Privatization of the Kibbutz' in Michal Palgi and Shulamit Reinharz (eds), *One Hundred Years of Kibbutz Life: A Century of Crisis and Reinvention* (Transaction Publishers, 2014) 33.

[205] Sarah Levi, 'The Revival of the Kibbutz: A Uniquely Israeli Institution', *The Jerusalem Post* (10 March 2018) www.jpost.com/magazine/a-uniquely-israeli-institution-543296; 'Kibbutz Reinvents Itself After 100 Years of History', *Taipei Times* (16 November 2010) www.taipeitimes.com/News/editorials/archives/2010/11/16/2003488628.

political, ideological and/or religious traditions and precepts. In doing so, they make claims of and for jurisdiction. Crucially, however, intentional communities do not use the language of statehood and do not aspire to international legal personality. Instead, intentional communities are typically content to operate within the state, albeit on a discrete basis. They do not purport to secede from the state, but largely wish to ignore it.

Evading the state is not always possible. In the United States and Canada, for example, most federal and state law applies in Anabaptist communities. The Amish pay income, property and sales taxes, follow workplace safety regulations, and must send their children to primary and middle school. However, they do not pay social security taxes and are not required to send children to school beyond the eighth grade.[206] Similarly, in Israel, state laws regulate and define kibbutzim. As intentional communities recognise, in the absence of formal legal independence, some regulatory or administrative relationship with the state is unavoidable.

Intentional communities are sometimes mistaken as making a claim for secession and independence. One such community is Freetown Christiania. Christiania is situated in south-eastern central Copenhagen, just over one kilometre from the Danish Royal Palace and Parliament. Stretching over 121 acres, the site consists of a former military barracks and portions of the old city's ramparts that were initially constructed in 1617 by King Christian IV. Although the city outgrew those fortifications, the barracks were not abandoned by the Ministry of Defence until the late 1960s.[207] In September 1971, residents of the neighbouring community pulled down some of the fencing to reclaim part of the disused site as a playground for their children. The actions of these residents were reported and popularised in the alternative magazine, *Hovedbladet*, widely distributed amongst the city's youth. By early 1972, some 300 people had flocked to the site, attracted by the community's utopian mission statement:

> The aim of Christiania is to create a self-governing society in which each individual may flourish while giving due regard to the interest of the

[206] *Wisconsin v Yoder*, 406 US 205 (1972).

[207] This material is drawn from René Karpantschof, 'Bargaining and Barricades – The Political Struggle over the Freetown Christiania 1971–2011' in Håkan Thörn, Cathrin Wasshede and Tomas Nilson (eds), *Space for Urban Alternatives? Christiania 1971–2011* (Gidlunds förlag, 2011) 38; Søren Flinch Midtgaard, '"But Suppose Everyone Did the Same" – The Case of the Danish Utopian Micro-Society of Christiania' (2007) 24 (3) *Journal of Applied Philosophy* 299; Päivi Rannila, 'Legal Diversity and the Strategies of Negotiating Public Spaces in Christiania' (2019) 41(5) *Journal of Urban Affairs* 602.

> community at large. The society in question must be financially independent. Furthermore, the common quest of the community must at all times be to show that physical and psychological pollution can be avoided.[208]

In May 1972, a group representing the community reached an agreement with the Ministry of Defence allowing them to use the area in exchange for agreeing to pay for electricity and water, prompting more squatters to move in. By 1975, around 800 people were living within the Freetown of Christiania, governing themselves through a form of collectivism and direct democracy.

In its fifty-year existence, the community has had a complex relationship with the Danish state. Asserting a right of autonomy, Christiania has long permitted activities prohibited under Danish law, sparking tensions with the Danish government and wider society. Most conspicuously, the community tolerated the sale of heroin until the late 1970s and continues to allow the open trade of cannabis. The frank flouting of Danish law has prompted both attempts to dissolve the community as well as efforts to maintain the unique collective. In more recent years, the relationship has been normalised to a degree. A 2004 law clarified that Danish law applied to the site, while in 2011 residents eventually agreed to collectively purchase the land from the state at below-market prices, transforming them from squatters to landowners.

The nature of Christiania has changed since 1971, but the community continues to claim a distinctive relationship with Denmark. At the same time, despite repeatedly maintaining the authority to govern itself, the community has never spoken in the language of statehood or asserted a right of sovereignty. On the contrary, in seeking to negotiate and protect its relationship with the state it has accepted Danish rule. Doing so makes it clear that Freetown Christiania does not belong on the statehood spectrum.

2.3.2 *Free Cities and Economic Zones*

Under international law, sovereign states may determine their own internal governance arrangements. For many states, the process of nation-building necessitated the development of a strong, central or unitary government that could promote a culturally bounded community. For others, geographic, ethnic, religious or cultural diversity

[208] Christianias Målsætning/Manifest (1971) www.christiania.org/.

encouraged federalism whereby sub-national units within the state were granted (or recognised to have) a degree of independent power and status. Irrespective of the particular arrangement, in all states laws and regulations enacted by a government are ordinarily expected to operate consistently throughout its jurisdiction. For unitary governments like those of the United Kingdom or France, that territorial scope encompasses the nation as a whole, while for sub-national governments like Texas or California, it applies only to the particular region. In some cases, however, a government may determine that a particular city or area within its jurisdiction should be permitted a larger or differential degree of autonomy. A diverse array of institutional forms can be considered, including charter cities, special economic zones and other innovative arrangements.

Charter cities developed in the Middle Ages. Where a monarch issued a Royal Charter to a settlement, its inhabitants were granted certain privileges. These could include the right to trade, establish guilds and other degrees of self-government. It could also remove the town from a feudal fiefdom and place its protection directly under the monarch.[209] Similar administrative models date back even further. During the Hellenistic and Imperial Roman periods, free cities such as Amphipolis and Athens enjoyed the special privilege of self-government and were permitted to follow their own laws and elect their own magistrates.[210] In the United States today, charter cities may be established by a state legislature or local election. In Texas, for example, once a city reaches a population of 5,000, voters may petition for an election for a city charter. If approved, the city is governed under home rule status that allows it to pass ordinances not inconsistent with state or federal laws.[211]

Special economic zones differ in important respects from charter cities. While charter cities may not enact ordinances inconsistent with state and federal legislation, special economic zones are geographically limited autonomous regions within states that operate under distinct

[209] Catherine Patterson, 'Town and City Government' in Robert Tittler and Norman Jones (eds), *A Companion to Tudor Britain* (Blackwell Publishing 2004) 116; James Lee, 'Urban Policy and Urban Political Culture: Henry VII and His Towns' (2009) 82(217) *Historical Research* 493.

[210] Anthony Spawforth, 'Free Cities' in Simon Hornblower, Anthony Spawforth and Ester Eidinow (eds), *The Oxford Classical Dictionary* (Oxford University Press, 4th ed, 2012).

[211] *Texas Constitution*, art XI, s 5; Local Government Code s 51.001.

rules.[212] In an effort to encourage foreign investment, trade and development, these zones are often governed under more business-friendly economic or financial regulation than other areas of the country. In some states, special economic zones are not permitted. Under the Australian Constitution, for example, the Australian Parliament may not enact laws with respect to taxation that discriminate between states or parts of states,[213] foreclosing the ability of the government to promote economic development by lowering taxation rates in certain regions. Other countries have more flexibility. The economic success of special economic zones in the People's Republic of China has popularised the concept and helped spread it to Latin America and Africa.[214] In 2016, one scholar found that around three-quarters of all countries host special economic zones.[215]

Quite clearly, charter cities and special economic zones are not independent states. Although these entities are empowered with a degree of self-government or operate under a different set of laws and regulations to the rest of the state, they are not sovereign entities. At all times they remain under the jurisdiction of the state. The rights accorded to the free cities of antiquity, for instance, were privileges: they were bestowed by the emperor and liable to be forfeited. Likewise, contemporary special economic zones are regulated and created by state law. In other words, special economic zones may operate under different rules, but those rules are set by the government of the state. What the state gives, the state may take away.

The same is true for entities like Hong Kong and Macau. Hong Kong and Macau have their own governments, legislatures, legal systems, police forces, immigration policies, national sports teams, customs territory and substantial competence in external affairs.[216] Under the 'one country, two systems' principle, each region possesses a degree of autonomy. However, they are formally part of the People's Republic of China.

[212] Thomas Farole and Gokhan Akinci, 'Introduction' in Thomas Farole and Gokhan Akinci (eds), *Special Economic Zones: Progress, Emerging Challenges, and Future Directions* (The World Bank, 2011) 1.

[213] Australian Constitution s 51(ii).

[214] Jin Wang, 'The Economic Impact of Special Economic Zones: Evidence from Chinese Municipalities' (2013) 101 *Journal of Development Economics* 133.

[215] Tom Bell, 'Special Economic Zones in the United States: From Colonial Charters, to Foreign Trade Zones, Toward USSEZs' (2016) 64(5) *Buffalo Law Review* 959, 968.

[216] See *Basic Law of the Hong Kong Special Administrative Region of the People's Republic of China* (1997); *Basic Law of the Macau Special Administrative Region of the People's Republic of China* (1999).

Each entity is characterised as a 'Special Administrative Region' (SAR). Article 31 of the Chinese Constitution empowers the state to establish SARs and clarifies that the ultimate authority rests with the National People's Congress. As the ongoing controversy over the Law of the People's Republic of China on Safeguarding National Security in the Hong Kong Special Administrative Region[217] demonstrates, the National People's Congress has the authority to unilaterally enact legislation for both regions in certain fields. Neither Hong Kong nor Macau is a sovereign state.

Distinctions are less clear with other institutional arrangements. Drawing on the financial success of Hong Kong and China's special economic zones, United States economist Paul Romer proposed that developing nations partner with foreign countries or corporations to create autonomous model cities. Under Romer's plan, host states would lease large tracts of undeveloped land to developed states who would administer the territory according to their own legal system. The city's residents would largely come from the developing state, but the administrators of the city would be appointed by (and accountable to) the developed state; residents could instead 'vote with their feet' by either migrating to or from the model city. Romer argues that such cities would attract significant international investment because their legal architecture would insulate them from any institutional and political turmoil present in their host state.[218] Romer envisages his model city as an extension of the special economic zone, 'increasing its size to the scale of a city and expanding the scope of its reforms'.[219] Notwithstanding strong neocolonial or neo-imperial resonances, several states have considered adopting Romer's proposition.

In 2008, Romer met with the Madagascan government to discuss his plan. President Ravalomanana proved receptive, and a plan was sketched. The idea was to lease a 'Connecticut-size tract of land' to the South

[217] 《中華人民共和國香港特別行政區維護國家安全法》 [Law of the People's Republic of China on Safeguarding National Security in the Hong Kong Special Administrative Region] (People's Republic of China) Standing Committee of the National People's Congress of the People's Republic of China, 1 July 2020; Government of the Hong Kong Special Administrative Region, *Gazette*, L.N. 136 of 2020, 1 July 2020.

[218] Paul Romer, 'Technologies, Rules, and Progress: The Case for Charter Cities' (The Center for Global Development, March 2010).

[219] Brandon Fuller and Paul Romer, 'Success and the City: How Charter Cities Could Transform the Developing World' (The MacDonald-Laurier Institute, 2012) 3. See further Rahul Sagar, 'Are Charter Cities Legitimate?' (2016) 24(4) *The Journal of Political Philosophy* 509.

Korean company, Daewoo, for ninety-nine years. Daewoo and Madagascar's neighbour, Mauritius, would jointly administer the export-processing zone. Despite a promising start, however, the plan was derailed after the opposition denounced it as treasonous and President Ravalomanana was forced from office in a coup d'état.[220]

More recently, Honduras has seriously contemplated Romer's idea.[221] In 2011, the Honduran Congress amended the nation's Constitution to facilitate the development of 'Special Development Regions' (Regiones Especiales de Desarrollo – REDs). Model cities built within nominated areas would not be subject to Honduran law or taxes but would be self-governing under a distinct legal framework. Under the proposed arrangement, disputes would be settled by Mauritian courts. As the ultimate appellate court in the Mauritian system is the Judicial Committee of the Privy Council in the United Kingdom, the model hoped to draw on the credibility of United Kingdom governance to attract investment. Despite signing an agreement with private investors led by American libertarian activist Michael Strong, the project soon stalled. The Indigenous Garífuna people noted that the chosen sites were not uninhabited but were in fact their homelands and they protested against their planned removal. When no developed country appeared interested in joining, Romer dropped out. More significant was an emerging legal problem. In October 2011, a five-member Constitutional Chamber of the Supreme Court declared the constitutional amendments enabling the development of REDs unconstitutional as breaching Honduran constitutional provisions protecting national sovereignty. In October 2012, that decision was affirmed by the Supreme Court en banc 13–1.[222]

The Honduran government has not been deterred. Following the Supreme Court decision, the Honduran Congress voted to remove the judges from the bench. In 2014, a newly constituted Supreme Court ruled similar constitutional amendments and legislation valid. Under the new law, an investor that builds infrastructure in a site designated as a Zone for

220 See Sebastian Mallaby, 'The Politically Incorrect Guide to Ending Poverty', *The Atlantic* (July/August 2010) www.theatlantic.com/magazine/archive/2010/07/the-politically-incorrect-guide-to-ending-poverty/308134/?single_page=true.

221 Michael Castle Miller, 'The Ciudades Modelo Project: Testing the Legality of Paul Romer's Charter Cities Concept by Analyzing the Constitutionality of the Honduran Zones for Employment and Economic Development' (2015) 22 *Willamette Journal of International Law and Dispute Resolution* 271; Lan Cao, 'Charter Cities' (2019) 27 *William and Mary Bill of Rights Journal* 717; Brian Doherty, 'The Blank Slate State', *Reason* (June 2013) https://reason.com/2013/05/13/the-blank-slate-state/.

222 Corte Suprema de Justicia, [Supreme Court] RI-769–11 (Honduras) (17 October 2012).

Employment and Economic Development (*Zonas de empleo y desarrollo económico* – ZEDE) will be granted quasi-sovereign authority.[223] The investing company will be permitted to impose and collect taxes, incur debts, establish its own education, health, civil service and social security systems, and impose property taxes.[224] In some areas, the scope of authority is reduced; unlike REDs, ZEDE are not authorised to directly engage in international relations. Overseeing all ZEDE is a committee appointed by the President that sets baseline rules and standards investors must follow. Reflecting the ideological backing of the idea, the first committee, announced in February 2014, was heavily comprised of libertarians and former advisers to United States President Ronald Reagan. These included Grover Norquist, Mark Klugmann, Richard Rahn, Loren Smith and Ronald's son Michael Reagan.[225] In 2020, the first ZEDE was launched, but it will take many years before development commences.[226]

Even if an autonomous model city is eventually established it remains clear that these entities are distinct from states. Despite their considerable autonomy, these cities and zones do not assert a right of sovereignty or a claim for statehood. In the case of the Honduran ZEDE, for example, 'the zones remain an inalienable part of Honduras, subject to its constitution and the national government on core issues of sovereignty such as territory, national defense, foreign affairs, and passports'.[227] Their backers are not interested in international legal personality but in commerce. They see free cities as a means to make money. Like the British East India Company before them, achieving statehood is unnecessary and perhaps a distraction from that primary goal.

2.3.3 *Sovereign Citizens*

Intentional communities, free cities and special economic zones enjoy varying degrees of internal autonomy, but none make a claim for

223 *Ley Orgánica de las Zonas de Empleo y Desarrollo Económico*, Decree No 33,222.

224 Bell (n 215) 973, 993–5; Tom Bell, *Your Next Government? From Nation State to Stateless Nations* (Cambridge University Press, 2018) 45–54.

225 Danielle Marie Mackey, '"I've Seen All Sorts of Horrific Things in My Times. But None as Detrimental to the Country as This."', *The New Republic* (15 December 2014) https://newrepublic.com/article/120559/honduras-charter-cities-spearheaded-us-conservatives-libertarians.

226 Paz Gómez, 'First Startup City Revives Honduran ZEDEs', *Econ Americas* (2 July 2020) https://econamericas.com/2020/07/first-charter-city-honduras-prospera-revives-zedes/.

227 Bell (n 215) 995.

sovereignty. The same is not true for sovereign citizens. Sovereign citizens are a loose group of individuals who are connected by a shared antagonism towards government and a convoluted and conspiratorial interpretation of the law. Estimated to number around 300,000 people in the United States alone, the movement emerged in the 1990s and has gained increasing attention during the COVID-19 pandemic.

Sovereign citizens represent the intersection of several overlapping groups with a longer history.[228] These include the Posse Comitatus, a radical right-wing Christian Identity sect that rejected all state authority higher than the county sheriff and enjoyed considerable support among farmers facing bankruptcy and foreclosure in the American Midwest in the 1970s and 1980s. It also includes more loosely organised right-wing Patriot or militia movements, whose members believe that federal government regulation concerning environmental protection and gun ownership, as well as taxation, interfere with constitutional liberties and amount to tyrannical rule. A third overlapping group is the common law court movement. Consistent with their rejection of state authority, individuals within this group establish their own local judicial systems – whether in private homes or community gathering places – and purport to apply common law principles to resolve disputes. While many of these courts appear to be 'sincere attempts by members to implement their beliefs by freeing themselves from state tyranny and holding public officials accountable to the people', others are more accurately seen as simple 'instruments of harassment'.[229] Finally, sovereign citizens are also related to a more disparate collection of anti-tax protestors. Although there are few strong political or ideological connections between anti-tax protestors and sovereign citizens, the latter have adopted and adapted the arguments of tax protestors in frequent – unsuccessful – challenges to the constitutionality of state authority. Indeed, despite protesting state authority, some sovereign citizens can be incredibly effective in utilising state judicial systems to hound and bully opponents.

[228] See, generally, Francis Sullivan, 'The "Usurping Octopus of Jurisdictional Authority": The Legal Theories of the Sovereign Citizen Movement' (1999) 4 *Wisconsin Law Review* 785, 786; James Evans, 'The "Flesh and Blood" Defense' (2012) 53(4) *William and Mary Quarterly* 1361; Caesar Kalinowski IV, 'A Legal Response to the Sovereign Citizen Movement' (2019) 80 *Montana Law Review* 153; Joshua Weir, 'Sovereign Citizens: A Reasoned Response to the Madness' (2015) 19(3) *Lewis & Clark Law Review* 829; Susan Koniak, 'When Law Risks Madness' (1996) 8 *Cardozo Studies in Law and Literature* 65.

[229] Sullivan (n 228) 792.

Articulating the precise beliefs of sovereign citizens is difficult. They have 'no leader, no central repository for ideas, and no unifying collective mission', with most adherents gaining 'their information through nebulous webpages or YouTube videos'.[230] Indeed, while sovereign citizens are 'surprisingly unified by their methodology and objectives' they are 'otherwise diverse', ranging from 'educated professionals to retired senior citizens', and consisting of both the wealthy and the poor.[231] They are also geographically diverse; although originating in the United States, sovereign citizens are now found all over the world.[232]

The logic of their arguments can be challenging to discern. As Justice James Judd of the Supreme Court of Victoria noted in a 2012 case, claims by sovereign citizens are often 'comprised of random, almost incomprehensible, statements, propositions, quotations, argument and references to other material ... lifted from other documents and randomly pasted into the pleading'.[233] In a lengthy exploration of sovereign citizen methods and ideologies, Associate Chief Justice Rooke of the Alberta Court of Queen's Bench admitted that following their reasoning is difficult: 'I would describe how these documents have the intended effect, except that the ... material I have reviewed has never made any sense, so I can only observe the "ingredients" and describe the intended "spell effect".'[234] Nonetheless, although the precise views of individual adherents may differ, sovereign citizens share a common core belief. At the root of their ideology is the position that government authority is illegitimate in the absence of individual consent. A bizarre and complex legal theory underlies this.

Sovereign citizens believe that there are two classes of citizen. On the one hand, there are 'natural' physical and tangible human beings, and on

[230] Kalinowski IV (n 228) 155.

[231] *Meads v Meads* 2012 ABQB 571; [2013] 3 WWR 419 [68].

[232] See, for example, the Reichsbürger movement in Germany, whose adherents believe that the German Reich and its 1919, 1937 or 1945 borders (opinions vary) continue to exist as the only sovereign authority in Germany. According to members, the victorious allies never signed a formal peace treaty with Germany at the cessation of hostilities at the conclusion of World War II. As such, the Federal Republic of Germany (itself a corporate entity) has usurped the Reich's authority and is an illegitimate colonial occupier: Timothy Wright, 'Germany's New Mini-Reichs', *Los Angeles Review of Books* (22 June 2019) https://lareviewofbooks.org/article/germanys-new-mini-reichs/; Linda Schlegel, '"Germany Does Not Exist!": Analysing the Reichsbürger Movement', *European Eye on Radicalisation* (17 May 2019) https://eeradicalization.com/germany-does-not-exist-analyzing-the-reichsburger-movement/.

[233] *National Australia Bank Ltd v Norman* [2012] VSC 14 [4] (Judd J).

[234] *Meads v Meads* 2012 ABQB 571 [536].

the other, there are 'artificial' persons who possess a separate legal personality.[235] They believe that every person born in the United States (or Australia, or Germany, etc.) is born as an individual sovereign, with natural and inalienable rights. Federal and state governments have no authority or jurisdiction over natural or 'flesh and blood' persons. When a baby is born, a birth certificate is issued, and the parents apply for a social security number. In that action, a duplicate 'artificial' person is created by the government. It is that 'strawman' over whom the government has jurisdiction. Sovereign citizens point to different legal instruments to justify their theory. The most popular account holds that artificial persons were created under the Fourteenth Amendment of the US Constitution, which is said to have established a federal United States citizenship. Others point to the birth certificate itself, which typically spells out the baby's name in all capitals. For example, JANE CITIZEN is the name of the strawman, while Jane Citizen is the flesh and blood person.

It is only by consenting to federal citizenship that an individual accepts the authority of the US government. On that basis, if an individual renounces their federal citizenship, and divests from their legally fictitious duplicate, they become free from the authority and jurisdiction of the government, and under no obligation to abide by its laws. This position is drawn from a misunderstanding of clause 39 of the Magna Carta, which reads that 'no freeman shall be taken or imprisoned or disseised [dispossessed of property] or exiled or in any way destroyed . . . except . . . by the law of the land'.[236]

Renouncing one's artificial personhood is difficult because it requires annulling any witting or unwitting contract that you may have with the government. Sovereign citizens purport to revoke their birth certificate, forfeit their social security number, destroy their driver's licence and close any account in a federally insured bank. They also avoid appearing to accept state authority in other instances, including when engaging with police or the judiciary. When forced to write their name on state documents they do so in non-standard ways. They may insert inappropriate punctuation or add obscure or obsolete legal (or quasi legalese) terminology, which is said to separate them from their artificial strawman. They may also sign documents using their thumb print made in red ink or blood.

[235] Material drawn from Kalinowski IV (n 228) 156, 158–164; Sullivan (n 228) 809–11.
[236] *Magna Carta 1215*, cl 39.

There is a reason why it is suggested the government creates an artificial duplicate of every person.[237] Sovereign citizens who believe in the 'redemption theory' assert that the US government went bankrupt in 1933 when it abandoned the gold standard as the basis of its monetary system. To secure its currency, the government began to use its citizens as collateral. For each artificial person, the government opens a secret bank account that contains between USD 600,000 to USD 20 million (opinion varies). By divesting themselves of their fictitious strawman and filing the 'correct combination of government documents', a person can supposedly redeem or reclaim their secret bank account and its funds.[238] When participants invariably find that they are worse off after attempting to engage in this process they are told that they have followed the procedure incorrectly.

If we put to one side the complicated (and bizarre) legal theory underpinning the movement, it becomes clear that sovereign citizens purport to act through their (incorrect) understanding of the law, rather than outside or in direct contravention of the law. In other words, although sovereign citizens 'misread, misconstrue, and misunderstand' the law,[239] they predicate their claims in law. Individuals rely on selective and spurious readings of legal texts to contest state authority and assert their own claims. Reflecting their emergence in the United States, sovereign citizens frequently cite articles of the US Constitution, or even the earlier Articles of Confederation.[240] Other foundational texts cited by sovereign citizens in the United States and globally include the Magna Carta, the 1688 English Bill of Rights, the Universal Declaration of Human Rights and the Bible.[241]

As should be clear, the claims of sovereign citizens have no basis in law. Courts in the United States have frequently ruled that their arguments are meritless.[242] In *United States v Schneider*, for instance, the Seventh Circuit of the United States Court of Appeals found that the defendant's argument that 'he is a free, sovereign citizen and as such not subject to the jurisdiction of the federal courts ... has no conceivable validity in

[237] Kalinowski IV (n 228) 156, 164–167.

[238] *Meads v Meads* 2012 ABQB 571 [536].

[239] Kalinowski IV (n 228) 154.

[240] Ibid 171.

[241] *National Australia Bank Ltd v Norman* [2012] VSC 14 [4] (Judd J); *Zeqaj v Deputy Commissioner of Taxation* [2020] FCA 1270 (4 September 2020); *R v Warman* (2001) BCCA 510 [9] (Hollinrake J).

[242] See Kalinowski IV (n 228) 194–209.

American law'.[243] Similarly, in *Augustinowicz v Nevelson*, the New Hampshire District Court dismissed a sovereign citizen's argument that property taxes cannot be imposed without the taxpayer's consent as defying common sense and 'foreclosed by New Hampshire case law'.[244] Likewise, in *Maxwell v Snow*, the District of Columbia Circuit of the United States Court of Appeals rejected Lawrence Maxwell's argument as frivolous and without merit that he was not subject to federal law because he was a 'sovereign citizen of the Union State of Texas', the United States was not a republican form of government and therefore must be abolished as unconstitutional, the Secretary of the Treasury's jurisdiction did not extend beyond the District of Columbia, and he was not a citizen of the United States.[245] The legal claims of sovereign citizens have also been dismissed in Canada,[246] Australia[247] and New Zealand.[248] No sovereign citizen claim has ever been upheld in a state-recognised court.

Two further points are worth noting. First, sovereign citizens challenge and contest state authority but they do not purport to secede and establish their own country. Sovereign citizens act in their individual capacity as a bearer of natural, common law or God-given rights. Their aim is to free themselves from government interference in the form of taxation, licensing or regulation of any sort. For some, engaging in these pseudolegal arguments may simply be a means to defer the bank foreclosing on their property. For others, it might be part of a get-rich-quick scheme. Although they may support each other with paperwork or socialise together in groups, they have no larger desire to achieve statehood or international legal personality.

Second, owing to their historical connections with far-right militia groups, sovereign citizens can be dangerous and confrontational. Many of their tactics revolve around filing false liens (a legal claim on property to secure the payment of a debt), frivolous lawsuits and fake letters of credit to intimidate and harass public officials. Such practices can be extensive. For example, following the loss of their home to foreclosure in 2009, Thomas and Lisa Eilerston filed more than USD 250 billion in liens,

243 910 F.2d 1569, 1570 (7th Cir. 1990).

244 *Augustinowicz v Nevelson*, No 10–cv–564–PB, 2011 WL 6300962 (D.N.H. December 16, 2011).

245 409 F.3d 354 (D.C. Cir. 2005).

246 *Meads v Meads* 2012 ABQB 571. See further Donald J Netolitzky, 'Organised Pseudolegal Commercial Arguments as Magic and Ceremony' (2018) 55(4) *Alberta Law Review* 1045, 1045.

247 *Agapis v Birmingham DCJ* [2013] WASC 329 (29 August 2013).

248 *France v Police* [2014] NZHC 2193 (10 September 2014).

demands for compensation and other claims against more than a dozen public officials in Hennepin County, Minnesota.[249] Even though these forms were eventually proven to be false, victims can incur significant emotional and financial distress in undertaking lengthy court action.[250] As Sheriff Richard Stanek, a victim of the Eilerston claims, explained, 'it affects your credit rating, it affected my wife, it affected my children. We spent countless hours trying to undo it'.[251] According to one state employee in Minnesota, 'it was scarier to engage with offenders who used sovereign citizen tactics than with murderers, given the prospect of facing lawsuits or fouled credit ratings'.[252]

Confrontation can extend beyond 'paper terrorism'.[253] The FBI has characterised sovereign citizens as 'anti-government extremists'[254] and classified the movement as a 'domestic terrorist threat'.[255] Members 'commit murder and physical assault; threaten judges, law enforcement professionals, and government personnel; impersonate police officers and diplomats; use fake currency, passports, license plates, and driver's licenses; and engineer various white-collar scams'.[256] Most infamously, sovereign citizen Terry Nichols was convicted of conspiring with Timothy McVeigh in the planning and preparation of the truck bombing of the Alfred P. Murrah Federal Building in Oklahoma City in 1995, which claimed the lives of 168 people. In 2018, the Southern Poverty Law Centre noted that at least six law enforcement officers had been murdered by sovereign citizens since 2005.[257] One of the more prominent incidents occurred in 2010. In May that year, father and son Jerry and Joseph Kane killed two police officers during a routine traffic stop outside

[249] Erica Goode, 'In Paper War, Flood of Liens Is the Weapon', *The New York Times* (23 August 2012) www.nytimes.com/2013/08/24/us/citizens-without-a-country-wage-battle-with-liens.html.

[250] Michael Mastrony, 'Common-Sense Responses to Radical Practices: Stifling Sovereign Citizens in Connecticut' (2016) 48(3) *Connecticut Law Review* 1015, 1027; Kalinowski IV (n 228) 155.

[251] Goode (n 249).

[252] Ibid.

[253] Christine Sartescshi, *Sovereign Citizens: A Psychological and Criminological Analysis* (Springer, 2020) 47–57.

[254] The Federal Bureau of Investigation, 'Domestic Terrorism: The Sovereign Citizen Movement' (13 April 2010) https://perma.cc/L8SQ-2K42.

[255] Ibid.

[256] Ibid.

[257] Raven Hodges and Adam Sommerstein, '42 Law Enforcement Officers Murdered by Domestic Extremists since 2005', *Southern Poverty Law Centre* (27 September 2018) www.splcenter.org/20180927/42-law-enforcement-officers-murdered-domestic-extremists-2005.

West Memphis, Arkansas. Jerry Kane was a sovereign citizen who travelled the country with his son, lecturing on alleged solutions to mortgage and foreclosure problems. He claimed that money and home loans are fictitious, and that people could live in their houses mortgage free by signing certain legal instruments.[258] Sovereign citizens can profit by selling hope to people facing difficult economic circumstances, but their disdain for government authority can sometimes turn violent.

2.4 Micronations

A broad diversity of political communities and actors exists across the globe. While the state remains the primary subject of international law, an array of state-like entities seek entry into the international plane. For many other communities, international legal personality and statehood are not sought. How do micronations fit into this picture? In this section, we outline our definition of micronations and explain where they are placed on the statehood spectrum.

2.4.1 What Are Micronations?

Micronations are often featured in colour supplements of newspapers, magazines and radio programs, but there are few accounts that develop a scholarly definition or deeper understanding. Perhaps, largely like the definition of a state and a microstate, you simply know it when you see it.[259] Micronations may be seen as nothing more than imaginary states ruled by eccentric men in faux royal garb with a bevy of pretend military medals on their chest. Though they assert their own independence, perhaps in a manner akin to sovereign citizens, they are largely harmless and generally keep to themselves. While this description may be accurate in some cases, micronationalism is far more diverse than this suggests. For this reason, while a rough and ready definition can be valuable, clarity is important in assessing the micronational challenge to statehood, sovereignty and international legal personality. In this section, we explore three non-legal definitions that provide an explanatory account of micronationalism, before offering our own.

[258] Shaila Dewan and John Hubbel, 'Arkansas Suspects Had Rage Toward Government', *The New York Times* (24 May 2010) www.nytimes.com/2010/05/24/us/24arkansas.html; Weir (n 228) 838–9.

[259] *Jacobellis v Ohio*, 378 US 184, 197 (1964) (Stewart J).

One of the few approaches to understanding micronations is provided by a geographer. In outlining the tourism potential of non-state entities, Dallen Timothy distinguishes between four entities, only two of which are properly considered micronations.[260] At one end of Timothy's spectrum sit internationally recognised, sovereign, non-state entities, like the Sovereign Military Order of Malta. As we noted earlier, these entities do not unequivocally meet the declarative criteria for statehood expressed in the Montevideo Convention but are nonetheless formally recognised (by at least other states) as de jure sovereign entities. For this reason, they are not strictly micronations but, usually, states with no control over physical territory. Timothy identifies his second type of entity as 'semi-legitimate places'. These entities have some historical foundation for claims of independence but, unlike the former category, have not been formally accepted or recognised by the international community. This group includes entities like the Republic of Somaliland.

Timothy's last two models are more traditionally understood as micronations. In the third, Timothy identifies places with little or no claim to historical legitimacy, but which have nonetheless 'earnestly attempted to lay claim to national independence'.[261] This archetype includes the most prominent micronations, like the Principality of Hutt River in Western Australia, and the Principality of Sealand off the coast of the United Kingdom, as well as lesser known wannabe states like Liberland on the Danube River and the Principality of Seborga in the Ligurian hills. Despite the absence of any legal basis for their statehood, these entities try to position themselves as de facto nations with a status similar to entities like the Sahrawi Arab Democratic Republic and the Turkish Republic of North Cyprus. Their hope is that a shift in international support will see them take their rightful place among the nations of the world.

Timothy's fourth example largely eschews control of significant physical territory. Increasingly prevalent, these are 'countries' that assert independence 'but are in fact little more than social clubs'.[262] While they engage in performative acts of sovereignty, this is conducted primarily for amusement or to seek attention rather than to actively challenge state sovereignty. Typically, the jurisdiction claimed extends to the real property owned by its founder, whether that is an apartment in

[260] Dallen Timothy, 'Where on Earth Is This Place? The Potential of Non-Nations as Tourist Destinations' (2003) 28 *Tourism Recreation Research* 93.

[261] Ibid 94.

[262] Ibid.

London (the Kingdom of Lovely), a flat in Sydney (the Empire of Atlantium) or a house in Nevada (the Republic of Molossia). These micronations are also known as 'simulationist' or 'virtual' nations. They extend to social media sites like Facebook, Reddit and MicroWiki, where communities share and discuss micronationalism, a practice they refer to as the social science of micropatriology. Though extensive – some online communities include thousands of members – they can raise different issues to more prominent secessionist or tangible micronations.

Timothy's typology usefully articulates major distinctions among micronations, as well as between micronations and other 'non-nations'. However, it does not clarify all variances between such entities. As we saw in the introduction, the claim for statehood made by some physical or secessionist micronations is more appropriately considered mischievous than earnest. It is not clear, for instance, that Dean Kamen actually desires statehood for his Kingdom of North Dumpling, but nor can it be said that the Kingdom is a mere social club. Rather it stands somewhere in the middle; used as a device to subvert government regulations, poke fun at state symbols and to promote Kamen and his endeavours. Similarly, in focusing on the tourism potential of non-nations, Timothy does not consider artistic projects that may or may not purport to assert jurisdiction over significant physical territory but are clearly aimed at critiquing and challenging state sovereignty. These and other forms of micronations are considered in more detail in Chapter 3.

Finnish artists Tellervo Kalleinen and Oliver Kochta-Kalleinen offer a more pronounced classification, distinguishing between three models: microstates, model-states and new country projects.[263] According to Kalleinen and Kochta-Kalleinen, microstates are very small countries whose territory is typically less than 20,000 square kilometres. Unlike our account of microstates explored earlier in the chapter, Kalleinen and Kochta-Kalleinen embrace unrecognised countries in their definition. They include the Vatican City, Monaco and San Marino as well as the Principalities of Hutt River and of Seborga. We disagree with this account because the former three entities are all recognised states even though they possess limited territory, while the latter two are not. We therefore place this group to one side.

[263] Tellervo Kalleinen and Oliver Kochta-Kalleinen, 'Introduction' in Tellervo Kalleinen and Oliver Kochta-Kalleinen (eds), *Protocols: Amorph!03Summit of Micronations* (Muu Artists' Association, 2005) 52.

Kalleinen and Kochta-Kalleinen's latter two categories are more helpful. On their view, model-states differ fundamentally from microstates. While microstates exercise (or purport to exercise) sovereignty over a small territorial expanse, model-states do not seek to establish legitimacy on the basis of territorial claims. Rather, model-states are 'experiments in forming a state with all of its political institutions' and symbols.[264] Like 'real' countries, model-states perform acts of sovereignty; they write constitutions, compose national anthems, design flags, issue stamps and currency, and conduct diplomatic relations with each other (and seek recognition from recognised nations). As the founder of the Principality of Nova Arcardia, Steven Scharff, has explained, model-states are a 'diplomatic version of a model railroad'.[265]

New country projects are similar to model-states in that they also engage in performative acts of sovereignty. However, while model-states generally do not lay claim to substantial physical territory, new country projects involve attempts to actually establish a viable state by 'acquiring or creating territory which does not belong to any existing state'.[266] This can involve sea steading initiatives in which floating structures are 'arranged into atolls and archipelagos' allowing individuals to settle on the high seas outside national jurisdiction,[267] like the Republic of Minerva, and the Floating Island Project's South Pacific city.[268] It can also include emerging efforts to develop permanent habitation on satellites like the Space Kingdom of Asgardia. As we explore in Chapter 3, many new country projects have been influenced by libertarian philosophies, and their founders have sought to develop and operate economic schemes prohibited in their homelands.[269] More recent initiatives, like Waveland and Asgardia, may also be inspired by cosmopolitan ideas of an integrated global pan-humanity. Nonetheless, even in these cases, new country projects can carry colonial overlays and resonances. In 2014, for instance, a United States man planted a flag in the Bir Tawil desert, asserting authority over 2,060 square kilometres of land claimed by

264 Ibid.

265 Steven Scharff, cited in Scott Neuman, 'Tiny Territories Mingle at MicroCon; Passports Optional', *NPR* (10 April 2015) www.npr.org/sections/thetwo-way/2015/04/10/398757610/molossia-heads-up-big-micro nation-summit-in-california.

266 Kalleinen and Kochta-Kalleinen (n 263) 52.

267 Surabhi Ranganathan, 'Seasteads, Land-Grabs and International Law' (2019) 32 *Leiden Journal of International Law* 205, 205.

268 The Seasteading Institute, 'The Floating Island Project: French Polynesia' www.seasteading.org/floating-city-project/.

269 Kalleinen and Kochta-Kalleinen (n 263) 52.

neither Sudan nor Egypt to establish a kingdom and fulfil a promise to his daughter to make her a princess.[270]

The typologies advanced by Timothy, and Kalleinen and Kochta-Kalleinen, are helpful in identifying distinctions between different forms of micronation. However, they also make clear that there are 'incredible differences' and 'no clear sense of unity' among this diverse practice.[271] Acknowledging this, sociologist Judy Lattas adopts a simpler definition. Lattas defines micronations as 'tiny countries declared by ordinary people in an act that repeats the establishment of sovereign nations, at least in some of its protocols'.[272] Lattas' approach is valuable as it more clearly identifies what makes micronations distinct from similar entities. Nonetheless, it still fails to capture what we understand by micronations within the context of our analysis. After all, some micronations are established by prominent political actors rather than ordinary people. Other micronations might have only a very small resident population but may claim authority over large areas of land, or even outer space. Furthermore, spurred by the growth of the internet, some micronations claim hundreds of thousands of citizens, significantly more than many recognised states.

This demonstrates the need to adopt a different definition that identifies the strengths of the above attempts, combined with more nuanced understanding of statehood and how international law and international political systems define and classify different communities. We define micronations as self-declared nations that perform and mimic acts of sovereignty, and adopt many of the protocols of nations, but lack a foundation in domestic and international law for their existence and are not recognised as nations in domestic or international forums. This definition simply and accurately encompasses the diversity of micronations; it includes libertarian sea steading efforts, simulationist micronations on social media, experimental states formed within college dorm rooms, conceptual art projects, as well as states established to publicise political agendas. It also excludes similar but distinct phenomena, such as

[270] Enjoli Liston, 'American Plans to Use "His" Piece of Africa for Advancement of Science', *The Guardian* (16 July 2014) www.theguardian.com/world/2014/jul/16/american-claim-africa-science-jeremiah-heaton-egypt-sudan.

[271] Judy Lattas cited in Mark Johanson, 'Masters of Micronations: Meet People Who Started Their Own Countries', *CNN* (24 May 2017) https://edition.cnn.com/travel/article/micronations/index.html.

[272] Judy Lattas, 'Queer Sovereignty: The Gay & Lesbian Kingdom of the Coral Sea Islands' (2009) 1 *Cosmopolitan Civil Societies Journal* 128, 129.

secessionist movements, Indigenous nations, microstates and intentional communities. As we have already outlined, secessionist movements and Indigenous nations enjoy some historical foundation for their assertions of independence, whether or not that claim has been formally recognised by domestic law or the international community. Similarly, despite their small size microstates are recognised as independent sovereign states. Finally, although intentional communities govern themselves according to their own precepts, they do not use the language of statehood, instead seeking to operate within the state.

2.4.2 Where Do Micronations Sit on the Statehood Spectrum?

The Montevideo Convention definition allows room for a variety of entities to qualify as states. Founders and proponents of micronations see that flexibility as promising. If Monaco can be regarded as a state, why not the Principality of Hutt River? If the Vatican City, why not the Kingdom of North Dumpling? Unfortunately for Leonard Casley, Dean Kamen and other would-be visionaries, micronations do not meet the Montevideo Convention criteria and are not states. In fact, in view of the complete absence of legitimacy, they do not sit on the statehood spectrum at all. Rather, micronations are a free-wheeling and variable combination of disparate elements such as (though not limited to) sovereign citizen legal theory, free city political philosophy and intentional community psychology.

Every micronation will fail for its own unique reasons. The Principality of Sealand, for example, falls at the first hurdle. While artificial islands constitute territory at international law, artificial installations and structures attached to the sea-bed do not.[273] The anti-aircraft platform that Roy Bates took possession of in 1967 is therefore not 'territory' for the purposes of international law. Arguably, the Principality also fails the second condition. While the Vatican City shows that there is no minimum requirement as to the number of people who call a state home, for a group of individuals to constitute a permanent population for the purposes of the Montevideo Convention, they must form a cohesive and vibrant community. Such a community is more than 'a loose association aimed at the furtherance of common hobbies and interests' but must be

[273] *In re Duchy of Sealand*, Administrative Court of Cologne, 3 May 1978 (1989) 80 ILR 683 ('*Duchy of Sealand*'); Imogen Saunders, 'Artificial Islands and Territory in International Law' (2019) 52 *Vanderbilt Journal of International Law* 643, 648–9, 653.

aimed 'at the maintenance of an essentially permanent form of communal life in the sense of sharing a common destiny'.[274] It is unlikely that the twenty or so people who have ever resided in Sealand at one time meet this standard.

Even more significant is the third condition. In his seminal examination of the creation of states in international law, Crawford considers that the key to statehood is 'governing power with respect to territory'.[275] That is, 'to be a state, an entity must possess a government or system of government in general control of its territory, to the exclusion of other entities not claiming through or under it'.[276] This position reflects the distinction between ownership of land (dominium) and the authority to exercise jurisdiction or sovereignty over that land (imperium). It is a distinction that is frequently identified by jurists as a key to statehood. In *Deutsch Continental Gas Gesellschaft*, for example, the German-Polish Mixed Arbitral Tribunal held that a state 'does not exist unless it fulfils the conditions of possessing a territory, a people inhabiting that territory, and a public power that is exercised over the people and the territory'.[277] Similarly, in the *Island of Palmas Case*, arbitrator Max Huber explained that '[s]overeignty in the relations between states signifies independence. Independence in regard to a portion of the globe is the right to exercise therein, to the exclusion of any other state, the functions of a state'.[278]

The key point here is that a state is independent or sovereign when it is not 'under the legal authority of another state'.[279] It is at this limb that micronations are most likely to fail. Micronations may declare their independence, but they are unable to do so to the exclusion of other entities. The lack of any legitimate foundation for their claim means that their assertion of jurisdictional authority over territory is legally contested by recognised states and not recognised in domestic and international forums, even if their actual occupation of that territory is permitted. Prince Leonard may have been the lawful owner of his

274 *Duchy of Sealand* (n 273).

275 Crawford (n 11) 56, 254. See also Lowe (n 131) 138.

276 Crawford (n 11) 59.

277 *Deutsche Continental* (n 40).

278 2 RIAA (1928) 829, 838.

279 *Austro-German Customs Union Case* [1931] PCIJ (ser A/B) No 41, 57–8 (Anzilotti J). This judgment was in minority in the case but is regarded as the 'classic statement': Crawford (n 11) 65.

wheat farm, but he did not possess sovereignty over that land. Despite his purported secession and declaration of independence, the Australian state possessed jurisdiction and sovereignty over the property at all times.

Could our understanding of what a state is evolve to encompass micronations? It is worth recalling that 'states are not innate or physical truths, but rather are recursively created by human social action and interaction'.[280] There is no reason that this must always exclude micronations. This, however, would seem highly unlikely, at least in the short term. No such evolution is evident, and no support for such a change has been expressed, apart from micronations themselves.

If understandings of statehood are unlikely to adapt to include micronations, is it possible that a micronation could become a state? Again, this is unlikely, but nonetheless a possibility remains. As we explore in the following chapters, libertarian-inspired micronations often prioritise the creation of an effective (albeit limited) government. In some cases, they do so on land or sea over which, they claim, no state exercises lawful authority, either because the area is unoccupied, or because the micronation has reclaimed land in international waters. Assuming that their legal basis for possession is correct and that they build a functioning government capable of exercising legitimate authority over defined territory, the micronation may come to constitute a state. Reflecting the declaratory theory of statehood, this is a question of fact.[281] Whether another state recognises an entity as a state or not is immaterial to its status. Hence, if a micronation can satisfy the criteria of statehood, non-recognition would not foreclose its status.

The likelihood of any transition remains remote. Consider the experience of the Global Country of World Peace (GCWP). The GCWP is a not-for-profit organisation incorporated in Iowa, United States, that promotes Transcendental Meditation. Inaugurated by Maharishi Mahesh Yogi, the founder of Transcendental Meditation, in October 2000, the GCWP styles itself as 'a nation without borders',[282] and – in its tax statements – describes its mission as the creation of

[280] Tom Sparks, 'State' in Jean D'Aspremont and Sahib Singh (eds), *Concepts for International Law: Contributions to Disciplinary Thought* (Edward Elgar, 2019) 838, 840.

[281] Jean D'Aspremont, 'The International Law of Statehood: Craftsmanship for the Elucidation and Regulation of Births and Deaths in the International Society' (2014) 29 *Connecticut Journal of International Law* 201, 205; *Montevideo Convention* (n 45) art 3.

[282] Global Country of World Peace www.globalcountry.org/wp/.

world peace 'by unifying all nations in happiness prosperity, invincibility, and perfect health'.[283] The GCWP has issued its own currency (the 'Raam') and sought diplomatic relations with many states. For several years, the GCWP also sought to establish a sovereign state by purchasing land from recognised states across the globe. In June 2001, for example, the GCWP offered Suriname USD 1.3 billion over three years for a 200-year lease of 3,500 acres of rural land.[284] The following month, reports stated that Tuvalu had, 'after careful consideration', rejected a proposal to create a 'Vatican-like sovereign city state' for a payment of USD 2 million per year.[285] In 2002, the GCWP tried again, proposing to establish its headquarters and invest USD 1 billion in the 85-square-kilometre island of Rota in the United States Commonwealth of the Northern Mariana Islands, on the condition that the island seceded and became independent. Rota declined.[286] A few months later, the GCWP was expelled from Costa Rica after it was discovered that the organisation was paying members of the Talamanca reservation USD 250 a month in return for the right to appoint a king of the reserve.[287] Chastened, it appears that the GCWP is now content to remain in Iowa – and remain a micronation.

The consequence of a micronation becoming a state is that it acquires a legal foundation for its existence. As a result, the entity would cease to be a micronation because an inherent characteristic of micronations is that they lack any such legal basis. This reveals how micronations and states should be conceived as mutually exclusive entities. It may be possible for an entity to shift its status between the two, and even perhaps for a state to become a micronation, but an entity cannot enjoy the status of both at the same time. A micronation is, by its nature, a non-state entity that adopts the trappings of a state, perhaps as a parody of a state or perhaps in defiance of it.

[283] Oshrat Carmiel, 'Wall Street Meditation Group Cuts Landmark Building Price 33%', *Bloomberg* (28 December 2009).

[284] Jan McGirk, 'Yogi's Disciples Want to Create New Utopia', *The Independent* (8 June 2001) www.independent.co.uk/news/world/americas/yogis-disciples-want-to-create-new-utopia-9200910.html.

[285] Freedom House, *Freedom in the World – Tuvalu (2002)* (18 December 2001) www.refworld.org/docid/473c53fbc.html.

[286] 'Rota Islanders Make the Right Decision', *Honolulu Advertiser* (13 April 2002) http://the.honoluluadvertiser.com/article/2002/Apr/13/op/op02a.html.

[287] 'Costa Rica Expels Foreigners for Naming King of Remote Indian Reservation', *CNN* (21 July 2002).

2.5 Conclusion

In this chapter we have developed the first account of how statehood interacts with micronations. We have done so by exploring the concept of statehood and comparing and contrasting micronations to similar non-state and state-like entities. We have found that micronations are self-declared nations that perform and mimic acts of sovereignty, and adopt many of the protocols of nations, but lack a foundation in domestic and international law for their existence and are not recognised as states in domestic or international forums. In Chapter 3, we expand further on this definition by exploring the myriad reasons why a person or group decides to establish their own country.

3

Motivations

Micronations share a status as non-state entities that lack any domestic or international legal basis for statehood and yet perform or mimic acts of sovereignty. Beyond this they are incredibly diverse. Some micronations are speculative experiments in statehood, perhaps utopian examples of how nations could or should be organised. Others are established for personal entertainment, fantasy or artistic expression. Where a town or small community supports the idea, micronationalism can even promote tourism and deliver an economic boost to a region. Others still are formed to challenge and critique statehood and sovereign authority or as a way to make quick money by fair or foul means. Some of the more enduring micronations emerge as personal grievances that take on a political dimension as anger, frustration and desperation push individuals into taking extreme action.

In this chapter, we undertake a survey of some of the most prominent micronations by focusing on the myriad of (often overlapping) motivations for their creation. This study complements our definition and conceptual framework, explored in the previous chapter, by expanding our knowledge of the justifications provided for micronations and the assorted rationales that underlie their assertions of statehood.

3.1 Libertarianism

A primary driver for the formation of many micronations is frustration with state authority, whether manifested in resistance to taxation or regulation.[1] Indeed, as Oliver Kochta-Kalleinen has succinctly noted, 'to understand micronations, one has to understand libertarianism'.[2]

[1] Judy Lattas, 'DIY Sovereignty and the Popular Right in Australia' (Paper presented at the Conference of the Centre for Research on Social Inclusion, Macquarie University, 2004) 6.

[2] Oliver Kochta-Kalleinen, 'Micronations – From Utopian Communities to Space Settlements' in Tellervo Kalleinen and Oliver Kochta-Kalleinen (eds), *Protocols: Amorph!03Summit of Micronations* (Muu Artists' Association, 2005) 38, 42

Libertarianism is a broad branch of political philosophy, but its adherents generally ascribe to a few common values. The most important of these is the idea that all persons are autonomous individuals of equal moral worth. Described by some as a form of 'self-ownership' and grounded by others in our nature as purposive beings, this principle means that we all have the right to determine what we do with our person, and as a corollary, that we are not entitled to do anything to another person without their consent.[3]

This position can promote certain liberal values, such as women's bodily autonomy and drug harm minimization programmes, but it can also be used to attack progressive taxation and other forms of income redistribution. Robert Nozick, for example, described redistribution in the form of compulsory taxation as 'morally on par with forced labor'.[4] As this might suggest, libertarians are sceptical of the state and political authority more generally.[5] Because libertarians place great weight on a strong moral notion of consent, they can regard the exercise of coercive state powers as illegitimate. Their ideal society is one predicated on independent persons relating to each other on a voluntary and consensual basis. If the state exists, it is minimal and limited to functions like the enforcement and protection of individual rights. It does not provide social welfare, nor does it limit individual freedom in any capacity.

A right-libertarian utopian ideal lay behind the ill-fated creation of the Republic of Minerva in the 1970s. Michael Oliver,[6] a wealthy Nevadan real estate mogul and Lithuanian-born Communist émigré, sought to establish an offshore tax haven. Inspired by the libertarian economist Ludwig von Mises, author Ayn Rand and philosopher Andrew Galambos, Oliver was alarmed about the apparent creeping tide of socialism in his new country. Perhaps Oliver's sensitivity was understandable – he had spent four years in a Nazi concentration camp and believed the social revolution reverberating throughout the United States in the 1960s was a precursor to an impending political uprising.

[3] Robert Nozick, *Anarchy, State, and Utopia* (Basic Books, 1974); Gerald A Cohen, *Self-Ownership, Freedom, and Equality* (Cambridge University Press, 1995); Eric Mack, 'The Natural Right to Property' (2010) 27 *Social Philosophy and Policy* 53.

[4] Nozick (n 3) 169.

[5] Mike Huemer, *The Problem of Political Authority: An Examination of the Right to Coerce and the Duty to Obery* (Palgrave Macmillan, 2012).

[6] For a background on Oliver and a summary of his committed attempts to found his libertarian paradise see Erwin Strauss, *How to Start Your Own Country* (Paladin Press, 3rd ed, 1999) 113–23.

Concerned that the US Constitution contained 'enough collectivist clauses to ensure a steady drift toward totalitarianism',[7] Oliver drafted a political manifesto and constitution for his laissez-faire paradise. *A New Constitution for a New Country* became a 'genuine underground best-seller, selling over 20,000 copies'.[8] For several years, Oliver travelled or sent representatives all over the world in search of a suitable site on which he could realise his vision. Following disappointments as far afield as the New Hebrides (Vanuatu), Costa Rica, French Guyana and the Bahamas, Oliver determined that the project's success required more than a status as a tax haven; 'a new libertarian polity needed its own sovereign powers'.[9] Eventually, Oliver settled on the Minerva Reefs, two submerged atolls in the Pacific Ocean.

The Minerva Reefs, also known as Ongo Teleki in Tongan, are remote. The reefs are situated around 500 kilometres south-west of the southern-most group of Tongan islands called the Tongatapu Group, and about 700 kilometres south-east of Fiji's main islands. Taking their name from a New South Wales whaling ship that ran aground on the southern shoal in 1829, the reefs had long been visited by Tongan and Fijian fishermen, but no state had ever asserted sovereignty over the atolls.[10] This may have been because permanent settlement was impossible; at high tide the reefs found themselves several feet under water. Even so, such a minor inconvenience would not prevent Oliver from seeking to realise his life's ambitions.

In August 1971, Oliver and a group of supporters calling themselves the Ocean Life Research Foundation entered the 29-kilometre-wide lagoon that separates the north and south reefs. Sailing on a chartered 54-foot pleasure yacht from Fiji,[11] the group immediately set about their plans. The party

[7] Raymond Craib, 'Escape Geographies and Libertarian Enclosures' (Paper presented at Yale's Program in Agrarian Studies, February 2015) 7.

[8] Anthony van Fossen, *Tax Havens and Sovereignty in the Pacific Islands* (University of Queensland ePress, 2012) 110.

[9] Ibid 110–11. See further Peter du Bois, 'Utopia on the Rocks: Or, the Short, Unhappy Life of the Republic of Minerva' (26 March 1973) 53(3) *Barron's National Business and Financial Weekly* 5, 5.

[10] Lili Song, 'The Curious History of the Minerva Reefs: Tracing the Origin of Tongan and Fijian Claims Over the Minerva Reefs' (2019) 54(3) *The Journal of Pacific History* 417, 417–18.

[11] Lawrence Horn, 'To Be or Not to Be: The Republic of Minerva: Nation Founding by Individuals' (1973) 12 *Columbia Journal of Transnational Law* 520, 520–8; Samuel Menefee, '"Republics of the Reefs": Nation-Building on the Continental Shelf and in the Worlds Oceans' (1994) 25 *Case Western International Law Journal* 81, 95–102.

> Dredge[d] up two hummocks of land, coral wrapped in seven layers of chicken wire and encased in reinforced concrete, to above mean high water. They erected twenty-six foot high markers replete with beacons and radar reflectors and topped by a flag with a gold torch inside a gold circle on a solid blue background, representing the Republic of Minerva – 'Land of the Rising Atoll'.[12]

Over the remainder of the year, sand was ferried on barges from Fiji to raise the reefs above sea level and rudimentary construction began. Although they did not get this far, the plans envisioned the creation of 2,500 acres of habitable land elevated around two and a half to three metres above mean high tide, floating cities established within the lagoon and a sea wall to protect the site from rough weather. On 19 January 1972, the Republic announced its independence. Quickly adopting the conventional formal protocols of statehood, it minted currency, elected a provisional President and issued a Declaration of Sovereignty, which it sent to more than 100 nations, including the United States. Interestingly, contemporaneous accounts suggest that 'only one head of state, His Majesty The Sultan of Occussi-Ambeno … bothered to reply'.[13] Reflecting the bizarre environment in which micronations operate, the Sultanate itself was a hoax; the creation of New Zealand anarchist and philatelist, Bruce Henderson.[14]

Consistent with his desire to establish 'a new land to escape from high taxes, riots, drugs and crime',[15] Oliver's vision was that government in the Republic would be limited to only one function: protection against force and fraud. Oliver expounded in his political manifesto:

> Government, under this constitution, can be construed as a private corporation, which is to be *hired* by participants on a *voluntary* basis, for the specific purpose of protecting their personal rights. Regardless of majority vote, no person, entity, or governmental agency may take away these rights from others.[16]

It would levy no taxation and expend no social welfare. There would be no free education and no social security. Citizens could, however, pay

12 Horn (n 11) 521.

13 du Bois (n 9); Horn (n 11) 526; van Fossen (n 8) 113.

14 See nn 137–140.

15 Editorial, 'South Sea Reef Proclaimed a Republic by 3 Americans', *The New York Times* (30 January 1972) 11.

16 Michael Oliver, *A New Constitution for a New Country* (Fine Arts Press, 1968) 105 (emphasis in original).

a voluntary annual premium for the ability to initiate court action, similar to an insurance policy taken out with the state. All laws would automatically expire after five years. Morris Davis, the provisional President, explained further:

> [P]eople will be free to do as they damn well please. Nothing will be illegal so long it does not infringe on the rights of others. If a citizen wishes to open a tavern, set up gambling or make pornographic films, the government will not interfere.[17]

Oliver considered that the state would eventually become a lucrative investment. He imagined that 'the new nation could compete with Liberia and Panama in becoming a "flag of convenience" for owners of merchant ships. In time, multinational companies looking for a tax haven might want to establish a base there.'[18] Although Oliver envisioned a 'new Venice' of perhaps 30,000 settlers,[19] he expected that most citizens would not be residents. Instead, people would be more interested in the tax advantages that citizenship would offer. The residents themselves would largely be Tongan or Fijian laborers, but it is not clear whether they would be offered (or allowed to take up) citizenship.[20]

All was not well, however. 'Alarmed by the prospect of unwelcome neighbors on numerous reefs in the area', a coalition of South Pacific nations raised the issue at the South Pacific Forum with Australia and New Zealand.[21] As we will see in Chapter 5, Tonga's sovereign claim over the reefs was eventually accepted, and it commenced a series of actions to substantiate its claim. Oliver and his followers left later that year, though Davis and another group of American libertarians attempted to reassert the Republic in 1982. Once again, they were thwarted by the Tongan military.[22] Today, Minerva has been 'more or less reclaimed by the sea'.[23]

Oliver did not resile from his dream. Instead, he began another strategy; this time seeking to create a new libertarian state by supporting

[17] Cited in Mark Parsons, 'Ashes to Ashes' (July 1981) 101 *The New Internationalist* https://newint.org/features/1981/07/01/phoenix.

[18] du Bois (n 9) 24.

[19] Reason Staff, 'Designing a Free Country: An Interview with Mike Oliver' (December 1972) 4(8) *Reason* 5.

[20] van Fossen (n 8) 111–12.

[21] Robert Trumbull, 'Pacific Islanders Fight Reef Plan', *The New York Times* (27 February 1972).

[22] Philip Hayward, 'Oecusse and the Sultanate of Occussi-Ambeno: Pranksterism, Misrepresentation and Micronationality' (2019) 2(2) *Small States & Territories* 183, 188.

[23] Katherine Mangu-Ward, 'Hope Floats' (August/September 2008) 40(4) *Reason* 72.

(and instigating) secessionist movements in already inhabited islands.[24] Learning from his experiences with the Republic of Minerva, it is likely that Oliver recognised that international law would more readily accept the right of a secessionist movement to assert statehood than an artificial island in international waters settled by wealthy Americans. Nonetheless, fomenting political rebellion has its own challenges.

In 1973, Oliver financed a nascent independence movement on Abaco island in the Bahamas. The plan appeared to be going well. Agents provocateurs drew on local political concerns to create an artificial independence party and manipulate public opinion towards secession. Local militia were flown to facilities in Florida and Georgia to undergo military training and learn propaganda techniques under the auspices of American millionaire arms dealer Mitchell WerBell III. Another associate, Robert Hamilton, the thirteenth Baron of Belhaven and Stenton, was even able to gain assurances in the House of Lords that the United Kingdom (UK), the former colonial power, would not intervene to prevent the 'harassed' Abaconians from seeking their independence if they so determined.[25] However, Oliver's plans soon fell apart. WerBell attracted the US Senate's attention as evidence about his apparent connection to targeted assassinations became public. Later suggestions that WerBell may also have been connected to the Watergate break-in forced him to reduce his activities, leaving the incipient independence movement to collapse.[26]

Undeterred, Oliver and his supporters quickly turned their attention to Vanuatu. After several years, it appeared their dreams were at hand. In 1980, the messianic Jimmy Stevens and his New Hebrides Autonomy Movement seized the northern island of Espiritu Santo and declared the new Republic of Vemarana. In return for USD 250,000, weapons and a radio, Stevens promised Oliver tax concessions to build a casino. The casino was never built. Vanuatu appealed for support from Papua New Guinea who arrived to put down the rebellion, while Oliver was interrogated in the United States over allegedly interfering in other countries' internal affairs and was permanently banned from entering Vanuatu.[27]

[24] van Fossen (n 8) 114–15.

[25] United Kingdom, *Parliamentary Debates*, House of Lords, 10 June 1974, vol 352, col 227–230.

[26] van Fossen (n 8) 115–16; John Beasant, *The Santo Rebellion: An Imperial Reckoning* (University of Hawaii Press, 1984) 54; Lynn Kinsky and Robert Poole, 'Abaco: Birth of a New Country?' (October 1974) 10(1) *Reason* 14.

[27] van Fossen (n 8) 126; 'Vemarana in a Nut Shell', *The New York Times* (8 June 1980) 18.

Recurrent failures to foment rebellion left Oliver looking wistfully once more towards the sea. In the early 1990s, he proposed an artificial, floating city off the coat of Panama. As advertised, Oceania promised to free residents from governments 'entangled in bureaucracy, corruption, and the free lunch philosophy'.[28] Once again, the project failed. This time for lack of funds.

Oceania may have failed, but the idea of building floating structures on the high seas is alluring to many people seeking respite from regulation and taxation. In the 1960s, several American businessmen sought to establish independent states upon coral reefs off the coasts of California and Florida. One group of entrepreneurs purchased the *SS Jalisco*, a World War II-era surplus troop ship, towed it out to the Cortes Bank some 170 kilometres west of San Diego, moored on a shallow ridge and opened the sea cocks to sink the vessel. Their plan was to then haul rocks and rubbish from the city of Los Angeles to create a base on top of the sunken ship from which they could build a habitable structure and a new country. The nation of Abalonia was to be a tax-free processing plant to harvest the abundant abalone and lobster of the area. There is some suggestion that a casino and aircraft runway were also planned. Unfortunately, rough seas broke the mooring line and the vessel was scuttled in deeper waters. Abalonia was sunk and the group were threatened with the charge of creating a navigational hazard.[29] The US Department of the Interior agreed not to sue the promoters on the condition that they agree not to return to the Cortes Bank.[30] A similar project backed by a group from Seattle, Washington to develop three islands on the Cortes Bank and create the nation of Taluga, dissipated after pressure from the US Army Corps of Engineers.[31]

Despite these failures, wealthy libertarians continue to explore and finance such projects. On 13 April 1999, American businessmen Lazarus Long (also known as Howard Turney) proclaimed the formation of the

[28] Chris Baker, 'Live Free or Drown: Floating Utopias on the Cheap' (February 2009) 17(2) *Wired* 58; van Fossen (n 8) 135.

[29] Sherry Eckhardt, 'Recent Cases: International Law – Continental Shelf – Proprietary Interest of United States in Continental Shelf Precludes Claims of Acquisition by Private Entrepreneurs. *United States v. Ray* (S.D. Fla. 1969)' (1969) 6 *San Diego Law Review* 487, 498–499; Menefee (n 11) 102–3; 'Seas Batter Abalonia', *Los Angeles Times* (20 November 1966) 99; 'Island "Nation" Being Planned', *Los Angeles Times* (24 November 1966) 3.

[30] Menefee (n 11) 103.

[31] Ibid 103–4; David Phillip Stang, 'Wet Land: The Unavailable Resources of the Outer Continental Shelf' (1968) 2 *Journal of Law and Economic Development* 153, 184–5.

Principality of New Utopia, located on the Misteriosa Bank, a 322-square -kilometre submerged atoll in the Caribbean Sea around 350 kilometres from Mexico, Honduras and Cuba. Long anchored a buoy to the seabed and planned to erect a glittering city that would 'out Cayman the Caymans'; 'a free-market oasis without government constraints where money can be made and stashed and the taxman never calls'.[32] Unfortunately for Long, the US Securities and Exchange Commission (SEC) did call. In 2000, the US District Court held that in offering and selling securities over the Internet purportedly to fund the development of New Utopia, Long made material misrepresentations and omissions concerning the status of construction of the project, the safety of the investment and the status of the SEC's investigation into his activities.[33] Long died in 2012, but his vision is being carried on by his widow.

More recently, attention has focused on the California-based Sea Steading Institute. Founded in 2008 by Patri Freidman, grandson of libertarian economist Milton Friedman, and initially financed by Silicon Valley billionaire Peter Thiel, the Sea Steading Institute aims to succeed where earlier efforts at building habitable structures on the high seas have failed.[34] Although their website suggests that sea steading could offer significant benefits to humanity globally, it is clear that the quest for profit and material advancement free of regulatory burden is the primary motivation. Backers are interested in sea steading's potential to 'peacefully test new ideas for governance' so that 'the most successful can then inspire change in governments around the world'.[35] It is not always clear whether proponents conceive sea steads as entirely new states or as enclaves within existing states.[36] So far, technological and financial challenges have meant that the latter has been prioritised. However, negotiations with French Polynesia for the development of proof-of-concept floating cities within their territorial waters stalled when community

[32] Tim Hulse, 'Prince Lazarus Rules the Waves', *The Independent* (31 May 1998) www.independent.co.uk/arts-entertainment/prince-lazarus-rules-the-waves-1157051.html.

[33] *Securities and Exchange Commission v Lazarus R. Long (a/k/a Howard Turney individually and doing business as New Utopia)* USDC/NDOK/TULSA Ca No 99CV 0257BU(M).

[34] See discussion in Surabhi Ranganathan, 'Seasteads, Land-Grabs and International Law' (2019) 32(2) *Leiden Journal of International Law* 205.

[35] The Sea Steading Institute, 'Vision/Strategy' (2019) www.seasteading.org/about_archive/vision-strategy/. See further Patri Friedman and Brad Taylor, 'Seasteading: Competitive Governments on the Ocean' (2012) 65(2) *Kyklos* 218.

[36] Philip Steinberg, Elizabeth Nyman and Mauro Caraccioli , 'Atlas Swam: Freedom, Capital and Floating Sovereignties in the Seasteading Vision' (2012) 44(4) *Antipode* 1532, 1544.

pressure forced the government to withdraw from the project.[37] Many wondered whether '"facilitating the tax evasion of the world's greatest fortunes" would actually be beneficial for the islands'.[38]

Friedman and Thiel are now looking to buy land in developing nations to establish semi-autonomous cities.[39] In this effort they join a long line of libertarian-inspired micronations. In 2001, for instance, the Principality of Freedonia, a micronation initially established by University of Texas student John Kyle, sought to lease territory in Somaliland to create its 'tax-free, business-friendly utopia'.[40] If Friedman and Thiel secure their libertarian dream in these new locales they will not be micronations but special economic zones, though they likely will not care much for the distinction.

Even if libertarianism as a political ideology was not the overriding factor, general frustration with government and regulation has been a key element in the establishment of several other prominent micronations, including the Principality of Sealand. In the United Kingdom, the British Broadcasting Corporation (BBC) had enjoyed a formal monopoly on radio broadcasting since its establishment in the 1920s. This allowed the BBC to carry out what its first Director-General, Lord Reith, regarded as its educative or civilising mission. To Reith, the purpose of the BBC was 'cultural improvement'; its broadcasts upheld the rhythm of the Church calendar, and it endeavoured to inform and educate the public by offering a carefully curated selection of programming. That programming was financed by a broadcast licence levied on all those who listened.[41]

From the very beginning, enterprising individuals sought to evade both the licensing fees and the BBC's territorial monopoly. Several substantial commercial radio stations were set up in continental Europe in places like Normandy and Luxembourg, but others adopted more

[37] Ranganathan (n 34); 'Hundreds March in Tahiti against Building of Floating Islands', *Radio New Zealand* (9 April 2018) www.rnz.co.nz/international/pacific-news/354491/hundreds-march-in-tahiti-against-building-of-floating-islands.

[38] Alexandre Taliercio cited in Dylan Taylor-Lehman, *Sealand: The True Story of the World's Most Stubborn Micronation* (Icon Books, 2020) 176.

[39] Lizette Chapman, 'The Hottest New Thing in Seasteading Is Land', *Bloomberg Business Week* (20 December 2019) www.bloomberg.com/news/articles/2019-12-20/silicon-valley-seasteaders-go-looking-for-low-tax-sites-on-land.

[40] John Ryan, George Dunford and Simon Sellars, *Micronations: The Lonely Planet Guide to Home-Made Nations* (Lonely Planet, 2006) 56–9; Stephen Mihm, 'Utopian Rulers, and Spoofs, Stake Out Territory Online', *The New York Times* (25 May 2000) G7.

[41] Adrian Johns, *Death of a Pirate: British Radio and the Making of the Information Age* (W. W. Norton & Co, 2011) ch 1; Taylor-Lehman (n 38) ch 3.

imaginative activities. In 1928, for instance, the *Daily Mail* newspaper installed a radio transmitter on a chartered sailing vessel called the *Ceto*, intending to broadcast music and advertisements into the country from outside the United Kingdom's territorial waters. Climatic and weather conditions prevented the apparatus from working effectively so the plan was adapted. The transmitter was replaced by four gigantic loudspeakers and the *Ceto* toured the United Kingdom, anchoring off holiday resorts and coastal towns blasting gramophone records. Despite being a 'technical failure', the experiment proved to be a 'publicity coup'.[42]

Whether or not inspired by the *Ceto*, a number of ships transmitting radio broadcasts into Northern Europe began operating in the late 1950s. By 1964, the first such ship broadcasting into the United Kingdom, *Radio Caroline*, had been established, followed a week later by *Radio Atlanta*. The pirate radio stations distinguished themselves from the BBC by offering pop music, as well as more traditional fare. They had another advantage. The 1956 Copyright Act prevented the BBC from broadcasting more than 28 hours of records across its stations each week; *Radio Caroline* and *Radio Atlanta* broadcast more than 12 hours of records each day. Ten more pirate radio stations would emerge over the next two years,[43] attracted by the considerable advertising revenue; 'some stations were said to individually bring in upwards of £20,000 each month (no less than £368,000 in 2019)'.[44] Dylan Taylor-Lehman notes: 'the enterprise also became so popular that the pirate radio was said to influence the outcomes of local elections, and the Beatles even recorded Christmas greetings for Radio London and Radio Caroline'.[45] Their popularity placed government in a political bind; Cabinet papers imply that even Prime Minister Harold Wilson listened.[46] As one government official remarked, 'they are beyond territorial waters. To stop them we will have to send a torpedo, but that's a bit drastic, isn't it?'[47]

Into this electric atmosphere stepped Roy Bates. Unlike many of his competitors who operated from ships, Bates transmitted *Radio Essex* from an abandoned World War II-era anti-aircraft gun platform called Knock John, located at the mouth of the Thames estuary. Securing the

[42] Johns (n 41) 38.
[43] Ibid 119–143.
[44] Taylor-Lehman (n 38) 27.
[45] Ibid.
[46] Johns (n 41) 225.
[47] Bernard Jordan, 'I Go Aboard the Pirate Pop Ship', *Daily Mail* (31 March 1964). Cited in John Venmore-Rowland, *Radio Caroline* (Landmark Press, 1967) 37.

site was not simple; Bates first had to eject the staff of a rival operator, *Radio City*.[48]

Radio Essex did not survive for long. Although the UK government had largely tolerated the existence of pirate radio operators, in part because public opinion supported their less staid programming, the government felt compelled to act in the aftermath of the highly publicised shooting of one entrepreneur by another. The government began enforcing the 1949 Wireless Telegraphy Act which prohibited unlicensed broadcasts within the United Kingdom's three-mile territorial zone. Unfortunately for Bates, Knock John was located only one and a half miles from the coast. Served with a summons, Bates was found in violation of the Act in November 1966 and fined £100; his appeal was dismissed the following year.[49] Bates did not give up. On Christmas Day 1966, he dismantled the equipment on Knock John and moved to another decommissioned offshore naval fort, Roughs Tower, located seven miles off the coast of Suffolk.[50]

Roughs Tower may have been decommissioned but it was not abandoned. Recognising that government intended to step up enforcement actions against pirate radio operators, the operators of *Radio Caroline* had already relocated to the remote fort. Over the first half of 1967, Bates and the staff of *Radio Caroline* struggled to wrest control. Bates eventually triumphed, evicting the crew from the tower, and repulsing their repeated attempts to return with an air-rifle, Molotov cocktails and perhaps even a flamethrower.[51] *The Times* reported one such incident:

> Mr. Bates said that Tuesday night's raid, in which a party of boarders was fought off, was 'a mere tickle' compared with the usual goings on. He said there had been several raids on the tower in the past three months. In one raid, Mr. Bates said, 'there were about 30 of them in foreign-looking boats, rather like Dutchmen, armed with knives and guns trying to take over. But they were repelled. After all, there is only one way up the ladder, and if you are at the top you are in a pretty good position. Some tried to swim with snorkels but they were spotted and given short shrift with a flame thrower.'[52]

48 Johns (n 41) 176-177; Taylor-Lehman (n 38) 28; James Grimmelmann, 'Sealand, Havenco, and the Rule of Law' (2012) 2 *University of Illinois Law Review* 405, 415.

49 *R v Kent Justices, Ex parte Lye* [1967] 2 QB 153.

50 Grimmelmann (n 48) 416.

51 Taylor-Lehman (n 38) 36–8.

52 'Sea Fort Repels Boarders: Raiders Faced Flamethrower', *The Times* (London, 30 June 1967) 2.

After another incident, 'one man was left hanging over the North Sea on a rope ladder for several hours' before being rescued by a lifeboat.[53] Unsurprisingly, the government faced questioning in Parliament over what it intended to do 'to end gang warfare on pirate radio stations'.[54]

In July, the government made its move. The 1967 Marine & Broadcasting (Offences) Act closed the legal loophole that allowed pirate radio stations to operate. The Act prohibited British citizens from operating or participating or assisting in broadcasts from the high seas and banned advertising on such broadcasts.[55] Rather than continue *Radio Essex*, Bates declared himself the ruler of the Principality of Sealand on 2 September 1967. It was a move he had foreshadowed earlier that year. Indeed, in June he had told *The Times*:

> 'My solicitors are studying the legal aspects of the entire affair', Mr. Bates said. 'This will entail international law and until they have completed their work I do not intend saying what my plans are. They have nothing to do with commercial radio, although I have all my equipment on board.'[56]

The Principality of Sealand continues to exist today.

The micronations or attempted micronations discussed thus far have all centred on peripheral territory. That is, land unclaimed, unsettled or abandoned by sovereign states. The proponents of these initiatives have adopted this strategy for pragmatic reasons; the vast majority, if not all, of the globe's habitable landmass has already been claimed, meaning that those looking to establish their own country must search further afield. For various reasons, however, some land has not been claimed.

One such area is Bir Tawil, a 2,060-square-kilometre uninhabited and unclaimed area along the Egyptian and Sudanese border. The land is claimed by neither Egypt nor Sudan because of a discrepancy between the 1899 political boundary and the 1902 administrative boundary that separates the two states. Egypt asserts the political boundary, which runs along the 22nd parallel and places Bir Tawil within Sudan (and the much larger Halayib Triangle within Egypt). For its part, Sudan adopts the administrative boundary, which was drawn to follow the actual use of land by the tribes in the region and places Bir Tawil within

[53] 'Struggle for Sea Fort', *The Times* (London, 28 June 1967) 1; '100GNS Health Trips to Sea Fort', *The Times* (London, 29 June 1967) 2; 'Commandos Set to Seize Fort', *The Times* (London, 8 August 1967) 1.

[54] United Kingdom, *Parliamentary Debates*, House of Commons, 3 July 1967, vol 749, col 191.

[55] *Marine & Broadcasting (Offences) Act 1967* (UK) c 47, ss 3–5.

[56] 'Sea Fort Repels Boarders' (n 52).

Egypt (and the Halayib Triangle within Sudan). In June 2014, Jeremiah Heaton, a 38-year-old Virginian farmer who had become aware of this anomaly, reached Bir Tawil and proclaimed the Kingdom of North Sudan. Ostensibly, Heaton claimed the territory to fulfil a promise to his daughter Emily to make her a princess (film rights to the story have been bought by Disney).[57] However, it appears that Heaton has other motivations. In conversations with a journalist from the *Guardian*, Heaton expanded on the advantages of statehood, arguing that his Kingdom 'could offer the world's great innovators a place to develop their products unencumbered by taxes and regulation, a place where private enterprise faces no socially prescribed borders of its own'.[58] Despite applying for observer status at the United Nations and appointing several ambassadors across Europe, no state has recognised the Kingdom. Prospects of any such recognition also appear dim.

Bir Tawil illustrates both the artificiality of borders and their significance to the exercise of legitimate political authority in the international state system. However, the diversity of the human experience belies the promise that clear lines on maps can resolve tensions between political communities. Another recent example comes from Europe and consists of a small, seven-square-kilometre portion of territory on the western bank of the Danube River. On 13 April 2015, Czech politician Vit Jedlička set foot on the territory, claimed by neither Croatia nor Serbia, and announced the establishment of the Free Republic of Liberland[59] with the intention of developing a libertarian utopia free of government regulation and taxation.[60] Jedlička also raised a flag, sent a diplomatic note to both neighbouring states and sought recognition across the globe. Liberland and the Kingdom of North Sudan formally recognise each

[57] Joe Jackson, 'Creating the Kingdom of North Sudan', *Al Jazeera* (11 May 2015) www.aljazeera.com/features/2015/5/11/creating-the-kingdom-of-north-sudan.

[58] Jack Shenker, 'Welcome to the Land that No Country Wants', *The Guardian* (3 March 2016) www.theguardian.com/world/2016/mar/03/welcome-to-the-land-that-no-country-wants-bir-tawil.

[59] Gideon Lewis-Kraus, 'The Birth Pangs of a Libertarian Paradise', *The New York Times Magazine* (16 August 2015) 46.

[60] Gabriel Rossman, 'Extremely Loud and Incredible Close (But Still So Far): Assessing Liberland's Claim of Statehood' (2016) 17(1) *Chicago Journal of International Law* 306, 308; Ryan Gorman, 'This New Microcountry Wants to Be a Big Tax Haven', *Business Insider* (23 April 2015) www.businessinsider.com.au/liberland-this-newly-declared-microcountry-wants-to-become-the-worlds-foremost-tax-haven-2015-4. See further, Christopher Balch, 'An Argument for the International Recognition of Liberland' (2016) *Michigan Journal of International Law Online* www.mjilonline.org/an-argument-for-the-international-recognition-of-liberland/.

other, but as we explore in Chapter 5, no sovereign state has responded positively.

3.2 Acts of Resistance

Libertarianism may be a driving force behind many declarations of independence, but it is not always sufficient. The financial challenges and psychological resources involved in acquiring territory and continually performing (unrecognised) acts of sovereignty over many years mean something more can be required. As Judy Lattas explains, that something more is the transformation of a personal grievance into a political grievance, a 'sense of being cheated out of some sort of natural right' that develops into a 'feeling about a loss of sovereignty'.[61] Lattas emphasises that for micronations founded by these individuals, secession is:

> not an act of withdrawing the self, but of presenting and re-presenting the self, in courts of law, in administrative tribunals, in bureaucratic offices and all the theatres within which may be played out a contesting of the authority to manage. The gesture of secession is one of refusing to withdraw oneself, refusing to cease, pushing oneself forward, getting 'in your face'. Micronationalists feature strongly among those 'vexatious litigants' whose obdurate presence in the courtroom and the corridor threatens to jam up the system, making it unmanageable.[62]

These are 'not utopian communes', Lattas reiterates, but rather an 'imaginative way of articulating resistance to bureaucracy'.[63]

The combination of ideological resistance to state authority and bureaucracy and a strong sense of injustice helps account for the founding of the Principality of Hutt River. Considered 'something of a template for modern micronations',[64] the Principality emerged out of a dispute over a wheat harvest. A similar combination of motivations sheds light on many other Australian micronations. For example, in 1993, George and Stephanie Muirhead founded the Principality of Malborough as a means to avoid repossession of their 20,000-acre cattle and grain farm in the State of Queensland. The Muirheads sent a copy of their 100-page

[61] Judy Lattas cited in ABC Radio National, *Micronations* (15 April 2010) www.abc.net.au/radionational/programs/lifematters/micronations/3039654.

[62] Judy Lattas, 'Queer Sovereignty: The Gay & Lesbian Kingdom of the Coral Sea Islands' (2009) 1 *Cosmopolitan Civil Societies Journal* 128, 130.

[63] Judy Lattas cited in Matt Siegel, 'The Royal Me: What's with Australia's Secession Obsession?' (April 2012) 309(3) *The Atlantic* 21, 22.

[64] Ryan, Dunford and Sellars (n 40) 22.

secession document to the Queen, the Governor-General, representatives of each of Australia's six states and the United Nations. Proclaiming himself the Duke of Malborough, George Muirhead presided over a ceremony marking the occasion in which four flags were raised; the Australian, the UN, the Australian Aboriginal flag and the flag of Scotland to represent his ancestors. The Principality survived only eleven days before they and thirty supporters were evicted by the Queensland Police.[65] Ten years later, Prince Paul and Princess Helena established the Snake Hill Principality, located near Mudgee in the State of New South Wales, following a long-running dispute with their bank. Unlike the short-lived Principality of Malborough, Snake Hill appears to be a going concern, though now ruled solely by Princess Helena following her husband's passing.

For many micronations, the trigger is a dispute with the local council. For instance, after several rejected planning applications on his property in Port Stephens, 215 kilometres north of Sydney, Australia, Peter Gillies proclaimed the independence of the Principality of United Oceania.[66] In a separate court action seeking payment of several thousand dollars in council rates, Gillies was declared bankrupt and his property auctioned, though fortuitously it was bought by another person sympathetic to the Principality.[67] Gillies took his fight to the United Kingdom where he has had no success persuading British courts that Australia is a colony and has no jurisdiction over his land.[68]

The curiously named Bible Based Christians of the Call can also trace their history to a long-running council dispute. In 2014, Julius Kudrynski declared his home in west Wollongong (100 kilometres south of Sydney) the world's newest country. Kudrynski claimed that he had 'no choice but to go to the International Court [of Justice]' to continue his forty-year fight against Wollongong City Council.[69] The council had successfully

[65] Robert Milliken, 'Outback "Duke" Takes on the Bank', *The Independent* (11 June 1993) www.independent.co.uk/news/world/outback-duke-takes-on-the-bank-a-queensland-man-has-defied-australia-by-creating-a-principality-to-1490896.html.

[66] Viva Goldner, 'Prince Finds If All Else Fails, Secede', *The Daily Telegraph* (24 July 2003) 20.

[67] Mike Scanlon, 'Breakaway Bushland Sold Off, Council Gets Back Rates', *Newcastle Herald* (5 March 2005) 14.

[68] See for example a submission that Gillies made to the Australian Parliament: Peter Gillies, Submission No 258 to Senate Standing Committee on Legal and Constitutional Affairs, *Inquiry into the Provisions of the Anti-Terrorism Bill (No. 2) 2005* (November 2005).

[69] Joshua Butler, 'Julius' Bid to Declare Himself a Micronation', *Illawarra Mercury* (5 September 2014).

secured a court order requiring Kudrynski to demolish and remove a host of unapproved structures in his backyard, including a 30-metre swimming pool, an archery range and 'piles of lawnmowers and stacks of fridges'.[70] It is not clear whether this micronation remains active.

The same is true for the Principality of Dubeldeka, once situated in the New South Wales Southern Highlands. Vas and Doreen Khanderkar, the owners of Braemar Lodge, purported to secede in 2001 in an effort 'to overcome bureaucratic interference'.[71] The Khanderkars claimed that council installation of a sewerage system interrupted their business and damaged the heritage building. Despite an update in 2010,[72] little recent information is available on this principality.

The Principality of Wy in the North Sydney suburb of Mosman shares a similar story. Following an eleven-year dispute with the local council over the construction of a driveway, Prince Paul opted to secede. In November 2004 he held a ceremony at Mosman Town Hall, where, dressed in full regalia, he presented a declaration of independence to the mayor of Mosman.[73] Although a change in the local environment plan in 2012 facilitated the approval and construction of the driveway,[74] Prince Paul maintains the Principality of Wy 'as a beacon of hope to all those oppressed by bureaucracy'.[75]

State governments can also serve as a catalyst. In 1979, Thomas Barnes founded the Independent State of Rainbow Creek as part of a decades-long compensation dispute between Victorian farmers and the state government's State Rivers and Water Supply Commission (SRWSC).[76] In the 1930s, a road bridge was built over the Thompson River at the town of Cowwarr in the Victorian Alps. The bridge was poorly sited. During a particularly strong flood in 1952, the bridge impeded the flow of debris, forcing the river to carve a new course around the edge of the structure. This breakaway, later named Rainbow Creek, passed through

70 Ibid. See also *Wollongong City Council v Kudrynski* [2013] NSWLEC 4 (29 January 2013).

71 'Lodge Secedes to Form New Country', *Southern Highland News* (9 October 2001).

72 Derek Henkle, 'Australians Fed Up with Government Creating Their Own Micronations', *Voice of America* (6 May 2010) www.voanews.com/east-asia/australians-fed-up-with-government-creating-their-own-micro nations.

73 The Principality of Wy, 'History' (2010) http://principalityofwy.com/history/.

74 Simone Roberts, 'Cars May Roll Down Royal Driveway: Delprat's Application Moves Forward', *Mosman Daily* (25 October 2012) 5.

75 Matthew Benns, 'Urban Prince Poised for Win Over Council', *The Sun-Herald* (6 May 2007) 32.

76 John Wells, 'The Shire of Rainbow Creek', *Warragul and Drouin Gazette* (14 July 2020) 20.

several private farms causing significant damage. The affected farmers began using water from the creek to irrigate their properties, but local and state authorities charged levies for water use. Farmers had to pay one levy to the local council for land now underwater because their title deeds did not show the existence of the creek, a second levy to the SRWSC for using creek water for irrigation purposes and a third levy to the Thompson River Improvement Trust which went towards preventing further erosion. Remedial action did not help and by the late 1970s, Rainbow Creek was eight metres deep and 50 metres wide. In 1978, a particularly strong flood washed away several bridges that affected farmers had privately funded. After their claim for compensation was dismissed, Barnes and around thirty supporters decided to take action. On 16 January 1979, the group served a declaration of war on the Victorian Governor. A few months later, on 23 July, Barnes seceded from Australia and swore allegiance to Queen Elizabeth II of the United Kingdom. He raised a flag, and lodged secession documents with Australian Governors, Buckingham Palace and the International Court of Justice.

Not all acts of resistance appear as justified. In the 1990s, the Rigoli family purported to secede and declare the formation of the Principality of Ponderosa, in protest of the Department of Agriculture bulldozing an infected fruit crop on their property at Shepperton, around 165 kilometres north of Melbourne. The family built a moat around their 60-acre property, fiercely guarded the entrance and required visitors to show their passport. After several years Philip Rigoli left the property, describing his family as 'strange and toxic', but father Virgilio and brother Joe continued to develop their nation, maintaining that it was the only valid response to a government purportedly discriminating against 'Christians, white Anglo-Saxons and capitalists'. Both were later convicted of tax evasion,[77] though the conviction was overturned on appeal.[78]

Australians are not the only people who can become sufficiently frustrated with government – such a sentiment is universal. In 1971,

[77] 'Ponderosa "Prince" in Court over Fraud', *The Sydney Morning Herald* (19 July 2005) www.smh.com.au/national/ponderosa-prince-in-court-over-fraud-20050719-gdlpov.html; David Fickling, 'Passport to Pimlico – Aussie Style', *The Guardian* (20 November 2002) www.theguardian.com/world/2002/nov/20/australia.davidfickling.

[78] Peter Gregory, '"Prince" Free as Tax Fraud Overturned', *The Age* (26 January 2006) www.theage.com.au/national/prince-free-as-tax-fraud-overturned-20060126-ge1n0s.html.

artist Edwin Lipburger erected a ball-shaped house in the small Austrian town of Katzelsdorf. Following several years of confrontation with state authorities over building permits, Lipburger declared the independence of the Republic of Kugelmugel in 1976 (the republic takes its name from the German word for ball or sphere (*kugel*) and the Austrian-German expression for 'hill on a field' (*mugel*)). Like other micronations, Kugelmugel raised a flag, minted currency and issued stamps. Lipburger went further, however, and constructed handmade street signs that he placed around the house, giving the flavour of a real separate republic. Unfortunately, in 1979 Lipburger was convicted of erecting unapproved street signs and jailed for ten weeks. Following a change of heart, the government later invited Lipburger to move his construction to Vienna's Prater Park, where it still sits today.

Other examples can be noted. On April Fool's Day 1977, Richard Booth 'strode down the high street of Hay-on-Wye, Powys [Wales], dressed in a home-made crown and fake ermine robe' to found the Kingdom of Hay-on-Wye.[79] Proclaiming himself King, he appointed his horse Prime Minister and issued passports and currency. Aiming to attract attention and tourism, Booth was keen to 'shake off the bureaucratic grip of a central government which showed little or no practical interest in re-vitalizing the clearly decaying market town'.[80] Similar motivations lay behind the formation of the Hajdučka Republika Mijata Tomića (The Hajduk Republic of Mijat Tomić), a micronation located in the middle of the Blidinje Nature Park in Bosnia and Herzegovina. Founded in 2002 by motel owner Vinko Vukoja–Lastvić, the Hajduk Republic owes its existence to bureaucratic inertia. In this case, the failure of local government to connect Vukoja–Lastvić's property to the electrical grid. Uncertain demarcation meant that three municipalities – Posušje, Tomislavgrad and Jablanica – could not agree under whose responsibility the area fell. So, none acted; NATO led peacekeeping forces were initially alarmed, but quickly realised the Republic had no secessionist ambitions.[81]

Ladonia also owes its existence to a long-running dispute between an artist and local government. In 1980, Swedish artist Lars Vilks built two

[79] Oliver Balch, 'Richard Booth Obituary', *The Guardian* (23 August 2019) www.theguardian.com/books/2019/aug/22/richard-booth-obituary.

[80] Richard King of Hay, 'History of the Hay Peerage' www.richardkingofhay.com/history-of-the-hay-peerage.html.

[81] See 'Čije Je Blidinje: Dok hajduci vladaju, tri općine se spore', *Tomislavcity.com* (13 August 2007).

large sculptures in an inaccessible nature reserve near Skåne, in southern Sweden. When the local authorities discovered the sculptures several years later, they ordered their destruction, reasoning that buildings were prohibited in the reserve. Vilks unsuccessfully appealed the decision all the way to the Supreme Court of Sweden. However, although the structures were determined illegal constructions, no action was ever taken to remove them.[82] In 1996, the Swedish Chancellor of Justice criticised the local authorities over the failure to enforce the court judgment. Seizing the moment, Vilks proclaimed the establishment of Ladonia,[83] named for the Greek dragon appointed to guard the golden apples in the Garden of Hesperides. Today, the micronation claims more than 22,000 citizens from fifty countries – though none, of course, live in Ladonia. The micronation waives any residency requirement and confers citizenship over the Internet.

Not all micronations are created by ordinary people. Consider the conceptual nation of Nutopia. In April 1973, John Lennon and Yoko Ono introduced the world to Nutopia at a press conference in New York City:

> We announce the birth of a conceptual country, NUTOPIA. Citizenship of the country can be obtained by declaration of your awareness of NUTOPIA. NUTOPIA has no land, no boundaries, no passports, only people. NUTOPIA has no laws other than cosmic. All people of NUTOPIA are ambassadors of the country. As two ambassadors of NUTOPIA, we ask for diplomatic immunity and recognition in the United Nations of our country and its people.[84]

Diplomatic immunity was important. Lennon had previously been denied permanent residence in the United States. In March 1973, a US Immigration Service Judge had ruled that Lennon could be deported unless he voluntarily left within sixty days on the basis of a British conviction for possession of hashish.[85] At the press conference, Lennon waved a white tissue, exclaiming: 'This is the flag of Nutipia – we

[82] Vicente Bicudo de Castro and Ralph Kober, 'The Royal Republic of Ladonia: A Micronation Built of Driftwood, Concrete and Bytes' (2019) 13(1) *Shima: The International Journal of Research into Island Cultures* 115, 120.

[83] Lars Vilks, 'Ladonia' in Tellervo Kalleinen and Oliver Kochta-Kalleinen (eds), *Protocols: Amorph!03Summit of Micronations* (2005) 76, 76. See also Ladonia, 'Ladonia' (2019) www.ladonia.org/history/.

[84] 'Declaration of Nutopia' (Nutopian Embassy, New York, 1 April 1973) https://twitter.com/johnlennon/status/980473627303927810/photo/2.

[85] Laurie Johnston, 'Lennon Sees a Wide Impact in Ouster', *The New York Times* (3 April 1973) 40.

surrender, to peace and to love.' A *New York Times* reporter noted that Lennon blew his nose on the tissue.[86]

Communities and towns buffeted by political decisions from state and federal governments sometimes also seek the safety of secession. In 2011, the Italian village of Filettino, located about 68 kilometres east of Rome, declared its independence. The decision was prompted by austerity measures enacted by the Italian government which aimed at cutting local administrative costs by forcing villages with less than 1,000 residents to merge with their neighbours. As Luca Sellari, the town mayor and founder of the new Principality of Filettino noted, 'Italy was once made up of dozens of principalities and dukedoms. . . . the landlocked republic of San Marino still manages to survive, so why not Filettino?'[87]

3.3 Personal Expression and Attention Seeking

The Republic of Kugelmugel and Ladonia reveal that micronations are not always so serious. For many founders and citizens, micronations are 'designed to be funny',[88] and simply a 'bit of a laugh'.[89] Widespread use of faux-regal titles, European-inspired heraldry and made-up military medals suggests personal expression and attention seeking can be a primary motivator behind the formation of micronations.

The rise of hobbyist or humorous micronations has risen in line with the growth of the Internet. The mid-1990s saw 'a sudden increase in interest' in the phenomenon, as the ease with which micronations could be established and promoted increased.[90] Today, many contemporary micronations exist only 'within extended social media spaces'.[91] While

[86] Ibid.

[87] David Willey, 'Italian Town Filettino declares Independence', *BBC News* (3 September 2011) www.bbc.com/news/world-asia-pacific-14774526; Elisabetta Povoledo, 'In an Italian Town, Dreams of Freedom on a Princely Scale', *The New York Times* (30 August 2011) A.10.

[88] Adam Grydehøj, 'Captain Calamity's Sovereign State of Forvik' (2014) 8 *Shima: The International Journal of Research into Island Cultures* 34, 35.

[89] Volker von Prittwitz, 'State, Size and Democracy: A Brief Comparative Survey of Micro-, Meso-, and Macronations' in Tellervo Kalleinen and Oliver Kochta-Kalleinen (eds), *Protocols: Amorph!03Summit of Micronations* (2005) 26, 28.

[90] Lattas (n 1) 1.

[91] Philip Hayward, 'Secessionism, Submergence and Site-Responsive Art: The Embassy of the Commonwealth of New Bayswater at the 1st Fremantle Biennale' (2018) 12 *Shima: The International Journal of Research into Island Cultures* 160, 161. See also Philip Hayward and Susie Khamis, 'Fleeting and Partial Autonomy: A Historical Account of Quasi-Micronational Initiatives on Lundy Island and Their Contemporary

others claim to exercise physical territory, their extent is limited. The Republic of Molossia, for instance, consists of three properties owned by President Kevin Baugh in the United States, with its capital, Baughston, located near Dayton, Nevada. The Republic is not a money-making exercise. As Baugh explains, 'It's an expression of personal sovereignty, creativity, imagination, and political satire … It's a nice way to look around the world. You can see what countries are doing and say, "I can do that".'[92]

Like other micronations, the Republic has its own flag, national anthem and currency, but also its own system of dates.[93] Molossia has 'played an unparalleled role in micronational development';[94] inaugurating the Intermicronational Olympic Movement in 2000, and establishing MicroCon, a biennial convention of micronation governments held since 2015.[95] It also claims to be at war with East Germany. In 1983, Baugh was stationed in West Germany while serving in the US Army. Military exercises conducted by the German Democratic Republic (GDR) often kept him awake at night, which he considered a declaration of war. Although the GDR formally ceased to exist in 1990 following the Treaty on the Final Settlement with Respect to Germany, Baugh claims that the war is ongoing. The Treaty does not mention Ernst Thälmann Island, a Cuban possession which Fidel Castro promised to donate to East Germany in the 1970s. While both Cuba and Germany maintain that the gift was merely symbolic, Baugh asserts that it remains East German land and so the war continues.[96]

Reflecting the growth of interest in and popular fascination with micronations, some have been established by documentary film-makers exploring the phenomenon. In the 2005 BBC documentary series, *How to Start Your Own Country*, Danny Wallace formed the Kingdom of Lovely. Asserting sovereignty over his apartment in East London, Wallace

Reconfiguration on MicroWiki' (2015) 9 *Shima: The International Journal of Research into Island Cultures* 69–84; Ruth Wedgwood, 'Cyber-Nations' (2000) 88 *Kentucky Law Journal* 957.

92 Carmen Machado, 'The Imaginary Republic of Molossia', *Vice* (27 April 2013) www.vice.com/en_us/article/vdywxm/the-imaginary-republic-of-molossia.

93 Ryan, Dunford and Sellars (n 40) 62–8.

94 Ibid 63.

95 MicroCon 2015 (Anaheim, CA, 11 April 2015) www.molossia.org/microcon/microcon2015.html.

96 'Castro's Caribbean Island Gift to East Germany', *Deutsche Weller* (27 November 2016) www.dw.com/en/castros-caribbean-island-gift-to-east-germany/a-36539460; Machado (n 92).

designed a flag, coat of arms and Latin motto ('Die Dulchi Freure' – Have a Nice Day). Thanks to the Internet and the popularity of his TV series, some 58,000 people registered as citizens – more than many recognized sovereign states. Around the same time, Canadian television news cameraman Christopher Beyette established the Kingdom of Vikesland in Manitoba as part of a documentary film he was working on.

Micronations exist only for so long as their proponents continue to engage in statehood rituals. For this reason, those established by individuals as a hobby or as a means of personal expression and attention seeking often do not survive for lengthy periods of time. Playing a nation can be time-consuming – King Robert of Talossa estimated he spent up to eight hours a week serving as monarch.[97] It may also distance a founder from their family and friends who could consider the activity strange or bemusing. Prince Paul of Wy acknowledges that his adult children are 'somewhat embarrassed' by the royal titles he has conferred upon them.[98] For this reason, many micronations established with these motivations, even those that started with a bang, quickly become defunct.

Consider the Principality of Outer Baldonia. Asserting jurisdiction over around four acres of Outer Bald Tusket Island, eight nautical miles off the southern tip of the Canadian province of Nova Scotia, the Principality was founded by American lawyer Russel Arundel in 1949. A keen recreational fisherman, Arundel bought the island for USD 750 to use as a base during the sport fishing season. After a particularly heavy drinking session, he and a group of friends conceived, drafted, approved and published the Declaration of Independence of Outer Baldonia:

> Let these facts be submitted to a candid world. That fishermen are a race alone. That fishermen are endowed with the following inalienable rights: The right of freedom from question, nagging, shaving, interruption, women, taxes, politics, wars, monologues, cant and inhibitions . . . The right to swear, lie, drink, gamble . . . The right to sleep all day and stay up all night . . .

Although never recognised by any sovereign state, the Principality managed to acquire attention on the international stage. The Washington Chesapeake and Potomac Telephone Company listed Arundel's

97 Alex Blumberg, 'It's Good to Be King' (March 2000) 8(3) *Wired* 132.

98 Kelly Burke, 'Why, Willoughby Begins with a W, Wy Begins with a W, It's All Quite Wonderful My Dear!', *Daily Telegraph* (14 April 2017) www.dailytelegraph.com.au/news/nsw/prince-paul-vs-mosman-council-maintaining-a-right-royal-rage/news-story/6f3204a38a81f431e2b0eb9b0a8dc9ef.

Washington office phone number as the Baldonian legation, and Arundel began receiving routine US State Department calls that went to all diplomatic missions inviting him to attend functions. In time, he began issuing press releases on the major international affairs of the day, including the Cold War. These press releases soon attracted the attention of the USSR. In 1952, the Soviet literary magazine *Literaturnaya Gazeta* published a scathing critique of Outer Baldonia. Quoting heavily from its Declaration of Independence, the article was incredulous that Arundel had 'granted his subjects the "unrestricted right" to tell lies, to be rude . . . In a word, the "right" not to adhere to the ethical and moral laws which have been established by civilized mankind'.[99] The author also sketched parallels with Baldonia and American capitalism and imperialism. While it may have been satire, international newspapers covered the story and Arundel was insulted. When the Soviet government did not reply to Arundel's invitation to visit his nation, he declared war on the USSR. The Soviets again did not respond, and Arundel claimed victory.[100] In 1973, Arundel sold the island to the Nova Scotia Bird Society for USD 1 and retired the Principality.

The Kingdom of Talossa has also been dissolved. Founded by 14-year-old Milwaukee resident Robert Madison in 1979 following the death of his mother, the Kingdom initially claimed jurisdiction over Madison's bedroom. The Kingdom was active – though small – throughout the 1980s, largely consisting of his family and friends. In the mid-1990s, however, media reports in *The New York Times* and elsewhere drew attention to Talossa, and many more people clamoured to attain citizenship. Over the years, King Robert developed Talossan symbols and artefacts, including a newspaper, flag, emblem and crown (a former Milwaukee fire department dress hat). He also invented a sophisticated Talossan language (*el glheþ Talossan*)[101] of over 28,000 words that purportedly traces its origins to a fifth-century sect of Latin-speaking North African Berbers.[102] In 2005, the Kingdom was disestablished by Madison, but it continues to operate today without Madison's involvement.

[99] Cited in Lachlan Mackinnon, '"Give Me Fish, Not Federalism": Outer Baldonia and Performances of Micronationality' (2014) 8(2) *Shima: The International Journal of Research into Island Cultures* 105.

[100] Andreas Schroeder, *Scams, Scandals and Skulduggery: A Selection of the World's Most Outrageous Frauds* (McClelland & Stewart, 1996) 62–8.

[101] Mihm (n 40); Roberta Smiths, 'We Could Have Invited Everyone', *The New York Times* (15 July 2005) E.32.

[102] Blumberg (n 97).

If a founder wants to ensure the sustainability of their micronation it helps to convince the local community to back their project. One particularly successful micronation is the Republic of Parva Domus Magna Quies, located in the Uruguayan capital of Montevideo. Founded in 1878 by a group of fishermen seeking great rest in a little house (where the Latin name for their nation comes from), the Principality is today based around a neoclassical residence on Punta Brava in the south of the city. Perhaps owing to its longevity, Uruguayan officials have sometimes treated it with faux recognition. In 2003, the Uruguayan Postal Service issued a postage stamp in honour of the Republic's 125th anniversary.[103] The Kingdom of Elleore on the Danish island of the same name has also outlasted many sovereign states. Established by a group of Copenhagen schoolteachers during the German occupation of Denmark in 1944, the Kingdom parodies the royal traditions and government structure of Denmark. Today, the Kingdom is only occupied for a one-week celebration each year.[104]

3.4 Tourism

Declaring independence and forming a new nation may start as a theatrical act to draw attention or as an act of personal expression, but many small towns soon recognise economic advantages in micronationalism. In a crowded marketplace, a mark of distinction can be valuable. What better way to attract tourists and visitors to your city than by hosting independence celebrations, selling fake stamps and faux currency? Nonetheless, the challenges of creating and sustaining a country are significant. It often takes much more than a simple desire to boost tourism to perform and re-perform acts of sovereignty. Hence, while tourism is a primary motivation for many founders and proponents, it is frequently accompanied by other impulses, including attention seeking, acts of resistance or political protest.

One such micronation is the Principality of Seborga. The vast majority of micronations are relatively young, but several purport to trace their history back hundreds of years in an effort to legitimate their claims. The Principality of Seborga traces its history to the tenth century. Located in the north Italian province of Imperia in Liguria, the town of Seborga is about 35 kilometres from Monaco. Its claim as an independent state rests

[103] See www.freestampcatalogue.com/surp2753-parva-domus-magna-quies-1v.
[104] Ryan, Dunford and Sellars (n 40) 42–7.

on the failure to properly register a contract. As the story goes, in 954 the Counts of Ventimiglia bestowed the village to the Benedictine monks of Lérins.[105] A century later, the monastery's abbot was made a prince in the Holy Roman Empire and was granted temporal authority over the Principality of Seborga. In 1729, the Principality was allegedly sold to the King of Sardinia, and it consequently became part of the Kingdom of Italy following the 1861 Act of Unification. However, the people of Seborga argue that the 1729 sale was not registered and point to the fact that Seborga is not mentioned in either the 1861 Act of Unification or the 1944 Declaration of the Italian Republic.[106] Bolstering their claim is Benito Mussolini's 1934 apocryphal statement acknowledging that 'for sure the Principato di Seborga does not belong to Italy'.[107]

In the 1950s, head of the flower-growers co-op Giorgio Carbone began exploring the history of the town. In 1963, he convinced his friends and colleagues of this history, and they voted to declare themselves the Principality of Seborga. Following the Benedictine monastic tradition, the town decided to elect its leader; Giorgio was duly elected with 304 out of a possible 308 votes and invested as His Tremendousness Giorgio I, Prince of Seborga.[108] His Tremendousness was apparently relatively successful: in addition to writing their Constitution, designing a flag and minting currency, Carbone purports to have 'convince[d] around 20 states to recognize Seborga' and maintains consular representation in ten countries.[109] Prince Giorgio I reigned until his death in 2009. Prince Marcello I was subsequently elected for a seven-year term.[110]

The Principality continues to exist today. Nina Menegatto, Marcello I's wife, who was elected Princess of Seborga in 2019, explains why:

> [The village] lives off agriculture and the flower business, these are the main sources of income ... But for tourism obviously the story of the principality helps. The restaurants and the souvenir shops, for example,

[105] Viktoriya Serzhanova, 'Concept and Status of Fictional States' (2014) 17 *Annales Universitatis Apulensis Series Jurisprudentia* 82, 85.

[106] Ryan, Dunford and Sellars (n 40) 55.

[107] Ibid.

[108] Serzhanova (n 105) 85.

[109] 'His Tremendousness Giorgio Carbone', *The Daily Telegraph* (27 November 2009) www.telegraph. co.uk/news/obituaries/royalty-obituaries/6671765/His-Tremendousness-Giorgio-Carbone.html.

[110] Nick Squires, 'Tiny Italian Principality Announces New Monarch Called "His Tremendousness"', *The Daily Telegraph* (27 April 2010) www.telegraph.co.uk/news/worldnews/europe/italy/7639617/Tiny-Italian-principality-announces-new-monarch-called-His-Tremendousness.html.

> they live off tourism. People are curious so they come up to check us out – 'why is this a principality, what's going on here?' . . . We have Japanese tourists in Seborga now which we never used to have before.[111]

In the 1980s, a quick-thinking mayor and city council in the United States also recognised the financial advantages of independence. In 1982, the US Border Patrol set up a roadblock and inspection point on the road between the Florida Keys and the mainland to curb drug smuggling and undocumented immigration. The inspection point resulted in a 27-kilometre traffic jam, severely inconveniencing residents and hurting Key West's tourism industry, but the city council was unable to secure an injunction or persuade the federal government to remove the roadblock. Determining that the federal government had essentially established a border station as if they were a foreign nation, the mayor declared Key West's independence on 23 April 1982. Like many micronations, the Conch Republic immediately declared war on its (much) larger neighbour. The Republic's intentions were financial rather than militaristic, however. After only one minute, the Conch Republic issued a declaration of surrender, before requesting a Marshall Plan style USD 1 billion in foreign aid to restore the local economy.[112]

The Conch Republic's tongue in cheek secession and independence was explicitly framed as being consistent with American values. As Peter Anderson, who served as Secretary-General of the Republic until his death in 2014, explained, the Conch Republic is a manifestation of the American spirit:

> of the experience that people aren't afraid to stand up to government gone mad with power, and to do it with humor and aplomb, and to actually win the day . . . . [The Conch Republic independence proclamation] is one of the quintessentially American documents that's been written.[113]

Nonetheless, while the event was and continues to be presented as 'the counterculture versus the establishment', a different impetus predominated. William Barnett notes that 'it was a conservative public relations effort by the Mayor, Chamber of Commerce, and Tourist Development

[111] Tristan Kennedy, 'Welcome to Seborga: The Extraordinary Story of the Italian Village that Thinks It's a Country', *Amuse* (24 January 2020) https://amuse.vice.com/en_us/article/yw4b9m/seborga-italian-village-claiming-independence.

[112] 'Key West, in Protest on Aliens, "Secedes"', *The New York Times* (25 April 1982) 12.

[113] Cited in Philip Steinberg and Thomas Chapman, 'Key West's Conch Republic: Building Sovereignties of Connection' (2009) 28 *Political Geography* 283, 285.

Board to defend tourism because the roadblock discouraged motorists from visiting the Keys'.[114] The group was successful in at least two ways. Drawing attention to the concerns of the city, the roadblock was moved. More significantly, the Republic's annual national ten-day celebrations attract many tourists each year.

Light-hearted acts of resistance can take on a momentum of their own. This is what happened to the Republic of Whangamōmona, located on the North Island of New Zealand. In 1989, the boundaries of New Zealand's Regional Councils were redrawn. The revised maps moved the forty-person township of Whangamōmona from the Taranaki Region into the Manawatu-Wanganui Region. Upset about potentially having to play rugby union for their rivals, residents objected; they decided to secede from New Zealand and declared themselves a republic on 1 November 1989.[115] Although initially a symbolic act aimed at drawing political and media attention to their concerns through humour, the motivation has shifted over time. Republic Day is now commemorated biennially in January, attracting thousands of visitors from across the North Island.[116] Nonetheless, revealing the spirit in which secession was undertaken, elected Presidents have included a goat (1999–2001) and a poodle (2003–04).[117] Like all democratic elections, controversy is not far from the surface; some residents speculate that Billy Gumboot (the goat) secured victory only after eating his opponent's ballots.

The Republic of Whangamōmona shares similarities with the Republic of Rathnelly, a neighbourhood of Toronto, Canada. In the 1960s, concerns over the proposed development of an expressway through their homes led residents to band together. During celebration of Canada's centennial on 1 July 1967, the residents declared the formation of the Republic of Rathnelly. They elected a Queen, issued passports, and organised a parade. In 1969, they wrote to Canadian Prime Minister Pierre Trudeau seeking foreign aid to build a playground, in exchange for letting the city use the Republic's parkland:

[114] William Barnett, 'Inventing the Conch Republic: The Creation of Key West as an Escape from Modern America' (2009) 88(2) *The Florida Historical Quarterly* 139, 171.

[115] Ryan, Dunford and Sellars (n 40) 35.

[116] Visit Taranaki, 'Whangamōmona Republic Day 2017' https://visit.taranaki.info/visit/news/whangamomona-republic-day-2017.aspx; 'Being a "Republic" Means Whanga Is Far from Forgotten', *Taranaki Daily Herald* (19 January 2017) 8.

[117] Ryan, Dunford and Sellars (n 40) 36.

> Unless immediate action is taken on your part we shall have no alternative but to regard your occupation as the commencement of hostilities and we shall therefore order total mobilization of our citizenry.[118]

The Prime Minister's secretary responded congratulating Rathnelly 'on the evident success' of its republic, but suggested it write to Toronto for funding.[119] The neighbourhood has changed dramatically since 1967, but Rathnelly Day continues to be celebrated every second June.[120]

Tourism was one of several factors in the micronations discussed earlier, but in some cases, it may be the overriding or sole motivation for the establishment of a new country. Indeed, communities as far afield as North America, Asia and Europe have created micronations in an explicit effort to promote tourism to their region. In 1947, the Republic of Saugeais was proclaimed in eastern France, when a hotelier jokingly asked a state official whether he had a permit to enter the territory. The official promptly appointed the hotelier the President of the Free Republic. Although the first President has since passed away, his successors continue today to promote tourism to the region. In 1963, residents in the Swedish county of Jämtland protested against the central government's plan to merge the county with neighbouring Västernorrland county. Establishing a Liberation Movement, proponents drew on the region's historic status as an independent polity in the tenth to twelfth centuries to mobilize the community and proclaim the formation of the Republic of Jämtland. Described as '51 per cent a joke and 49 per cent serious', the Republic is largely focused on promoting regional Jämtlandic culture throughout the country.[121]

Similarly, in 1997, the small village of L'Anse-Saint-Jean in Quebec voted in a referendum to secede from Canada and become Le Royaume de L'Anse-Saint-Jean (The Kingdom of L'Anse-Saint-Jean) as a means of boosting tourism which had been negatively affected by a flood the previous year. Likewise, in 2006, a tourism company operating on a privately owned island in South Korea declared its 'cultural independence' from the state. The Naminara Republic acquired its own flag, insignia, passports, stamps and coins and now requires all visitors to

118 Azzura Lalani, 'Rebellious "Republic of Rathnelly" Celebrates 50 Year', *Toronto Star* (12 June 2017) www.thestar.com/news/gta/2017/06/12/rebellious-republic-of-rathnelly-celebrates-50-years.html.

119 Ibid.

120 Republic of Rathnelly, 'Rathnelly Day' www.rathnellyrepublic.com/rathnelly-day/.

121 Kiara Suneson and Kristian Bengtsson, 'The Joke Republic of Jämtland Isn't Really a Joke Anymore', *Vice* (1 October 2010) www.vice.com/en_us/article/kwgb8e/the-joke-republic-568-v17n10.

the island and amusement park to purchase a Naminara passport on arrival.[122] Most recently, in 2011, two citizens of Aigues-Mortes, a small medieval town in southern France, claimed to be a royal couple in an effort to revitalize their town which had been damaged by the economic recession. Styling themselves as Prince and Princess, they 'function as vehicle for initiatives favouring the local economy and social events to rebuild the area's damaged social fabric'.[123]

3.5 Critiques of Statehood

The Principality of Aigues-Mortes is a useful drawcard for a small French town to gain media attention and boost tourism, but micronations are also established for more critical reasons. In their form and function, micronations 'mimic and in many ways, parody established sovereign nation-states', allowing 'for playful and critical approaches to sovereignty'.[124] Indeed, as Philip Hayward has noted, assertions of secession are often 'highly performative and/or rhetorical', and for this reason several micronations 'have been formed by artists in response to local issues and/or as components of broader artistic projects'.[125]

Consider the State of Neue Slowenische Kunst (NSK), for example. Originating in Slovenia in 1984, the political art collective NSK is known for its controversial practice of reappropriating totalitarian imagery and symbols from extreme nationalist movements. In 1991, following the dissolution of Yugoslavia, they claimed to establish themselves as a sovereign state as a means to explore statehood and statelessness. NSK describes itself as a 'State in Time', without a nation or territory and it 'denies the principle of national borders'. As NSK Ambassador Slavoj Žižek explains, the 'uniqueness of NSK is this idea of the "stateless state"'.[126] Many other conceptual art projects develop micronational

[122] Mark Johanson, 'Masters of Micronations: Meet People Who Started Their Own Tiny Countries', *CNN* (24 May 2017) https://edition.cnn.com/travel/article/micronations/index.html.

[123] Julien Oeuillet, 'Springtime of Micronations Spearheaded by Belgian "Grand-Duke" Niels', *The Brussels Times* (29 July 2020) www.brusselstimes.com/all-news/magazine/35805/springtime-of-micronations-spearheaded-by-belgian-grand-duke-niels/.

[124] Fiona McConnell, Terri Moreau and Jason Dittmer , 'Mimicking State Diplomacy: The Legitimizing Strategies of Unofficial Diplomacies' (2013) 43 *Geoform* 804, 810.

[125] Hayward (n 91) 160.

[126] Cited in Benjamin Ramm, 'A Passport from a Country that Doesn't Exist', *BBC* (16 May 2017) www.bbc.com/culture/article/20170515-a-passport-from-a-country-that-doesnt-exist.

claims as a way to challenge statehood. For instance, the Kingdom of Elgaland & Vargaland (KREV) was developed by Swedish artists Carl Michael von Hausswolff and Leif Elggren in 1992. Like other micronations, KREV has a flag and national anthem, and issues passports and stamps on request.[127] However, KREV claims sovereignty over 'all border frontier areas between all countries on earth, and all areas (up to a width of 10 nautical miles) existing outside all countries' territorial waters'.[128] This expansive claim is intended to challenge the concept of the nation-state. As King Michael I explains, 'the nation state is bullshit in our opinion . . . it barely has any power. The multinational companies have the economic power and the economic power runs everything else'.[129] In later years, KREV has also asserted authority over other 'interstitial territories', such as the transition from being asleep to wakefulness.

The Kingdom's assertion of physical territory is intended to critique state sovereignty, but other conceptual art-inspired micronations have firmer physical territory, even if their claims for sovereignty are similarly weak. The State of Sabotage (SOS), for example, began entirely as an art project aimed at challenging 'the condition of statehood'.[130] Founded in 2003 by Czech artist Robert Jelinek as part of the *Amorph! Festival of Micronations*, SOS subsequently bought land near Tenterfield on the New South Wales/Queensland border in Australia. As Jelinek explains, this location was chosen because in 1889 Henry Parkes delivered the Tenterfield Oration, advocating the federation of the Australian colonies, and as such, the town is considered the 'birthplace of [the] nation'.[131] The transformation of SOS from conceptual art piece to proprietor of real property shows how micronations can develop and evolve in their motivations and form.

By their very nature micronations critique conventional practices of statehood, but not all are so deeply theoretical. The Republic of Zaqistan in Box Elder County, Utah, for example, has gradually evolved in that

127 Kingdoms of Elgaland-Vargaland https://elgaland-vargaland.org/. Discussed in Mika Hannula, 'Nightmares Fallen from the Tree' in Tellervo Kalleinen and Oliver Kochta-Kalleinen (eds), *Protocols: Amorph!03Summit of Micronations* (2005) 19–20.

128 Ibid, 66.

129 King Michael I cited in 'Round Table Talks' in Tellervo Kalleinen and Oliver Kochta-Kalleinen (eds), *Protocols: Amorph!03Summit of Micronations* (2005) 141.

130 Robert Jelinek 'Summit of Egonations – How Not to Start Your Own Country' in Tellervo Kalleinen and Oliver Kochta-Kalleinen (eds), *Protocols: Amorph!03Summit of Micronations* (2005) 126, 127.

131 Robert Jelinek, 'Notes of Seduction' in Tellervo Kalleinen and Oliver Kochta-Kalleinen (eds), *Protocols: Amorph!03Summit of Micronations* (2005) 128, 129.

direction. In 2005, Brooklyn sculptor Zaq Landsberg bought the two-acre remote property, almost 100 kilometres from the nearest town, on eBay. When he visited for the first time, he erected a flag so he could locate it on future visits, and later decided to establish a state. As he explains, his decision was sparked by frustration with the government's management of and response to the Iraq War and Hurricane Katrina; Landsberg thought 'I can run a country better than these clowns'.[132] Although he acknowledges that it is not a sovereign country, his intention is to push the boundaries of ownership and sovereignty: 'My goal is to, like, probe those little areas ... To try and find what that does mean'.[133] Landsberg continues:

> Zaqistan works best as a probing of what is real. I mean, is Iraq a real country? It is from maps and borders or whatever, but effectively it's way more complicated than that. What about Kurdistan? Is IT a real nation? If not, why not?
>
> ...
>
> Zaqistan *is* real. These are real monuments, even if they're completely ridiculous. Zaqistani passports *are* real. They're not fake or counterfeit. They exist. They're simply not-quite-legitimate things existing in a legitimate space.[134]

The Empire of Atlantium is also interested in examining ideas of statehood and sovereignty. Initially established by three Australian teenagers in 1981, the micronation was revived by George Cruickshank when he purchased an apartment in Potts Point, an inner-city suburb of Sydney in the 1990s. Although the Empire now has interest in three plots of land, it does not maintain any formal territorial claims, instead conceiving itself as a 'non-territorial' state. In line with this designation, the Empire has welcomed over 3,000 citizens from over 100 countries. As His Imperial Majesty George II explains:

132 Cathy Free, 'New Yorker Zaq Landsberg Creates His Own Country Called Zaqistan in Remote Utah Desert – But He Doesn't Live There', *People* (27 October 2015) https://people.com/celebrity/new-yorker-zaq-landsberg-creates-his-own-slice-of-nothing-called-zaqistan/.

133 Alex Cabrero, 'New York Man Creates "Sovereign Nation" in Box Elder County', *KSL.com* (19 October 2015) www.ksl.com/article/37022657.

134 Mike Abu, 'A Trip to Zaqistan, One Man's "Sovereign Nation" in the Middle of the Utah Desert', *Vice* (30 October 2015) www.vice.com/en_us/article/exqqpk/a-visit-to-zaqistan-the-sovereign-nation-in-the-middle-of-the-utah-desert-1028 (emphasis added).

> The purpose of Atlantium is to promote the idea that sovereignty in the modern world need not necessarily be linked to geography, and that all human beings can and should have the right to choose their country of citizenship irrespective of where they were born, or where they live.[135]

In this sense, the Empire of Atlantium is 'a type of sustained performance art project'.[136]

Another long-running project aimed at challenging conventional understandings of the state is Bruce Henderson (also known as Bruce Grenville)'s Sultanate of Occussi-Ambeno. Devised with a group of friends in Auckland, New Zealand in 1968, the Sultanate was explicitly framed as a 'parody' of statehood. As Grenville explained in a 1985 statement,

> To anarchists, the idea of something as bizarrely improbable as 'The State' actually being taken seriously by most of the dwellers on this planet, would elicit considerable humour were it not so lethal an institution.[137]

Occussi-Ambeno is a real place. Today known as Oecusse, it is an East Timorese exclave located on the western part of the island of Timor and surrounded by Indonesia and the Savu Sea. The Sultanate is thus a relatively unusual example of a micronation claiming defined territory of a pre-existing administrative region with which its founder has no connection. Grenville later explained that he located the Sultanate in an actual place because 'in 1968 no one had ever heard of Timor, much less of our exotic enclave!'.[138] Of course, Grenville means that knowledge or awareness of Occussi-Ambeno was limited among westerners, rather than the Timorese. In this, he proved correct. Using their Sultanate as a means to further their art practice, Grenville and others developed their graphic design techniques by printing stamps, letter heads and other miscellaneous items. Over time, articles on the Sultanate of Occussi-Ambeno's stamps began appearing in philatelic magazines, and the project delivered a small but steady income from mail-order stamps. In 1977, their practice received a significant boost:

135 Atlantium, 'Frequently Asked Questions' www.atlantium.org/faq.html.

136 Ewan Gilbert, 'Empire of Atlantium: Take a Glimpse into Australia's Smallest Micronation', *ABC News* (18 October 2015) www.abc.net.au/news/2015-10-18/micronation-the-empire-atlantium-boorowa-nsw/6856468.

137 Bruce Grenville, 'Ocussi-Ambeno: A Modern Satirical State' (1985) 6 *Phlogiston* 17, 17.

138 Cited in Hayward (n 22) 191.

> [A] European consortium wrote to the Occussi-Ambeno Consulate in New Zealand (Occussi-Ambeno's only contact address at that time) offering substantial graft payments if we would induce the Sultan to sign a contract giving them the exclusive rights to produce and sell Occussi-Ambeno stamps to collectors throughout the planet. Obviously, we were quite happy to be subsidised by the rich in this manner, which also upgraded our stamps from single-colour letterpress productions to being full-colour glossy offset designs. The consortium produced several designs over the next year: Medieval sailing ships, Asian birds and Airships being among the best. We were paid about $US 40,000 as graft on these stamps, and as well, made a considerable income from selling our portions to collectors. A year later they cancelled the contract after some press articles in the US questioned Occussi-Ambeno's legitimacy – leading to the financiers concluding that they may have been taken for a ride![139]

During the 1970s and 1980s, the Sultanate sought to establish diplomatic relations with sovereign states. Grenville claims to have received a response from several recognised nations, including Monaco and Liechtenstein, but several micronations also replied, including the Republic of Mevo putatively located on the island of South Georgia in the Southern Atlantic Ocean and the Republic of Morac-Songhrati-Meads in the Philippines. Illustrating the confusion that Grenville sought to instil, the Sultanate was also the only group to recognise the Republic of Minerva, drawing considerable media attention.[140] While the Sultanate of Occussi-Ambeno is no longer active, Grenville continued to develop his artistic stamp practice, creating an entire alternative universe of artistamp countries.

3.6 Political Protest

Micronations do not just challenge existing understandings of nationalism and globalism. Rather, in asserting sovereignty over a defined physical territory, writing constitutions, regulating citizenship status and performing other acts of sovereignty, micronations are 'active political agents … [whose] … experimental politics'[141] can have 'a real transformative force'.[142] For this reason, micronations are often founded as

[139] Grenville (n 137) 17–18.

[140] Ibid 17. See also Hayward (n 22) 188.

[141] Anastasiya Astapova and Vasil Navumau, 'Veyshnoria: A Fake Country in the Midst of Real Information Warfare' (2018) 131 *The Journal of American Folklore* 435, 442.

[142] Tellervo Kalleinen and Oliver Kochta-Kalleinen, 'Foreword' in Tellervo Kalleinen and Oliver Kochta-Kalleinen (eds), *Protocols: Amorph!03Summit of Micronations* (2005) 6, 6.

a mechanism to protest government policy or state actions, and not just with frustration at the administrative state or as a challenge to orthodox accounts of sovereignty. For example, the online Republic of Veyshnoria emerged in 2017 as a political riposte to the autocratic Belarusian state conducting joint military exercises with Russia in Western Belarus.[143] Similarly, residents in the Užupis neighbourhood of Vilnius, Lithuania declared themselves a republic on April Fools' Day in 1998. While the tongue-in-cheek secession suggests that personal expression was a key impulse, the Republic's flag hints at more serious concerns; it consists of a blue hand with a hole in the middle, making it unable to accept bribes.[144]

One of the more prominent micronations established entirely for political protest is the Gay and Lesbian Kingdom of the Coral Sea Islands. The Kingdom was founded in 2004 at the passage of Australian legislation prohibiting same-sex marriage.[145] Self-styled Emperor Dale Anderson sailed to the uninhabited island of Cato, east of the Great Barrier Reef, planted a flag, issued a Declaration of Independence and laid a memorial plaque.[146] Emperor Dale explained his motivations:

> [O]nly sovereign states and territories can access an international court. So . . . we can't as a community take on Iran and say, look, why did you, you know, kill those two teenage boys last month because they were gay . . . we thought, if we have a sovereign, if we have some type of sovereignty that could access the courts and give gay people a voice on the international stage, whether it be through the UN or [whatever] . . . then why not look at doing that?[147]

Reflecting its existence as a political statement, Emperor Dale dissolved the Kingdom in 2017 following the legalisation of same-sex marriage in Australia.[148]

Many other micronations have been formed as vehicles for political protest. In 1977, residents of Freston Road in west London sought to secede and create the Free and Independent Republic of Frestonia. The majority of the residents were squatters whom the Greater London

143 Astapova and Navumau (n 141) 440.

144 Erin Rhone, 'Užupis: A Tiny Republic of Free Spirits', *BBC* (15 October 2018) www.bbc.com/travel/story/20181014-uupis-a-tiny-republic-of-free-spirits.

145 *Marriage Amendment Act 2004* (Cth).

146 Ryan, Dunford and Sellars (n 40) 39.

147 Interview with Emperor Dale Anderson, cited in Lattas (n 62) 133.

148 *Marriage Amendment (Definition and Religious Freedoms) Act 2017* (Cth), amending the *Marriage Act 1961* (Cth).

Council (GLC) had threatened to evict to transform the area into an industrial estate. At a public meeting, one of the residents, Nicholas Albery, proposed that the residents declare the street independent of the United Kingdom. Albery had been inspired by the feature film *Passport to Pimlico*, in which a small section of the London suburb is found to be legally a part of Burgundy, and a previous visit to the intentional community of Freetown Christiania in Copenhagen. His suggestion was accepted. In a referendum, 94 per cent of the residents supported the plan, and a further 73 per cent voted to join the European Economic Community. Border guards were installed, passports issued and an application for membership of the UN posted (complete with request for a peacekeeping force).[149]

The Shadow Chancellor of the Exchequer, Sir Geoffrey Howe, even expressed his support. Sir Geoffrey wrote to Albery (who had renamed himself Nicholas Exelby-Bramley), 'I can hardly fail to be moved by your aspirations', though he also noted that 'my training as an international lawyer (and a former Law Officer of the Crown) is bound to induce a degree of scepticism about your aspirations for international status'.[150] Nonetheless, the endeavour paid off. Photographer and Freston Road squatter Tony Sleep explained:

> [I]t was a snowball that started rolling, and getting bigger. Normally, squatters had terrible, terrible press. But journalists found this really amusing. The tabloids loved it. They came down here and starting [sic] interviewing people, and before you knew it, it was a big story. Then as word got around, the streets started filling up with Japanese and Danish TV crews. The great thing about Frestonia being a joke was that it was non-threatening. . . . If we'd turned it into a riot, we'd just have got beaten over the head and thrown out. But the GLC found it hugely embarrassing: 'Why the hell have you got all these people living in all these ridiculously empty houses that you've done nothing with, and why do you now want to turn it into a load of rubble and make all these people homeless?'.[151]

149 Letter from David Rappaport-Bramley, Minister of State for Foreign Affairs, to the United Nations, 30 October 1977, 4 www.frestonia.org/application-to-the-united-nations/. See further AO Sulzberger Jr, 'A New Nation in London?' *The Evening Standard* (Union Town, Pennsylvania, 5 November 1977) 20.

150 Letter from the Rt Hon Sir Geoffrey Howe to Nicholas Exelby-Bramley, 20 July 1978 www.frestonia.org/letter-from-the-rt-hon-sir-geoffrey-howe-qc-mp/.

151 John Harris, 'Freedom for Frestonia: The London Commune that Cut Loose from the UK', *The Guardian* (30 October 2017) www.theguardian.com/cities/2017/oct/30/frestonia-london-commune-squatters.

The GLC decided to negotiate. In 1982, the residents formed the Bramleys Housing Co-operative, which partnered with the Notting Hill Housing Trust to redevelop the site in collaboration. The decrepit houses were replaced with safe and liveable homes.

The Free and Independent Republic of Frestonia may have inspired similar community-level forays into micronationalism. In the 1970s, an aluminium smelter was proposed at the small coastal settlement of Aramoana in New Zealand's South Island. The plan required the destruction of the villages of Aramoana and nearby Te Ngaru, and also threatened a local wildlife reserve. In December 1980, following several years of community activism, the residents announced their secession from New Zealand. They established a border post, travelling embassy, and printed passports, citizenship certificates and stamps, with the aim of drawing on the publicity to build a national grassroots campaign opposing the smelter. Their campaign was successful, forcing the government to back down from its plan and causing one of the companies involved in the project to withdraw. The failure of the smelter plan eventually paved the way for the Independent State of Aramoana to reintegrate with New Zealand.[152] The Free Republic of Wendland was less successful. Founded a few months earlier, on 3 May 1980, the republic was devised as a protest against the proposed establishment of a nuclear waste dump in the town of Gorleben, West Germany. After a thirty-three-day sit-in, during which the Lower-Saxony Minister of the Interior decried the purported declaration of independence as an act of high treason, 3,500 police evicted the 2,000 non-violent Wendlandians.[153]

These early community-driven experiments in environmentally inspired micronations have been repeated at a larger scale in more recent years. In 1997, for instance, Greenpeace activists landed on a small uninhabitable granite islet over 300 kilometres west of Scotland's St Kilda islands. Claiming the 780-square metre rock and its adjacent seas 'for the planet and all its peoples',[154] Greenpeace declared the outcrop the capital of the new global

[152] David Downes, 'The New Zealand Environmental Movement and the Politics of Inclusion' (2000) 35(3) *Australian Journal of Political Science* 471, 475; Roger Wilson, *From Manapouri to Aramoana: The Battle for New Zealand's Environment* (Earthworks Press, 1982); Angela Findlay, '"Vive Aramoana": The Save Aramoana Campaign, 1974–1983' (University of Otaho, MA Thesis, 2004).

[153] Andrew Blowers, *The Legacy of Nuclear Power* (Routledge, 2016) ch 5; Ullrich Kockel, 'Toward an Ethnoecology of Place and Displacement' in Ullrich Kockel, Máiréad Nic Craith and Jonas Frykman (eds), *A Companion to the Anthropology of Europe* (Blackwell, 2012) 551, 553–4.

[154] Stephen Royle, '"This Mere Speck in the Surface of the Waters": Rockall aka Waveland' (2014) 8 *Shima: The International Journal of Research into Island Cultures* 72, 79.

state of Waveland. Around 15,000 people across the world registered as citizens, attracted by its founders' stated aspiration 'to protect the global commons rather than to exploit it',[155] and its commitment to block fisheries and oil exploration. The UK government ignored the development; Greenpeace's occupation ended after forty-two days, and Waveland has since ceased to exist. The idea has not dissipated, however. In March 2014, Greenpeace activists proclaimed the formation of the Glacier Republic in Chile. Claiming all 23,000 square kilometres of Chilean glaciers, the Republic aims to 'draw attention to glacier retreat and global warming' and encourage Chile to enact environmental laws protecting glaciers. Consisting of over 165,000 citizens, the Republic has pledged to maintain its assertion of sovereignty until all mining near glaciated areas is abandoned.[156]

Individuals have also created micronations to draw attention to environmental concerns. At least two micronations assert jurisdiction over portions of Antarctica with the goal of raising media attention to significant conservation issues. The Grand Duchy of Westarctica was founded in 2001 and claims Marie Byrd Land, while the Grand Duchy of Flandrensis, which asserts authority over five Antarctic islands, was established in 2008. As we will explore more in Chapter 4, both maintain (incorrectly) that loopholes in the 1959 Antarctic Treaty mean that their claims are valid. The Grand Duke of Flandrensis, Niles Vermeersch, has explained what drove him towards micronationalism:

> I wanted it to be useful. I learned of micronations proclaiming territories in Antarctica so I did it, but as an ecological venture, to raise awareness on ice melting. Flandrensis is the only country that does not want citizens on its territory.[157]

Other micronations with environmental goals claim even more remote territory. The Angyalistan Empire, for instance, asserts sovereignty over the Great Pacific Garbage Patch making it the only country in the world 'that seeks its own destruction'.[158]

155 Ibid 80.

156 Jorge Daniel Taillant, *Glaciers: The Politics of Ice* (Oxford University Press, 2015) 224; Kristen French, 'Copper Versus Ice: Chilean Mine Would Excavate Five Glaciers', *Glacier Hub* (1 October 2014) https://glacierhub.org/tag/glacier-republic/.

157 Oeuillet (n 123).

158 Ibid; Oliver Touzeau, 'Everything You Wanted to Know About Angyalistan' (Paper presented at the 3rd International Conference on Micronations, Free Republic of Alcatraz, 4–5 July 2015) 4 www.angyalistan.com/includes/files/angyalistan-polination15.pdf; Corinne Nèves, 'Les (Faux) Princes, Empereurs et Marquis des Micronations Francophones en Sommet à Vincennes', *Le Parisien* (20 July 2018)

3.7 Scams

Micronations are non-state entities, but their purported legal status can negatively affect persons seeking in good faith to rely on this status. As we have seen at different times in this chapter, it can also be beneficial for fraudsters and other individuals seeking to avoid domestic and international regulation or interested in making some quick money. For instance, the now defunct New Age International University claimed to be 'a leading university of Seborga', licensed by the Principality's Department of Education.[159] However, admissions, licensing and certification were controlled by an institute in Kolkata, India, and the university was not accredited in Italy or any other European country. The university was a diploma mill established to sell illegitimate academic degrees.

More elaborate scams have also been devised. Consider the curious case of the Republic of Morac-Songhrati-Meads and the Kingdom of Humanity, located in the Spratly Islands in the South China Sea. According to an affidavit lodged at the American Embassy in the Philippines in late 1971, the islands were discovered by Captain James Meads in the late 1870s.[160] Meads named one of the major islands (called Itu Aba) after himself, designated the larger area the 'Humanity Sea' and staked a personal claim to several atolls. He then established a colony on Meads Island, described as the Republic of Morac-Songhrati-Meads. The colony apparently prospered, with title passing through several generations to his grandson Morton Meads. During World War II, some complications emerged, with Japanese troops occupying the island and evicting the inhabitants. Nonetheless, the islanders returned in 1946, at which time Morton Meads and another settler buried sovereignty markers on the main island of the archipelago in an effort to protect their claim. In the 1950s, a rival group emerged and formed the Kingdom of Humanity, though within several years the dispute was resolved and the two states merged peacefully.

Other reports differ. These suggest that the islands were in fact 'discovered' by Morton Meads either immediately before or after his discharge from the US Army in Manilla in 1946. Meads is said to have reached an

www.leparisien.fr/val-de-marne-94/les-faux-princes-empereurs-et-marquis-des-micronations-francophones-en-sommet-a-vincennes-20-07-2018-7827972.php.

159 Institute of Education Research and Development, 'Ph.D. Programme' www.webcitation.org/6CoUGqmYA?url=http://ierdworld.org/phd_programmeabroad.

160 The material in this section is drawn from Marwyn Samuels, *Contest for the South China Sea* (Routledge, 1982) 168–72; Menefee (n 11) 83–5.

agreement with others already living on the islands to act as a commercial agent for the group and help them develop projects to exploit the mineral resources and pearl beds of the area. In collaboration with them, he is said to have concocted the story of the founding of the Republic of Morac-Songhrati-Meads and the Kingdom of Humanity in order to lay a sovereign claim to the islands and to engage in a fake postage stamp enterprise to con philatelists across the world. For this and other reasons, Meads was arrested in Manila in 1955, but the charges were apparently dropped. Not much is known of Meads until he filed his affidavit in 1971, but that act prompted a flurry of claims. The following year, he wrote to President Marcos of the Philippines, President Chiang Kai-shek of Taiwan and the United Nations Secretary-General on behalf of his claim. No response was received, but soon a more devastating blow struck the Republic/Kingdom. In June 1972, Meads' collaborators were killed when their boat, the *E. Pluribus Unum* was struck by a typhoon and sunk west of Mindoro Island. Meads presumably abandoned his claim.

The veneer of statehood offers an attractive visage for those interested in committing financial crimes. Consider the example of Noah Musingku, who created a country to facilitate a pyramid scheme. Musingku is a Pentecostal Christian who, under the name King David Peii II, claims to rule the twin Kingdoms of Papaala and Me'ekamui on Bougainville Island. Musingku's success owes much to political and economic strife on Bougainville. Although part of the Solomon Islands archipelago, the island of Bougainville has been administered as part of Papua New Guinea (PNG) since 1949. That year, the island was incorporated into the Australian Territory of Papua to form the United Nations Trust Territory of Papua and New Guinea, which was administered by Australia. When PNG attained independence from Australia in 1975, Bougainville became part of the new state. Political tensions between Bougainville and the rest of PNG have long been a feature of the relationship. While a brief secessionist attempt in 1975 did not succeed, a decades-long conflict over independence and autonomy raged between 1988 and 1997.

Musingku's financial scams emerged at this time. In 1997, he established 'U-Vistract Financial Systems', promoting it as a 'Bank for Bougainvilleans' and 'drawing on Bougainville's sense of having been exploited by international capital'.[161] Initially U-Vistract attracted praise

[161] Nick Bainton and John Cox, 'Parallel States, Parallel Economies: Legitimacy and Prosperity in Papua New Guinea' (Research School of Pacific and Asian Studies, Discussion Paper 2009/5) 2.

and support from prominent Bougainvilleans in PNG, excited about the prospect of 'Bougainville's first international financier'.[162] U-Vistract was popular. Promising to double investors' money over a few months, it enticed thousands of people from across PNG, including members of the political elite, to invest. Within two years, however, the scheme had collapsed after failing to meet the government's demand that they present their financial records. Undeterred by several failed attempts to relaunch his plan in Port Moresby and Honiara, Musingku returned to his family village in South Bougainville in 2003. Once there, he sought an alliance with the Bougainville separatist leader Francis Ona, who had proclaimed his own independent Republic of Me'ekamui in 1998 in protest at the PNG peace settlement.[163] Around the same time, Musingku crowned himself ruler of the separate kingdom of Papala.

The alliance with Ona led Musingku to reshape U-Vistract and present it as 'the financial foundation of a new state'.[164] Musingku explained in his newsletter, the *Papala Chronicles*:

> We had to set up our own home-grown international government, monetary and banking system with the capability of resolving the crisis once and for all. At Bougainville national level we had Me'ekamui government as our hardware whilst Papala government provided the software. Internationally we established RAONK (Royal Assembly of Nations & Kingdoms) as our hardware whilst U-Vistract System provided the software. We then invited other nations, governments and kingdoms to seek affiliations with us.[165]

When Ona passed away suddenly in 2005, Musingku merged the two kingdoms. In circumstances where the Bougainville government is unable to project authority across the entire island without risking inflaming tensions, Musingku has operated out of south Bougainville since then.[166] Protected by a group of Fijian militia, the twin kingdoms possess the trappings of a state, including their own currency (graced with an image of Musingku's face). Reports note than even in 2020,

[162] John Cox, 'The Magic of Money and the Magic of the State: Fast Money Schemes in Papua New Guinea' (2013) 83(3) *Oceania* 175, 176. See further John Cox, *Fast Money Schemes: Hope and Deception in Papua New Guinea* (Indiana University Press, 2018) ch 2.

[163] Anna-Karina Hermkens, 'Like Moses Who Led His People to the Promised Land: Nation- and State-Building in Bougainville' (2013) 83(3) *Oceania* 192, 202.

[164] Cox, 'The Magic of Money' (n 162) 177.

[165] *Papala Chronicles* (2005) 3(9); cited in Cox (n 162).

[166] Volker Boege, 'Vying for Legitimacy in Post-Conflict Situations: The Bougainville Case' (2014) 23(2) *Peacebuilding* 237, 245–6.

'people are still visiting him to invest more money, or to ask for their promised returns'.[167]

The promise of a utopian community was key to the fraud allegedly perpetrated by German-Australian Paul Neuman. Claiming to have received the title Baron Neuman of Kara Bagh from the exiled former King Hassan III of Afghanistan,[168] Neuman founded the Sovereign State of Aeterna Lucina in 1978. Initially located in Byron Bay in northern New South Wales, Aeterna Lucina moved with Neuman to Curl Curl in Sydney, and later Cooma at the foothills of the Snowy Mountains in the southern part of the state. In a pamphlet entitled *A Promised Land*, Neuman sought to attract members to his new country. Aeterna Lucina was a land of 'unspoiled mountain character' where citizens would 'enjoy the purity of true fruit juices, mineral water, ice cream made from fresh cream and fruit, bread baked in brick ovens . . . [and] butter churned in the dairies of our alpine meadows'.[169] Coca-Cola, blue ice cream and cars were all banned. His advertisements were successful; individuals from as far as West Germany bought blocks of land in ¼, 1 and 10-acre lots, and became members of the community.

Many did so for idealistic reasons. West German computer technician Gunter Frick paid AUD 50,000 to move to Aeterna Lucina because he was 'sick of hearing about nuclear missiles, the daily poisoning of the environment and ruthless corporations'.[170] Unfortunately, Aeterna Lucina soon ran into trouble. Neuman had allegedly told members that because Aeterna Lucina was independent, Australian laws did not apply and land transactions could be completed internally by his government. This was not true. Aeterna Lucina had no basis for its existence and Australia did not recognise its independence. Australian law also did not recognise any land conveyances; all of the 1,400-hectare property remained registered in the name of Neuman and his wife.[171] Neuman

[167] Liam Fox, 'Bougainville's Conman "King" Still on the Run as Island Edges Closer to Independence', *ABC News* (15 November 2020) www.abc.net.au/news/2020-11-15/bougainville-conman-king-still-on-the-run-independence-png/12879932.

[168] Anabel Dean, 'Founder of "Sovereign State" in NSW Gives Evidence', *Sydney Morning Herald* (21 June 1989) 7.

[169] Alison McClymont, 'Trouble in Baron's "Peace State"', *Sydney Morning Herald* (26 August 1990) 22.

[170] Alison McClymont, '$50,000 Paid to Live in "Ideal" State, Claim', *Sydney Morning Herald* (2 September 1990) 23.

[171] Anabel Dean, 'Dreams of a Promised Land End in Court', *Sydney Morning Herald* (28 August 1990) 3.

was charged with obtaining AUD 144,000 by deception, but after a jury failed to reach a verdict, the case was abandoned.[172]

Perhaps the 'most audacious fraud in history' belongs to the Scottish General Gregor McGregor.[173] An officer in the British Army, McGregor served in the Peninsula War between Spain and Portugal before assisting the Republican forces in the Venezuelan War of Independence in 1812. In June 1817, purportedly under the commission of South American revolutionary hero Simón Bolívar, he captured Amelia Island in Spanish Florida on the border with Georgia and proclaimed a new 'Republic of the Floridas'. McGregor was less concerned with establishing republican institutions than with engaging in lucrative privateering and smuggling. Over the following months, USD 500,000 worth of African slaves stolen from Spanish slave ships were smuggled into the United States. Citing the 'body of [armed] Blacks from St Domino' along the border, United States President Monroe ordered troops to occupy the island in December.[174] The Republic may have met an untimely demise, but it appears to have given McGregor an idea.

When McGregor returned to Britain in 1821, he claimed that King George Frederic Augustus of the Mosquito Coast in the Gulf of Honduras had invested him Cazique of Poyais; a fictional territory larger than Wales, blessed with fertile soils, plentiful game and the flourishing seaside capital of St Joseph. Armed with a series of fabricated official-looking documents, McGregor announced that he intended to seek investment and immigrants for the new colony. He constructed an elaborate state to achieve his ruse. Poyais was apparently governed by a tricameral parliament with intricate and complicated constitutional arrangements. He also devised commercial and banking mechanisms, designed distinctive uniforms for each regiment of the army, and developed the country's own honours system, coat of arms, titles and flag.[175] Drawing on his exaggerated military achievements and natural charm, McGregor became a fixture in London society. By the end of 1821, Major William Richardson had provided his estate as a British base for the

[172] Malcolm Brown, 'Clouds Cleared on Baron's Reign', *Sydney Morning Herald* (24 June 1992) 10.

[173] David Sinclair, *The Land that Never Was: Sir Gregor McGregor and the Most Audacious Fraud in History* (Da Capo Press, 2003).

[174] Cited in Rafe Blaufarb, 'The Western Question: The Geopolitics of Latin American Independence' (2007) 112(3) *American Historical Review* 742, 752–3; Charles Bowman Jr, 'Vicente Pazos, Agent for the Amelia Island Filibusters, 1818' (1975) 53(4) *The Florida Historical Quarterly* 428.

[175] Sinclair (n 173) 319–20.

Poyaisian Royal Family. Richardson was rewarded with the Poyaisian Order of the Green Cross and appointed the top representative of Poyais in Britain. Richardson even presented his letter of credence to King George IV.[176]

McGregor's main aim was to secure profit, and he aggressively drummed up attention. He gave interviews in national newspapers, wrote a 355-page guidebook to the territory under a pseudonym, and paid for Poyais ballads to be sung on the streets of London, Edinburgh and Glasgow. It appeared that the climate suited him. The British economy was booming following the defeat of Napoleon and falling interest rates caused many people to look for higher returns on riskier investments. The collapse of the Spanish Empire meant that there were a range of new Latin American countries one could invest in at attractive rates; Mexican bonds paid 6 per cent; double the rate of the British government bond.[177] McGregor quickly floated £200,000 in bonds at 6 per cent – the equivalent of £3.6 billion today.[178] The 'founding father of securities fraud' convinced another 500 people to invest their life savings buying land at one, two and then four shillings per acre.[179] McGregor targeted Scots on the basis that they would be more likely to trust him, a fellow Scot.

In 1822 and 1823, two ships and 250 colonists set out. Upon arriving just under two months later they assumed that they were in the wrong place. There was no port, no bustling town and no roads; just a dense, mosquito-infested jungle. Over the following months, two-thirds of the settlers died, and fewer than fifty ever returned to Britain. By this stage, McGregor was in Paris attempting to raise £800,000 for another scheme. Although he persuaded sixty would-be colonists, Parisian authorities were alerted when no one could prove the country existed.[180] Arrested but acquitted, McGregor returned to Edinburgh before emigrating to Venezuela to escape angry and disappointed investors. McGregor was awarded a military pension for his participation in Venezuela's War of Independence, and after his death in 1845 was buried with full military honours in Caracas Cathedral.[181]

176 Ibid 39.

177 'The King of Con-Men', *The Economist* (22 December 2012).

178 Alfred Hasbrouck, 'Gregor McGregor and the Colonization of Poyais, between 1820 and 1824' (1927) 7(4) *The Hispanic American Historical Review* 438, 442.

179 Louis Straney, *Securities Fraud: Detection, Prevention, and Control* (Wiley, 2011) 35.

180 'The King of Con-Men' (n 177).

181 Frank Dawson, 'MacGregor, Gregor (1786–1845)', *Oxford Dictionary of National Biography* (Oxford University Press, 2004).

3.8 Conclusion

It is no wonder when the motivations of their founders differ so considerably that micronations are incredibly diverse in form and function. This chapter has provided a survey of the major justifications that lie behind an individual's decision to purport to secede and found their own country. In doing so, it has illustrated key distinctions between and among micronations. Some micronations seek to claim physical control and exercise jurisdiction over unclaimed land or develop structures in the high seas, while others intend (with varying degrees of seriousness) to usurp the authority of existing sovereign states. Still others may be better described as 'virtual' micronations. These entities do not appear to actually desire sovereignty but nonetheless perform and re-perform acts of statehood to challenge conventional understanding of international legal personality and legitimate political authority. In the next chapter, we take a closer look at how micronations assert their sovereignty in these and other ways.

4

Performing Sovereignty

Micronations challenge existing conceptions of statehood and international legal personality. They do so largely by engaging in the rituals of statehood rather than contesting them. In practice, this means that although usually unqualified or unskilled in law, proponents act through their understanding of the law rather than acting outside the law. For example, they are typically careful to declare their independence in a way that they consider, or at least argue, to be a lawful basis for their actions. Often meticulous in their planning and apparent justification, micronationalists send letters to government officials, foreign states and even the United Nations, informing them of their planned actions and explaining why those actions are lawful under their interpretation of domestic or international law.

In this chapter we explore in more detail how micronations assert and perform sovereignty. We examine the legal instruments that micronationalists identify when seeking to find a lawful basis to justify secession and proclaim their independence and outline their strained legal arguments. As we explain, the use of international covenants, principles and legal documents in an attempt to ground statehood is intended to create a façade of legality that can fool or confuse unsuspecting individuals. Micronations revel in ambiguity. Relying on the good faith of government actors or ordinary citizens they strive to create situations in which they can (mistakenly) be recognised as a sovereign state – even if only for a moment.

4.1 Search for Legitimacy

The Montevideo Convention on the Rights and Duties of States outlines four conditions for an entity to be considered a state.[1] As we explored in Chapter 2, international law has also developed additional criteria,

[1] *Convention on the Rights and Duties of States*, 165 L.N.T.S. 19, art 1 (signed 26 December 1933 and entered into force 26 December 1934) art 1 (‘*Montevideo Convention*’).

including that an entity will not be regarded as a state where it is established in violation of certain norms of international law.[2] Because micronations purport to act in accordance with the law rather than outside of the law, they are careful to attempt to meet these requirements. For this reason, they struggle to predicate their independence and statehood on a range of international legal instruments and principles. In this part, we examine some of their major arguments.

4.1.1 Magna Carta

Perhaps conscious of the fragility of their legal claim, some micronations strive to ground their independence and statehood on centuries-old legal instruments. In seeking to cloak their legally untenable actions in celebrated documents and enduring legal principles, micronationalists hope that their unsound or shaky legal status might be remedied. These efforts are also manipulative attempts to rely on the legal ignorance of ordinary citizens, who may have some familiarity with the existence of a foundational document but be unaware of its content, meaning or applicability. Because of its significance in Anglo-American law, the Magna Carta is often adopted for these purposes. One prominent example comes from Australia. In his formal notice of secession issued to the Australian government, Prince Leonard Casley of the Principality of Hutt River cited the Magna Carta as permitting individuals threatened with loss of economic livelihood to form a 'self-preservation government'.[3]

The Magna Carta was issued by King John of England in June 1215 at Runnymede, outside London. Designed to secure peace between the King and a group of rebel barons, the Magna Carta promised a suite of legal protections, many of which had been included in Royal charters issued as early as 1100.[4] Among other clauses, Magna Carta guaranteed the right of a freeman to trial by his peers before imprisonment, swift access to justice and limits on the feudal payments the King could demand from his

[2] *Accordance with International Law of the Unilateral Declaration of Independence in Respect of Kosovo (Advisory Opinion)* [2010] ICJ Rep 403, 437 [81]. See further *Legal Consequences of the Construction of a Wall in the Occupied Palestinian Territory (Advisory Opinion)* [2004] ICJ Rep 136, 171 [87].

[3] Letter from Leonard Casley to Sir David Brand (Premier, Western Australia) (21 April 1970).

[4] See Henry I's *Charter of Liberties*: Judith Green, '"A Lasting Memorial": The Charter of Liberties of Henry I' in Marie Flanagan and Judith Green (eds), *Charters and Charter Scholarship in Britain and Ireland* (Palgrave, 2005) 53.

barons.[5] It also included a number of now outdated provisions. Clause 54, for example, provided that 'no man is to be arrested or imprisoned on account of a woman's appeal for the death of anyone other than her own husband'. Clause 61 provided a method of enforcement. It stated that a council of twenty-five barons would be established to monitor the King's adherence to the charter. If the King failed to abide by his commitments within forty days of being notified of a transgression by the council, the twenty-five barons were empowered to seize the King's 'castles, lands and possessions' until they accepted that amends had been made. This provision proved unacceptable. On John's request, the Charter was annulled by Pope Innocent III in August 1215 and England descended into civil war. Following King John's death from illness in October the next year, his nine-year-old son Henry III took the throne. A revised Charter (without clause 61 and several others) was issued in the young King's name in an effort to secure peace. In 1225, when Henry III achieved majority, it was issued again.

The Charter has little direct legal application in the United Kingdom today. As befitting a document drafted in the thirteenth century to govern relations between the King and his barons, many of its clauses have fallen into obsolescence or have been superseded. By 1969, the whole Charter, save three provisions, had been repealed.[6] In Australia, only the prohibition on imprisonment without trial and the guarantee of swift justice survives in the law of each state and territory.[7] The situation is slightly different in the United States, where the Magna Carta was turned into a practical embodiment of limited government and served as inspiration for revolution.[8] In 1766, Benjamin Franklin referred directly to the instrument when asked by the British House of Commons on what basis the Pennsylvanian assembly could assert 'that laying a tax on them by the Stamp Act was an infringement of their rights?'. While Franklin acknowledged there was no specific provision within the colony's charter, he

5 *Magna Carta 1215*, cl 39, 40.

6 See Anthony Arlidge and Igor Judge, *Magna Carta Uncovered* (Hart Publishing, 2014).

7 David Clark, 'The Icon of Liberty: The Status and Role of the Magna Carta in Australian and New Zealand Law' (2000) 24(3) *Melbourne University Law Review* 866; Steven Rares, 'Why Magna Carta Still Matters' (Paper delivered to the Judicial Conference of Australia, Adelaide, 9 October 2015).

8 Renee Lettow Lerner, 'The Troublesome Inheritance of Americans in Magna Carta and Trial by Jury' in Robert Hazell, James Melton (eds), *Magna Carta and Its Modern Legacy* (Cambridge University Press, 2015) 77; Harry Dickinson, 'Magna Carta in the American Revolution' in Lawrence Goldman (ed), *Magna Carta: History, Context and Influence* (University of London Press, 2018) 79.

explained that they were justified by, 'the common rights of Englishmen, as declared by Magna Charta'.[9]

Echoing its invocation by Benjamin Franklin some 250 years ago, today the Magna Carta largely plays a symbolic role in contemporary society. While British judges have described it as 'the greatest constitutional document of all times – the foundation of the freedom of the individual against the arbitrary authority of the despot',[10] its real power and authority stems from its function as a political rallying cry. As United States Supreme Court Justice Benjamin Cardozo explained in 1931, shortly before he was appointed to the Court: 'what lives in the charter today is the myth that has gathered around it – the things that it has come to stand for in the thought of successive generations – not the pristine core within, but the incrustations that have formed without'.[11]

Prince Leonard's failure to identify what section or which aspect of the Magna Carta he drew upon in purporting to legitimate his government is immaterial. The strength of his claim relied simply on the invocation of the instrument, rather than any of its sixty-three provisions. He saw regulations inhibiting his capacity to harvest wheat as an infringement of his freedom. As an important symbol of liberty in Anglo-American law, he suggested that the Magna Carta could ground the lawful establishment of a new government.

Unfortunately for Prince Leonard, Australian courts disagree. As early as 1905, the High Court confirmed: 'The contention that a law of the Commonwealth is invalid because it is not in conformity with Magna Charta is not one for serious refutation'.[12] The same is true elsewhere. Although more than 170 decisions of the US Supreme Court have cited or referred to the Magna Carta,[13] it cannot displace the Constitution or laws duly passed by Congress. There is no basis upon

[9] Great Britain, House of Commons, *The Examination of Dr Benjamin Franklin, before an August Assembly, Relating to the Repeal of the Stamp Act* (Hall & Sellars, 1766) 15 https://quod.lib.umich.edu/e/evans/N08073.0001.001/1:1?rgn=div1;view=fulltext.

[10] Lord Denning cited in Lord Dyson, 'Strengthened by the Rule of Law: The Message of Magna Carta for Religions Today' in Robin Griffith-Jones and Mark Hill (eds), *Magna Carta, Religion and the Rule of Law* (Cambridge University Press, 2015) 334, 335.

[11] Cited in Stephen Rohde, 'From Discontented Barons to Predator Drones', *Los Angeles Review of Books* (14 June 2015) https://lareviewofbooks.org/article/magna-carta-from-discontented-barons-to-predator-drones/.

[12] *Chia Gee v Martin* (1905) 3 CLR 649, 653 (Griffith CJ).

[13] Stephen J Wermiel, 'Magna Carta in Supreme Court Jurisprudence' in Andrea Martinez, Daniel Magraw and Edmund Brownell II (eds), *Magna Carta and the Rule of Law* (American Bar Association, 2015) 111, 111.

which the Magna Carta can ground a claim for sovereignty and statehood.

4.1.2 Antarctic Treaty

Several micronations assert sovereignty over Antarctica. The coldest, driest and windiest continent, Antarctica may appear to be a strange territory to desire. However, its hostile environment, lack of easily accessible resources and isolation are alluring to the right person. The 14.2 million-square-kilometre continent is the only territory on earth without indigenous human inhabitants. It was also the last region to be discovered; the first recorded sighting occurred only in 1820, when a Russian expedition sighted the Fimbul ice shelf. Today, around 4,000 scientists and staff live in Antarctica during the summer months, with the population falling to about 1,000 over winter. In fact, the continent is not only extremely lightly populated; much of it is unclaimed and the sovereign claims of recognised states are largely in abeyance.

The human history of Antarctica is linked to whaling, scientific research and sovereignty. Seven states have made territorial claims to the continent. The earliest are those of Argentina and Chile, whose assertion of sovereignty is grounded in a series of 1493 papal bulls. In *Inter caetera*, *Inter caetera II* and *Dudum siquidem*, Pope Alexander VI purported to dismiss competing European claims and grant the Spanish monarchs Ferdinand and Isabella all lands to the 'west and south' of a pole-to-pole line 100 leagues west of any of the islands of the Azores or the Cape Verde islands. The following year in the Treaty of Tordesillas between Spain and Portugal, that line was shifted to 370 leagues west of the Cape Verde islands to accommodate Portuguese interests. The views of the Indigenous peoples of these territories were never considered, but other European powers dismissed the notion that the Pope could convey sovereignty over such a large portion of unexplored territory. Francis I of France is said to have replied to the Spanish ambassador in Paris: 'The sun shines for me the same as for others: I would like to see that clause in Adam's will that excluded me from the partition of the world'.[14] Nonetheless, the papal bulls and subsequent treaty served as the initial basis for Spanish claims in South America. Upon the break-up of the Spanish Empire, newly independent Argentina and Chile drew on the

[14] James Moltz, *The Politics of Space Security: Strategic Restraint and the Pursuit of National Interest* (Stanford University Press, 2008) 16.

international law principle of *uti possidetis* ('as you possess, thus may you possess') to claim their own title to the formerly Spanish territory – including all the way to the South Pole.[15]

The claims of other states are more recent in origin. In 1840, French explorer Jules Dumont d'Urville briefly landed on the Antarctic coastline, erected a flag and named a 432,000-square-kilometre territory Adélie Land after his wife. The United Kingdom had asserted sovereignty and maintained effective occupation over the Falkland Islands in the far South Atlantic Ocean since 1833. In 1908, the United Kingdom extended its claim by declaring sovereignty over all territories located south of the 50th parallel of south latitude and within the 20th and 80th degrees of west longitude. This significant claim was intended to enable the United Kingdom to regulate the whaling industry more effectively. Wishing to avoid British taxation, Norwegian whalers financed expeditions to the continent. In the 1930s, Norway claimed sovereignty over several islands and eventually a 2.7 million-square-kilometre region named Queen Maud Land in honour of the Norwegian Queen. That same decade, the United Kingdom transferred much of its claimed territory to Australia and New Zealand.

No other state has made a formal claim to Antarctica, though the situation is more complex than this would suggest. In 1938, Germany sought to claim sovereignty over a portion of land within Queen Maud Land that it called New Swabia. Pilot Alfred Ritscher flew a sea-plane across an area of around 350,000 square kilometres, surveying the territory and dropping darts inscribed with swastikas. However, Germany never constructed a permanent base nor made a formal claim. The United States, Russia and Brazil have also never formally made a territorial claim, though they maintain that they have reserved the right to make a claim in the future.

The relative stasis of territorial claims is a consequence of the Antarctic Treaty. Signed in Washington DC on 1 December 1959, the Treaty 'sought to suppress and contain sovereignty and sovereign practices such as flag planting and "effective occupation"'.[16] Article IV preserves the status quo. It provides that no acts or activities shall constitute a basis for asserting, supporting or denying a claim to territorial sovereignty in Antarctica, or create any rights of sovereignty in Antarctica. It also

[15] Benedetto Conforti, 'Territorial Claims in Antarctica: A Modern Way to Deal with an Old Problem' (1986) 19 *Cornell International Law Journal* 249, 255.

[16] Donald Rothwell, 'Sovereignty and the Antarctic Treaty' (2010) 46(1) *Polar Record* 17, 18.

prevents the assertion of new claims or enlargement of existing claims to territorial sovereignty.[17] Although arguably rewarding 'colonial occupation and annexation',[18] the Antarctic Treaty has prevented the assertion or enlargement of claims. This sometimes causes complications. For example, Japan continues to operate whaling fleets within the Australian Antarctic Territory, despite an Australian court finding such practices a violation of Australian law,[19] because Japan refuses to recognise Australian sovereignty in Antarctica.

The Antarctic Treaty has also left large portions of the continent unclaimed. This includes the 1.6-million-square kilometre Marie Byrd Land, which remains the largest unclaimed territory on Earth. Unclaimed by recognised states that is – a number of micronations assert their sovereignty over Marie Byrd Land, and other parts of Antarctica, on the basis of a supposed loophole in the Antarctic Treaty. The 'loophole' was first discovered by American Travis McHenry. According to McHenry, while the Treaty precludes states from making territorial claims, it does not prohibit claims made by individuals.[20] Discovering that Marie Byrd Land had not been claimed by any state, McHenry claimed it for himself – and then established a state to rule over the land. On 2 November 2001, McHenry wrote letters to each of the twelve original signatories of the Antarctic Treaty announcing his formal claim and the creation of the Grand Duchy of Westarctica. His letter was ignored, but the Grand Duke continues to assert and exercise Westarctican sovereignty by contacting states across the globe and requesting formal diplomatic relations. While no internationally recognised state has yet accepted, the Duchy has entered into a treaty of mutual recognition, cooperation and friendship with the Republic of Molossia, a fellow micronation.[21]

Many other micronations have followed the Grand Duke's lead. MicroWiki lists ten active micronations that claim land in Antarctica along with twenty-one further Antarctic micronations that have since

[17] *The Antarctic Treaty* 402 UNTS 71 (opened for signature 1 December 1959 and entered into force 23 June 1961) art IV.

[18] Klaus Dodds, 'Post-Colonial Antarctica: An Emerging Engagement' (2006) 42(1) *Polar Record* 59, 63. See also comments made by Pakistan, Ghana, Zambia and Malaysia in the United Nations in the 1980s: Moritaka Hayashi, 'The Antarctica Question in the United Nations' (1986) 19 *Cornell International Law Journal* 275, 280.

[19] *Humane Society International Inc v Kyodo Senpaku Kaisha Ltd* (2008) 165 FCR 510.

[20] John Ryan, George Dunford and Simon Sellars, *Micronations: The Lonely Planet Guide to Home-Made Nations* (Lonely Planet, 2006) 111.

[21] Ibid 112.

been abandoned. Perhaps reflecting the tenuousness of their hold of territory, several Antarctic micronations have mimicked recognised states by engaging in international diplomacy to consolidate their claims and regulate rival micronational claims to the continent. In 2009, the Grand Duchy of Flandrensis, the Kingdom of Finismund and Marie State signed a treaty to establish a supra-micronational organisation – The Antarctic Micronational Union (AMU).[22] As of November 2020, the AMU comprised nine members.

4.1.3 Law of the Sea

Antarctica may be largely uninhabited and unclaimed, but it also has downsides. Its remote location, harsh environment and legal regime that prohibits sovereign claims make it difficult to establish a functional or effective government. Many micronations seeking to create a new state have therefore looked for alternative sites. Some of the more prominent micronations have sought to establish sovereign claims over coral reefs, rocky outcrops and even artificial islands in the high seas. These attempts are often based on the law of the sea.

American libertarians have been particularly interested in the possibility of creating states on artificial islands or reclaimed land on coral atolls. In the previous chapter we examined Michael Oliver's ill-fated Republic of Minerva and touched on Lazarus Long's Principality of New Utopia, as well as Abalonia and Taluga. Here, we note two more attempts. In 1962, two competing groups endeavoured to establish states on a series of reefs 16 kilometres off the coast of South Florida.[23]

William Anderson purported to have 'discovered' the reefs. Despite their close proximity to the US mainland, it appears that the question of sovereignty had never been raised. Anderson wrote to the Florida government and was apparently told that the reefs were 'outside the Constitutional Boundaries of the State of Florida and therefore, not within the jurisdiction' of the State.[24] The federal government was similarly uninterested. The Department of Interior replied to his letters, explaining

[22] *Antarctic Micronational Union Charter* (2020) https://amu.lostisland.org/charter/.

[23] Adam Clanton, 'The Men Who Would Be Kings: Forgotten Challenges to US Sovereignty' (2008) 26(1) *Pacific Basin Law Journal* 1, 12–15; Imogen Saunders, 'Artificial Islands and Territory in International Law' (2019) 52 *Vanderbilt Journal of Transnational Law* 655, 670–1.

[24] *Atlantis Development Corporation v United States*, 379 F.2d 818, 820 (5th Circuit 1967) ('*Atlantis Development Corporation*').

that it 'has no jurisdiction over land that is outside the territorial limits of the United States',[25] while a legal advisor with the State Department noted that 'the areas in question are outside of the jurisdiction of the United States and constitute a part of the high seas. The high seas are open to all nations and no state may validly subject any part of them to its sovereignty'.[26] Excited, Anderson gave public notice of his discovery in US and British newspapers, announced his intention to develop hotels and casinos and declared the formation of a new sovereign nation, 'Atlantis, Isle of Gold'.[27] Encouraging eighteen Miami Beach millionaires to tour the reefs, Anderson estimated he would need USD 250 million to build an island and construct government buildings.[28] Around the same time, Louisianan Louis Ray announced a similar plan, proposing the establishment of the 'Grand Capri Republic' on the same group of reefs.[29]

Neither Atlantis, Isle of Gold nor the Grand Capri Republic were built. While Ray commenced dredging work, and Anderson constructed four prefabricated buildings on the reefs, financial and technical impediments proved considerable. Ultimately, the US government dashed their ambitions. In April 1965, the US government charged Ray with trespass and construction without an Army Corp of Engineers permit and sought a permanent injunction against any further development on the reefs. Anderson intervened in the case, claiming superior title to Ray's claim based on his prior discovery.[30] Both Ray and Anderson argued that the reefs were islands, outside US jurisdiction and were therefore subject to colonisation under international law.[31] The Southern District Court of Florida disagreed. The court ruled that the reefs were not islands because they were submerged at high tide. Instead, they were part of the 'subsoil and seabed' of the outer continental shelf (as defined in the Geneva Convention on the Continental Shelf), and therefore 'subject to [United States] jurisdiction, control, and power of disposition'.[32] As the court explained, national security interests were also front of mind:

> The issues of this case are of great public interest, involving not only the preservation of rare natural resources, but the reservation of our very

[25] Ibid 821.
[26] Ibid.
[27] *United States v Ray*, 294 F.Supp. 532, 535 (S.D. Fla. 1969) ('*United States v Ray*').
[28] Ibid 535–6.
[29] Ibid 534–5.
[30] *Atlantis Development Corporation* (n 24) 822.
[31] *United States v Ray* (n 27) 538.
[32] Ibid; citing the *Outer Continental Shelf Lands Act* USC § 1332(a).

> security as a nation. If these reefs were available for private construction totally outside the control of the United States Government, they could conceivably support not only artificial islands and unpoliced gambling casinos, but even an alien missile base, all within a short distance of the Florida Coast. Congress has seen fit to claim this area so that it may be used for the Commonwealth rather than private gain.[33]

Not all island nations are built on libertarian philosophies. In 1964, Leicester Hemingway, the brother of Ernest Hemingway, constructed a raft and towed it into international waters, just under 10 kilometres off the coast of Jamaica.[34] Composed of bamboo, steel, iron piping and rock, the raft was anchored on a shallow ocean bank with an old Ford engine block. It measured two and half metres by nine metres. On July 4 – Independence Day – Hemingway announced the establishment of New Atlantis, claiming 'there's no law that says you can't start your own country'. Declaring his raft an island, he predicated his sovereign claims on the Guano Islands Act 1856 (US), which empowered US citizens to take possession of unclaimed islands containing guano deposits in the name of the United States. Apparently, Hemingway had discovered a small amount of guano on the raft; though just how that Act could found a new sovereign claim is unclear. In any event, Hemingway sought to reassure his larger neighbour, explaining that New Atlantis would be 'a peaceful power and would pose no threat to Jamaica'.[35]

Hemingway intended his new state to serve as 'a test tube for democracy'.[36] He was also interested in researching marine life in the Caribbean Sea. He formed the International Marine Research Society, an organisation headquartered on the raft, with the aim of furthering the study of marine biology. Initially, his project was funded through the publication of *My Brother, Ernest Hemingway*, but Hemingway planned to finance his operations through sovereign privileges, in particular the sale of stamps. Although he had already printed several batches of stamps, the international Universal Postal Union refused to recognise their validity.

33 *United States v Ray* (n 27) 542.

34 Russell McDougall, 'Micronations of the Caribbean' in Maria Cristina Fumagalli et al (eds), *Surveying the American Tropics: A Literary Geography from New York to Rio* (Oxford University Press, 2013) 231, 258–60; Russell Hale, 'Contents of a Country: Leicester Hemingway's Republic of New Atlantis', *Harry Ransom Center Magazine* (30 July 2015) https://sites.utexas.edu/ransomcentermagazine/2015/07/30/throwback-thursday-contents-of-a-country-leicester-hemingways-republic-of-new-atlantis/; 'The Old Man and the Sea', *The Michigan Daily* (9 July 1964) 1.

35 'New Atlantis Holds First Election', *The Daily Gleaner* (4 February 1965) 1.

36 McDougall (n 34) 260.

Undeterred, Hemingway mailed a stamp featuring President Lyndon B. Johnson to the White House and claimed international recognition when the reply letter from the US State Department addressed him as 'Acting President'. He also intended to mint coins, write books and scripts, and encourage tourism. Unfortunately, however, within a few years of establishment New Atlantis was destroyed by a hurricane.

Americans are not the only people interested in establishing nations on the high seas. As we discussed in the introduction, in 1967, Englishman Roy Bates declared himself the ruler of the new Principality of Sealand – an artificial naval installation located just outside the United Kingdom's territorial waters. The following year, two Italian citizens made a similar bid. Setting out from Rimini on the Adriatic Sea, the two entrepreneurs built a platform just under 300 metres outside Italian territorial waters and announced the formation of a new independent nation named *Isola Delle Rosa* – the Republic of Rose Island.[37] Mimicking the prerogatives of statehood, the newly formed Council of Government swiftly declared war on their neighbour. While their motivations were not clear, Italian authorities believed that the platform was a ploy to raise money from credulous tourists and avoid taxation. Uninterested in legal wrangling, the harbour office of Rimini issued a demolition order.

The President of the Republic, Giorgio Rosa, appealed to the Italian Council of State. Rosa's argument was predicated on the Geneva Convention on the High Seas, which Italy had ratified in 1964. According to Rosa, the Convention 'granted a right to the free use of the high seas both to States and to individuals'.[38] In fact, the Convention does no such thing. The Council of State accordingly dismissed this argument, holding that the Convention 'only creates rights and obligations of an international character for the Italian State with respect to other nations of the international community'.[39] One of those obligations was to prevent activities that may obstruct freedom of the high seas. The platform was demolished, but the Republic lived on. As a self-declared government-in-exile, the Republic issued several stamps portraying the Italian destruction of its homeland.[40]

[37] Samuel Pyeatt Menefee, '"Republics of the Reefs": Nation-Building on the Continental Shelf and in the World's Oceans' (1994) 25 *California Western International Law Journal* 81, 105. This story is now the subject of a movie: *L'incredibile storia dell'Isola delle Rose* (Groenlandia, 2020).

[38] *Chierici v Ministry of the Merchant Navy* (14 November 1969) (1986) 71 ILR 258, 259.

[39] Ibid. See also Menefee (n 37) 105–6; Saunders (n 23) 667.

[40] Esperanto Postage Stamps and Labels, 'Rose Island' https://alphabetilately.org/Esperanto/RoseI.html.

The 'reef republics' we have discussed thus far were all purportedly established in the 1960s and 1970s. This is not a coincidence for this period represents a gap between the signing of four international treaties on the law of sea that encouraged exploitation of ocean resources and developments in jurisprudence and state practice that clarified the scope and extent of coastal state authority. As Samuel Menefee notes, 'it was a period, if not of unclaimed islands, then of reefs and banks which had hitherto escaped the embrace of neighbouring States'.[41] It was not until the conclusion of the 1982 United Nations Convention on the Law of the Sea (UNCLOS) – a conference that first commenced in 1973 – that the scope of coastal state authority was confirmed. Entering into force in 1994, the UNCLOS provides for an expansive jurisdiction. All coastal states enjoy a 12-nautical-mile territorial sea within which they may set laws, regulate and use any resource; a further 12-nautical-mile contiguous zone, in which a state can continue to enforce laws in customs, taxation, immigration and pollution; and a 200-nautical-mile exclusive economic zone (EEZ), within which a coastal state has sole exploitation rights over natural resources. Coastal states also possess exclusive jurisdiction over mineral and non-mineral resources within their continental shelf – an area that may exceed beyond the 200-nautical-mile EEZ. The greatly increased scope of authority recognised for coastal states under the UNCLOS means that future micronations seeking to establish themselves on atolls or artificial structures must look far beyond the nearest state.

Even where the law of sea does not ground a claim of sovereignty, it can play a role in the purported establishment of a new micronation. In 1997, Greenpeace activists landed on a 780-square-metre rocky atoll that stretches 17 metres high, appropriately named Rockall. Located over 300 kilometres west of Scotland's St Kilda archipelago and around 420 kilometres north-west of Ireland, Rockall is remote. In 1971, Lord Kennet of the UK House of Lords described Rockall as 'a dreadful place', noting that '[t]here could be no place more desolate, more despairing and more awful to see in the whole world'.[42] A colleague in the House of Commons remarked the following month that 'more people have landed on the moon than have landed on Rockall by sea'.[43] While

[41] Menefee (n 37) 111.

[42] United Kingdom, *Parliamentary Debates*, House of Lords, vol 325, cols 754–755 (Lord Kennet) (18 November 1971).

[43] United Kingdom, *Parliamentary Debates*, House of Commons, vol 828, col 199 (William Ross) (13 December 1971).

known to the Vikings and documented in written records since the late sixteenth century,[44] the atoll first became significant during the Cold War.

Initially the subject of competing claims by Iceland, Ireland and Denmark, the United Kingdom annexed the tiny granite islet in 1955. The decision to annex Rockall was motivated by the desire to prevent the Soviet Union from using it to monitor British missile testing, and to use it as a base to further the United Kingdom's EEZ.[45] A three-man team landed on the island via helicopter, raised the Union Jack and cemented a brass plaque to stake the United Kingdom's claim. In 1972, the United Kingdom sought to perfect this claim by formally incorporating it into the Shire of Inverness.[46] As the UK Fleet Air Arm Officers Association records, this action was the final 'territorial expansion of the British empire'.[47]

This action may have been the last the world heard of Rockall. However, art 121 of the UNCLOS precludes uninhabitable rocks from sustaining an EEZ. When the United Kingdom signed the UNCLOS in 1997, it acknowledged that Rockall could not sustain human habitation and therefore lost its claim to a 200-mile EEZ.[48] In June 1997, Greenpeace landed.[49] Announcing that they rejected British sovereignty, they claimed the rock and adjacent seas 'for the planet and all its peoples', and declared Rockall the capital of the new global state of Waveland.[50] Around 15,000 people across the world registered as citizens, attracted by its founders' stated aspiration 'to protect the global commons rather than to exploit it',[51] and its commitment to block fisheries and oil exploration. The UK government ignored the development. Greenpeace's occupation ended after forty-two days and Waveland has since ceased to exist.

[44] George Sidney Holland and Richard Aylmer Gardiner, 'The First Map of Rockall' (1975) 141(1) *Geographical Journal* 94.

[45] Stephen Royle, '"This Mere Speck in the Surface of the Waters": Rockall aka Waveland' (2014) 8 *Shima: The International Journal of Research into Island Cultures* 72, 76.

[46] *Island of Rockall Act 1972* (c. 2) (UK).

[47] Fleet Air Arm Officers Association, 'On This Day 18 September 1955' (18 September 2014) www.fleetairarmoa.org/news/on-this-day-18-september-1955.

[48] Royle (n 45) 78.

[49] James Mellor, 'A Hard Place for a Protest as Invaders Raise the Flag on Rockall', *The Independent* (12 June 1997) www.independent.co.uk/news/a-hard-place-for-a-protest-as-invaders-raise-the-flag-on-rockall-1255452.html.

[50] Royle (n 45) 79–80.

[51] Ibid 80.

4.1.4 Terra Nullius

Rockall may not be inhabited but it is still legally part of the United Kingdom. Notwithstanding Greenpeace's occupation, Waveland had no legal basis for its formation. Perhaps it would be simpler for micronations to establish themselves on unclaimed land? The Free Republic of Liberland purports to ground its existence and authority on the international legal doctrine of *terra nullius* – literally, land belonging to no one. On 13 April 2015, Czech politician Vit Jedlička announced the establishment of the new state[52] with the intention of developing a libertarian utopia free of government regulation and taxation.[53]

Terra nullius is a principle of international law used to justify the legal acquisition of territory by occupation. In the modern context, the principle has fallen into disuse, in part because no vacant land capable of sustaining sovereign claims exists and also as a result of the principle's imperialist overtones.[54] *Terra nullius* had been used to justify European colonisation of large tracts of land inhabited by Indigenous peoples across the globe. As Judge Ammoun exclaimed in the International Court of Justice's *Western Sahara* Advisory Opinion, the principle today 'stands condemned'.[55] Nonetheless, Liberland maintains a claim of sovereignty and statehood on the basis of *terra nullius* in a non-colonial context.

Liberland is located on a small uninhabited parcel of land beside the Danube River. The land is claimed by no state because of a border dispute. In 1945, Yugoslavia appointed a commission to determine the internal boundaries between two of its constituent republics, Serbia and Croatia.[56] The Commission was required to draw the border along ethnic boundaries, which it did where possible. However, the ethnic composition of towns either side of the Danube River made this task exceedingly difficult along a 140-kilometre portion of the border. For this section, the Danube was adopted as the internal border, despite the fact that large

52 Gideon Lewis-Kraus, 'Welcome to Liberland, the World's Newest Country (Maybe)', *The New York Times* (11 August 2015) www.nytimes.com/2015/08/16/magazine/the-making-of-a-president.html.

53 Ryan Gorman, 'This New Microcountry Wants to Be a Big Tax Haven', *Business Insider* (23 April 2015) www.businessinsider.com.au/liberland-this-newly-declared-microcountry-wants-to-become-the-worlds-foremost-tax-haven-2015-4.

54 James Crawford, *Brownlie's Principles of Public International Law* (Oxford University Press, 9th ed, 2019) 208.

55 *Western Sahara (Advisory Opinion)* [1975] 12, 86 (Separate Opinion of Judge Ammoun).

56 Mladen Klemenčić and Clive Schofield, *War and Peace on the Danube: The Evolution of the Croatia-Serbia Boundary* (IBRU, 2006) 12.

Serbian populations existed on the Croatian side, and vice versa.[57] This fix was relatively unimportant until the dissolution of Yugoslavia in 1991. In August that year, the European Economic Community established the Badinter Commission to provide advice on where the Croatian and Serbian international border should lie. Adopting the international law principle of *uti possidetis*, the Badinter Commission concluded that the international boundary should be based on the existing internal border.[58] As a consequence, significant portions of historically Croatian land were assigned to Serbia, and historically Serbian land to Croatia.

On this basis, Liberland is officially part of Croatian territory. However, Croatia refuses to recognise its possession because to do so would imply that it accepts the Badinter Commission border, which gives significantly greater portions of historically Croatian lands to Serbia than vice versa.[59] Croatia thus insists that Liberland is Serbian. For its part, Serbia has issued a statement that Liberland would 'not theoretically impinge on its border'.[60] Despite this, as we explore in the following chapter, Liberland and its 500,000 online citizens have found it challenging to exercise its independence. Croatian authorities have frequently prevented Jedlička and other supporters from accessing the area.[61] It is likely that Croatian interference is sufficient to dismiss Liberland's claim. As the *Western Sahara* case found, *terra nullius* cannot be lightly assumed. Where it is said to occur because of abandonment or absence of authority, there must be a clear and 'definite renunciation'[62] on the part of the abandoning state. Abandonment is 'effected through the owner-state completely abandoning territory with the intention of withdrawing from it forever, thus relinquishing sovereignty over it'.[63]

57 Gabriel Rossman, 'Extremely Loud and Incredibly Close (But Still So Far): Assessing Liberland's Claim of Statehood' (2016) 17 *Chicago Journal of International Law* 306, 312.

58 Peter Radan, 'Post-Secession International Borders: A Critical Analysis of the Opinions of the Badinter Arbitration Commission' (2000) 24 *Melbourne University Law Review* 50, 52.

59 Rossman (n 57) 311–12.

60 Euan McKirdy, 'Liberland: Could the World's Newest Micronation Get Off the Ground?', *CNN* (29 April 2015) https://edition.cnn.com/2015/04/25/europe/liberland-worlds-newest-micronation/index.html.

61 Dusan Stojanovic, 'Police in the Balkans Block Inauguration of Europe's New "Mini-State"', *US News* (9 May 2015) www.usnews.com/news/business/articles/2015/05/09/microstate-tax-haven-in-the-balkans-not-that-easy.

62 *Legal Status of Eastern Greenland (Denmark v Norway) (Judgment)* [1933] PCIJ (ser A/B) No 53, 22, 47.

63 Zhiguo Gao and Bing Bing Jia, 'The Nine-Dash Line in the South China Sea: History, Status, and Implications' (2013) 107 *American Journal of International Law* 98, 111.

One year earlier, another micronation was purportedly established on the basis of *terra nullius*. In March 2014, Greenpeace activists planted a flag in a Chilean glacier and announced the creation of the new Glacier Republic. Echoing the formation of Waveland in 1997, the activists saw statehood and international legal personality as a means to draw attention to environmental causes; in this case, the absence of legislation protecting glaciers in Chile. They encouraged people from all over the world to take up citizenship, solemnised a marriage on the El Morado glacier near Santiago and set up embassies (operating out of Greenpeace offices) with more than forty countries. According to the activists, because neither the Constitution of Chile nor the Chilean Water Code specifies that glaciers are part of the national territory, they 'were in no man's land'.[64] On this basis, the executive director of Greenpeace Chile, Matias Asun, explained: 'We took possession of the entire surface area of glaciers in Chile and declared ourselves an independent republic'.[65] The legal status of the Glacier Republic is decidedly less secure than Asun would suggest.

4.1.5 Historic Legitimacy

There is not always an international covenant, principle or celebrated legal instrument with which one can ground a case for sovereignty and statehood. In many cases, micronations attempt to predicate their independence on an alternative history where an agreement between sovereign entities went unfulfilled in some manner; the Principality of Seborga, for instance, rests its claim as an independent state on the failure to properly register a contract. Although the world may have failed to notice, or perhaps even wilfully chosen to disregard this legal flaw, micronationalists can seek to take advantage of this by positioning themselves as truth tellers.

Marriage contracts are often identified. In medieval Europe, the relationship between a sovereign and territory was 'roughly analogous to the relationship between a property-owner and her land'.[66] Parcels of territory could be bought and sold or transferred by marriage and inheritance. Indeed, many dynastic marriages were sought on the basis of the lands that marriage partners brought with them. Famously, the Habsburg

64 Marianela Jarroud, 'Environment: Greenpeace Starts a Virtual "Republic" to Save Chile's Glaciers', *Global Information Network* (24 February 2015).

65 Ibid.

66 Margaret Moore, *Ethics of Nationalism* (Oxford University Press, 2001) 141.

Empire both protected and expanded their territorial holdings across eastern Europe through careful marriage policies.[67] For some micronations, the question is whether those marriage contracts were correctly fulfilled.

Consider Stuart Hill's claim for an independent Shetland. Shetland is a subarctic archipelago in the Northern Isles of Scotland, situated in the Northern Atlantic around 170 kilometres north of the Scottish mainland and 300 kilometres west of Norway. Initially inhabited during the Mesolithic period, Shetland came under Norse influence during the Viking expansion before becoming part of Scotland in the fifteenth century. Stuart Hill argues that this transfer was never properly constituted.

Hill first came to the attention of the British press in 2001. That year, he attempted to circumnavigate Britain in a four-and-a-half-metre dinghy but ran into trouble. In fact, he ran into considerable, repeated trouble, causing five lifeboat launches and two rescue helicopter callouts before he was conclusively shipwrecked off the coast of Shetland.[68] Dubbed 'Captain Calamity', he decided to settle in Shetland and became an active participant in the minor independence movement.[69] In 2008, Hill unilaterally declared Forewick Holm, a small 2.5-acre island in the Sound of Papa in Shetland, the Sovereign State of Forvick. Although the island had no inhabitants or permanent structures, he set out to begin construction. Hill sailed to the island on a homemade boat but was forced to call for a Coastguard helicopter and lifeboat after his 'ramshackle' vessel began to sink.[70] Undeterred, in 2010, he enlarged his claim to include independence of the entire Shetland Islands.

Hill predicates his claim on an agreement struck in 1469 between King Christian I of Denmark and King James III of Scotland, in which James married Christian's daughter Margaret. As part of the arrangement, Christian pawned Shetland (including Forewick Holm) to James to

[67] Paula Fichtner, 'Dynastic Marriage in Sixteenth-Century Habsburg Diplomacy and Statecraft: An Interdisciplinary Approach' (1976) 81(2) *The American Historical Review* 243.

[68] '"Captain Calamity" Returns to Sea', *BBC News* (21 July 2010) http://news.bbc.co.uk/2/hi/uk_news/1450230.stm.

[69] Adam Grydehøj, 'Captain Calamity's Sovereign State of Forvik: Micronations and the Failure of Cultural Nationalism' (2014) 8(1) *Shima: The International Journal of Research into Island Cultures* 34, 39.

[70] Bob Dow, '"Captain Calamity" Rescued for 8th Time after Setting Sail in "Floating Wardrobe"', *Daily Record* (16 September 2008) www.dailyrecord.co.uk/news/scottish-news/captain-calamity-rescued-for-8th-time-990567.

raise money for Margret's dowry. Hill argues that the agreement only pledged 'about 3 or 10 per cent of the land in Shetland' and left the remainder of the land in the 'outright ownership of the people of Shetland'.[71] The treaty also included a right of redemption. If Christian could repay the money, Shetland would be returned to him.[72] Hill argues that the possibility of redemption means that there was never a formal transfer of ownership or sovereignty; as such, Shetland never technically became part of Scotland or the United Kingdom.[73] Hill outlines his case in his *Stolen Isles: Shetland's True Status* (published by Forvik University Press).[74] As we will explore in Chapter 5, Scottish courts have dismissed his argument.

The Free Borough of Llanrwst does not trace its sovereign status to a marriage contract but a privilege granted by the last Welsh Prince of Wales. In 1276, Llywelyn ap Gruffudd (Llywelyn the Last) seized the town on the River Conwy and declared it a 'free borough' independent of the diocese of Llanelwy. Llywelyn was killed in battle in 1282 and the principality of Wales annexed by Edward I of England. According to the town council, however, Llanrwst retained their independent status, ripping down banners related to Edward I or the bishopric. Over time, the town has developed its own coat of arms, flag and motto, 'Cymru, Lloegr a Llanrwst' (Wales, England and Llanrwst). Independence is prized. In 1947, the town supposedly petitioned the United Nations Security Council for a seat in the General Assembly, arguing that Llanrwst was an independent state within Wales. The Llanrwst Historical Society have reportedly obtained proof of this petition,[75] but nothing is available in the United Nations records. In any event, while Llanrwst was unsuccessful, the town remains certain of its status. In 2019, Mayor Huw Prys Jones explained to incredulous journalists: 'As there is no record of the removal of that status given to the town by Llywelyn ap Gruffydd, we are pleased to reaffirm it.'[76]

[71] *The Royal Bank of Scotland Plc v Stuart Hill* [2012] CSOH 110, [19] (Lord Pentland).

[72] Katharine Anderson, 'Case Comment: *Royal Bank of Scotland v Stuart Hill*' (2013) 4 *Aberdeen Student Law Review* 105, 108.

[73] George Nelson, 'Meet "Captain Calamity", the Man Who Wants to Free Shetland from the UK's "Imperial Ruling Class"', *Vice UK* (29 April 2015) www.vice.com/en/article/nn9w88/captain-calamity-and-the-quest-for-shetlands-independence-930.

[74] Stuart Hill, *Stolen Isles: Shetland's True Status* (Forvik University Press, 2014).

[75] 'Talk of the Town', *BBC News* (28 April 2006) https://web.archive.org/web/20121111051636/http://www.bbc.co.uk/wales/northwest/sites/llanrwst/pages/history.shtml.

[76] Eryl Crump, 'National Eisteddfod Visitors to Be Offered Free "Passport" to Llanrwst', *Daily Post* (4 August 2019) www.dailypost.co.uk/news/north-wales-news/national-eisteddfod-visitors-offered-free-16696601.

Several micronations in the United States trace their independence to supposedly improperly executed treaties. One such case is the Dominion of British West Florida which emerged in 2005. The Dominion claims the territory of the eighteenth-century colony of West Florida, which includes land now part of Alabama, Louisiana, Mississippi and Florida. In 1763, Great Britain established the colonies of West and East Florida out of land acquired from France and Spain following the French and Indian War. During the American Revolution, both colonies remained loyal to the British Crown, but West Florida was captured by Spain. After the war, Britain ceded both Floridas to Spain in the Treaty of Paris. Over the next decades, a series of border disputes and confrontations between the United States and Spain ensued. In 1810, a group of British and Americans rebelled against Spanish rule and declared the formation of the Republic of West Florida. The Republic did not control the entirety of the colony of West Florida, but merely the western region, now Louisiana. It survived only two-and-a-half months before it was annexed by the United States. In 1819, Spain ceded the remainder of its territory to the United States in the Adams–Onís Treaty.

The Dominion of West Florida accepts this chain of events. However, they argue that Spain did not have the authority to cede West Florida in the 1819 Treaty. Instead, they assert that control of the colony defaulted to the United Kingdom in 1808, when Napoleon Bonaparte, the Emperor of France, forced Charles IV and his son, Ferdinand VII, to abdicate from the Spanish throne (Napoleon then invested his brother Joseph as King of Spain).[77] In reaching this conclusion, they draw on a speech given by the Governor of the short-lived Republic of West Florida, who exclaimed in 1810:

> When Charles the 4th, late sovereign of Spain, abdicated his throne, and was followed by the heir apparent, styled Ferdinand the 7th, to prefer an asylum in a foreign country, to defending the sovereign independence of his crown and subjects; the people of the Floridas, in common with the rest of the Spanish colonies, had they consisted of but one family, were restored to the original rights and natural charter of man; that of providing for their own preservation and government.
>
> We are then entitled to independence, and wherever the voice of justice and humanity can be heard, our declaration, and our just rights will be respected.[78]

[77] Ryan, Dunford and Sellars (n 20) 139.

[78] Governor Fulwar Skipwith, Speech to the Senate and House of Representatives of the State of West Florida (St Francisville, 29 November 1810).

Although Governor Fulwar Skipwith's speech called for the Republic to honour the 'genius of Washington' and return 'to the heart of our parent country',[79] the Dominion of British West Florida aspires to become part of the British Commonwealth.

Sometimes a simple land contract can ground a micronation's independence. The Grand Duchy of the Lagoan Isles was founded in 2005 by schoolteacher Louis Stephens. The Grand Duchy claims sovereignty over three small islands within Baffins Pond, in Portsmouth, southern England. Records of Baffins Farm (including the pond) date back to 1194. In 1912, it became a public park and in 1938 it was sold to the City of Portsmouth. According to the Grand Duke, however, because the pond's islands were not specifically mentioned in the 1938 land sale contract, they were not conveyed. Stephens sent a letter to Portsmouth Council announcing his claim and released a series of banknotes in an effort to substantiate his title.[80]

One of the stranger micronations that predicates its sovereignty on a supposed historic lineage is the Romanov Empire. Founded in 2011 by Russian businessman Anton Bakov, this micronation claims to be the successor state to the pre-revolutionary Russian Empire, which ceased to exist in 1917. As such, it claims authority over land and marine territory that belonged to the historic Russian Empire but was not absorbed into the Soviet Union. This encompasses the entire continent of Antarctica, as well as seventeen islands now under the jurisdiction of Japan, the United Kingdom and the United States. It does not, however, claim land that was part of the Russian Empire but is now Finland, Poland or other Eastern European countries. Bakov has designed state symbols, drafted a constitution and claims to have issued around 4,000 passports (at 1,000 rubles each). In 2014, Bakov announced that Prince Karl Emich of Leiningen, a descendent of the House of Romanov, had acceded to the throne as Nicholas III, Emperor of All Russia. The previous year, Prince Karl converted from Lutheranism to Eastern Orthodox Christianity to enable his accession.

The Romanov Empire has struggled to convince others of its legitimacy. Russian President Vladimir Putin declined to grant the Empire a plot of land in Yekaterinburg (the site of the 1918 Romanov assassination). Various attempts by Bakov to purchase land to develop a new state in

[79] Ibid.

[80] See The Grand Duchy of the Lagoan Isles, 'History of Our Nation' http://lagoan-isles.moonfruit.com/history-of-our-nation/4545798160.

Montenegro, Macedonia, Albania, the Gambia and Antigua and Barbuda have also so far failed.[81] In 2020, reports suggested that Bakov was planning to build artificial islands outside Venice.[82]

4.2 Mimicry of Statehood

Micronations do not only assert their sovereignty in the immediate act of secession. As we have noted, many founders enjoy sovereignty's performative aspects or rituals. Micronations mimic the actions of nation-states. They adopt the symbols and protocols of nations and engage in earnest or mock reproductions of statehood. As we explore in this part, these actions are further attempts to legitimate their status.

4.2.1 National Symbols

Sovereign states are not natural entities with preordained borders and boundaries. As Benedict Anderson explained in his examination of the emergence of nationalism, states are 'imagined communities',[83] constructed through collective cultural identities and shared iconography, 'symbols, memories, myths, values and traditions'.[84] National symbols, myths, ritual and political language are intended to unite diverse communities and peoples in a common cause by creating verbal, visual or iconic representations of the nation and state.

Micronations also create national symbols as a means to both imitate and critique statehood. They draft their own constitutions, compose their own national anthems and design their own flags. They also confer their founders with royal titles, issue stamps and mint currency. The paraphernalia of nationhood serve as visual representations of statehood, acting to confer a degree of legitimacy on the status of the micronation. Consider

[81] See, for example, Jonathan Pearlman, 'Russian Businessman Seeks to Restore Tsarist Empire Overthrown in 1917 on Pacific Atoll', *The Daily Telegraph* (30 January 2017) www.telegraph.co.uk/news/2017/01/30/russian-businessman-seeks-restore-tsarist-empire-overthrown/; 'Kiribati Mulls Proposal to "Restore Russian Monarchy"', *BBC News* (30 January 2017) www.bbc.com/news/blogs-news-from-elsewhere-38798535; 'Gambia Denies Hosting Russian Imperial Revival Bid', *BBC News* (12 December 2017) www.bbc.com/news/blogs-news-from-elsewhere-42324401.

[82] Dmitry Komarov, 'Anton Bakov Wants to Build a New State "Noah's Ark" Near Venice', *ZNAK* (29 April 2020) www.znak.com/2020-04-29/.

[83] Benedict Anderson, *Imagined Communities* (Verso, 1991).

[84] Anthony Smith, 'When Is a Nation?' (2002) 7(2) *Geopolitics* 5, 14–15.

the use of postage stamps as an example. Philatelic studies have long recognised postage stamps as 'vehicles for identity creation and propagation, and as mechanisms for regime legitimation'.[85] The postage stamp

> is a small but mighty symbolic emissary from one particular nation to the rest of the world. A functioning postal service, made visible in stamps, is an unmistakable expression of national legitimacy. Throughout their history, stamps have been prized by collectors for their unique ability to represent a political culture in miniature. As a result, the postage stamp is an excellent vehicle for spurious, tenuous, or completely fictitious states to declare their existence.[86]

Postage stamps reflect and construct national identity. For instance, the Province of Bumbunga, established in the mid-1970s in protest at Australia's apparent drift towards republicanism, always featured the British royal family in its stamps. Stamps issued by the Republic of Molossia frequently comprise portraits of his Excellency President Kevin Baugh, the Molossian flag and celebrated movements in the nation's history. Reflecting its pioneering spirit, the Principality of Sealand often features famous explorers, including Vasco de Gama, Christopher Columbus, Ferdinand Magellan and Captain James Cook.

The Principality of Sealand has adopted other prominent symbols of nationhood. Scholars have remarked on the connection between sport, national identity and state-building. Sport offers 'a uniquely effective medium for inculcating national feelings';[87] it can play a critical role in fostering unity between diverse communities, both reflecting and constructing political units,[88] for it is in sporting competition that 'the nation becomes tangible'.[89] Sport also has external state-legitimating functions. States gain prestige and soft power from hosting global sporting events,[90] while membership of international sporting bodies 'is the clearest signal

[85] Phil Deans and Hugo Dobson, 'East Asian Postage Stamps as Socio-Political Artefacts' (2005) 22(2) *East Asia* 3, 6.

[86] Laura Steward, 'Bogus Cinderella' (Outsider Art Fair New York, 2020) www.outsiderartfair.com /program-new-york/oaf-special-projects-bogus-cinderella.

[87] Grant Jarvie, 'Sport, Nationalism and Cultural Identity' in Lincoln Allison (ed), *The Changing Politics of Sport* (Manchester University Press, 1993) 58, 74.

[88] Roger Livermore, 'Sport's Role in Constructing the "Inter-State" Worldview' in Adrian Budd and Roger Livermore (eds), *Sport and International Relations: An Emerging Relationship* (Routledge, 2004) 16, 21.

[89] Richard Arnold, 'Nationalism and Sport: A Review of the Field' (2021) 49(1) *Nationalities Papers* 2, 4.

[90] Jonathon Grix and Paul Michael Brannagan, 'Of Mechanisms and Myths: Conceptualising States' "Soft Power" Strategies through Sports Mega-Events' (2016) 27 (2) *Diplomacy and Statecraft* 251.

that a country's status as a nation-state has been recognized by the international community'.[91] For entities with no or limited recognition, sport may hold the key for access to the international community. Indeed, as Kieran Pender explains, the German Democratic Republic was one of the first states to explicitly pursue this strategy:

> [L]acking widespread recognition it utilised 'diplomats in track suits' to establish de facto and then de jure recognition from other states. As a former head of the German Gymnastics and Sports Association acknowledged: 'Sport led the way in increasing the international prestige of our socialistic republic and led to its diplomatic recognition by a majority of the states of the world'.[92]

Drawing on interviews with key government officials and members of civil society, Pender explains that similar motivations lay behind the decision of Abkhazia to host a football world cup for unrecognised states in 2016.[93]

Conscious of these potential advantages, the Principality of Sealand founded the Sealand National Football Association in 2003. The following year the Sealand National Football team played its first official game against the Åland Islands, a Swedish-speaking autonomous region of Finland. Sealand is not a member of FIFA or UEFA but was a member of the Nouvelle Fédération Board – a federation of football associations that represented nations, dependences, unrecognised states, minorities, stateless peoples, regions and micronations not affiliated to FIFA. In this capacity it has competed against teams from the Chagos Islands, Alderney, Raetia, Tamil Eelam, Somaliland and Occitania, as well as the Principality of Seborga.[94] However, the future of the Sealand football team is uncertain. The Nouvelle Fédération Board became defunct in 2013, replaced by the Confederation of Independent Football Associations (CONIFA). Although CONIFA is based on the view that 'countries are often just historic flukes. One broad stroke on a map and

[91] John Sugden and Alan Tomlinson, 'Football and FIFA in the Postcolonial World' in John Bale and Mike Cronin (eds), *Sport and Postcolonialism* (Berg, 2003) 175, 179.

[92] Kieran Pender, 'More than a Game: Sport, Legitimacy and Unrecognised States' (BA Thesis, ANU, 2016) 49–50. Citing Andrew Strenk, 'Diplomats in Track Suits: The Role of Sports in the Foreign Policy of the German Democratic Republic' (1980) 4(1) *Journal of Sport and Social Issues* 34, 43.

[93] Pender (n 92) ch 3.

[94] James Baines, 'I Went to an International Football Match between Two Non-Countries', *Vice* (6 March 2014) www.vice.com/en/article/9bjnm5/chagos-islands-sealand-football-match.

a peace treaty a hundred years ago. Does that make a country?',[95] it has rejected Sealand's application to join the successor organisation as 'frivolous'.[96] For this reason Sealand did not participate in the most recent 2018 CONIFA World Cup (Kárpátalja, a team representing the Hungarian minority in Carpathian Ruthenia, defeated Northern Cyprus 3–2 on penalties).[97]

4.2.2 Diplomatic Relations

Under international law, diplomatic recognition is not constitutive of statehood. A state does not lose its status simply because it is not recognised by another state or the international community at large and a non-state actor does not become a state merely because it is treated as such by one or more states.[98] Even if not constitutive, however, diplomatic recognition and consular relations carry a legitimating function. In the absence of formal legal recognition, many micronations (and indeed, many non-state entities) attempt to engage in diplomatic practices and other 'language of stateness' to assert their claims.[99] They write letters to their former government justifying their secession and declaration of independence, as well as a range of other international actors, including Queen Elizabeth II, the United Nations and even the International Court of Justice.

The Nation of Celestial Space was particularly energised in the diplomatic sphere. Founded on 20 December 1948 by Illinois resident James Mangan, the micronation asserted sovereignty over the entirety of outer space in an effort to ensure that no other state might establish political hegemony there. In 1949, Mangan notified the United States, USSR, United Kingdom and the UN that the Nation of Celestial Space had banned all atmospheric nuclear tests. Later, as the space race got

[95] Dylan Taylor-Lehman, *Sealand: The True Story of the World's Most Stubborn Micronation* (Icon Books, 2020) 137.

[96] Matthew Engel, 'World Football Cup an Alternative to Fifa and a Lesson in Geopolitics', *The Guardian* (2 June 2018) www.theguardian.com/football/2018/jun/01/world-football-cup-alternative-fifa-lesson-geopolitics.

[97] Conifa, 'WFC 2018 Results and Tables' www.conifa.org/en/wfc-2018/wfc-results-tables-2/.

[98] *Montevideo Convention* (n 1) art 3; Arbitration Commission of the Hague Conference on Yugoslavia ('Badinter Commission'), *Opinion No 1* (1993) 92 ILR 162, 165.

[99] Thomas Blom Hansen and Finn Stepputat, 'Introduction: States of Imagination' in Thomas Blom Hansen and Finn Stepputat (eds), *States of Imagination: Ethnographic Explorations of the Postcolonial State* (Duke University Press, 2001) 1, 9.

underway in earnest, he sent letters of protest to the leaders of the USSR and United States on the occasions that their early space flights encroached upon his territory.[100] It is not known whether he received a response.

Micronational diplomacy is often 'opportunistic and experimental'.[101] Bruce Grenville founded the Sultanate of Occussi-Ambeno as a means to critique and satirise the concept of the state. Among many diplomatic engagements, the Sultanate wrote to the Albanian politician Enver Hoxha seeking release of political prisoners.[102] Other micronationalists may leverage personal relationships with members of government to engineer supposedly formal meetings. As we have noted, Dean Kamen used his relationship with President George H.W. Bush to sign a faux non-aggression pact between the United States and the Kingdom of North Dumpling,[103] while Igor Ashurbeyli trumpeted his friendship with Prince Michael of Kent – cousin to Queen Elizabeth II of the United Kingdom – as de facto recognition of the Space Kingdom of Asgardia.[104]

In other cases, micronations rely on the good faith, and ignorance, of state actors to push their claims. In the years immediately following the Principality of Hutt River's purported establishment, other countries 'were unaware of what was occurring, and timely exchange of information with Australian authorities was impossible'.[105] Several individuals took advantage of this.

In 1981, Hong Kong became the first government in the world to extend diplomatic recognition to Hutt River. In a public notice published in the Hong Kong Government *Gazette* it announced the appointment of 'a Mr Raymond Sacklyn as Ambassador for Hutt River Province', declaring that Mr Sacklyn 'enjoyed the special trust and confidence of the Prince as his personal representative in Hong Kong'. Following inquiries by journalists, 'embarrassed officials'

[100] See Virgiliu Pop, 'The Nation of Celestial Space' (2006) 22 *Space Policy* 205.

[101] Fiona McConnell, Terri Moreau and Jason Dittmer, 'Mimicking State Diplomacy: The Legitimating Strategies of Unofficial Diplomacies' (2012) 43 *Geoforum* 804, 805.

[102] Bruce Grenville, 'Ocussi-Ambeno: A Modern Satirical State' (1985) 6 *Phlogiston* 17, 19.

[103] Clarice Butkus, 'North Dumpling Island: Micronationality, the Media and the American Dream' (2014) 8 *Shima: The International Journal of Research into Island Cultures* 84.

[104] Ivan Cherbeko, 'Head of Nation Talks of Asgardia to Queen Elizabeth II's Cousin', *Asgardia* (8 March 2019) https://asgardia.space/en/news/Head of-Nation-talks-of-Asgardia-to-Queen-Elizabeths-II-Cousin.

[105] Vicente Bicudo de Castro and Ralph Kober, 'The Principality of Hutt River: A Territory Marooned in the Western Australian Outback' (2018) 12(1) *Shima: The International Journal of Research into Island Cultures* 143, 150.

in Hong Kong admitted that they had made 'a frightful mistake'. A special *Gazette* was issued ending the recognition of the Principality and Mr Sacklyn's tenure as Ambassador.[106]

Individuals also took advantage of the confusion. Some people who had taken out Hutt River citizenship and been awarded royal titles proclaimed it on their business cards. The 'response was incredible'; on international flights 'they are often upgraded to first class', while in hotels, 'they are moved from standard rooms to suites'.[107] Others claimed to use Hutt River passports to travel internationally. At Orly Airport in Paris, retired Australian detective and supposed Hutt River Ambassador, Sir Tom Ericksen, sought to enter on a diplomatic passport:

> 'Hutt River Province?' [the Immigration Officer] asked in heavily-accented English, his eyebrows rising to meet his cap. 'Where is Hutt River Province?'
>
> Ericksen recalls the conversation because he is fond of recalling it. 'It's 18 times bigger than Monaco,' he replied. 'Second-biggest country in Australia.'
>
> 'One moment,' said the passport officer, not at all happy with the green and gold embossed document in his hand, nor apparently with the knighthood it proclaimed for its 20-stone owner.
>
> Ericksen stood politely in the queue while the officer conferred with his superior. Presently the two men returned to the counter. 'Yes, excuse me, Your Excellency,' said the more senior man, ushering Ericksen through the desk and slapping his underling at the same time. 'Right this way, Your Excellency,' he said as he led Victoria's ambassador to Hutt River Province into France, pausing only to stamp his passport on the way through.[108]

Whether this story is true or not, it is difficult to imagine it occurring again. Following the September 11 attacks, the United States and other countries have significantly enhanced security requirements concerning international travel, thereby complicating the ability of people attempting to enter countries on non-state passports. Indigenous peoples who travel on non-state passports, like the Haudenosaunee, have faced the same difficulties.[109]

[106] Tony Walker, 'Hong Kong Accolade for Hutt River', *Sydney Morning Herald* (16 March 1982) 10.

[107] Jane Cadzow, 'Prince and the Pawpaws', *Sydney Morning Herald* (20 February 1993) 162.

[108] Phil Ackman, 'The Second Biggest Country in Australia: Hutt River Province', *Australian Penthouse* (August 1982) 83.

[109] See Brian Kolva, 'Lacrosse Players, Not Terrorists: The Effects of the Western Hemisphere Travel Initiative on Native American International Travel and Sovereignty' (2012) 40 *Journal of Law & Policy* 307. See further Justin Lindeboom, *The Quality of Nationalities of Countries that Don't Exist: Measuring the Value of Unrecognized Nationalities* (Quality of Nationality Index, 3rd ed, 2018).

It may be that the era of micronations mistakenly invited to state functions has also ended. As we discussed in the previous chapter, the Principality of Outer Baldonia was erroneously included in a US State Department list, and its representative was regularly invited to various events. The Dominion of Melchizedek had a similar experience. In 1995, the US Immigration and Naturalization Service sent a letter to its apparent embassy requesting 'some item of uniform insignia from your country's law enforcement services' to be displayed in an exhibition of global law enforcement badges at the Atlanta airport for the 1996 Olympics.[110] This was not the first time the Dominion received some form of international recognition. After its formation, individuals purporting to be members of the Dominion government wrote to sovereign states and the United Nations seeking recognition. The responses are proudly displayed on the Dominion's website. In most cases, these are simply letters acknowledging receipt and requesting more information 'especially with regard to its location, economic and political data, and the counties with which it has diplomatic relations and other information about the country which may be pertinent in the establishing of formal ties'.[111] However, a letter from the Central African Republic appears genuine:

> This letter has been drawn to set forth the Central African Republic's official and formal recognition of the government of the Dominion of Melchizedek, an Ecclesiastical Sovereignty.
>
> Therefore, the Dominion of Melchizedek is hereby invited to establish a Diplomatic Mission in our Republic and will be granted all the consummate and traditional rights and privileges delineated in the Vienna Convention on Diplomatic Relations.
>
> ...
>
> Finally, any Real Estate purchased by the Dominion of Melchizedek from our Republic shall be treated as Sovereign Territory of the Dominion of Melchizedek.[112]

The Washington Post reported at the time that 'you get the feeling that the Central African Republic would recognize the State of Denial if it had

[110] Richard Leiby and James Lileks, 'The Ruse that Roared', *The Washington Post* (5 November 1995).

[111] Letter from the Ministry of Foreign Affairs of Grenada to the Office of the President of the Dominion of Melchizedek, 6 August 1998 https://melchizedek.com/wp-content/uploads/2015/04/DoM-Grenada011.pdf.

[112] Letter from Général d'Armée André Kolingba (President, Central African Republic) to Branch Vinedresser (Minister Plenipotentiary, Embassy of the Dominion of Melchizedek), 3 June 1993 www.melchizedek.com/wp-content/uploads/2015/04/TPR-With-Central-African-Republic.pdf.

a letterhead'.[113] In a rare example of quasi-state recognition, in 2017 Somaliland opened formal diplomatic relations with Liberland.[114]

Micronations prize these instances of inadvertent recognition. Although of no legal import (and sometimes of questionable veracity), they can be used to add a veneer of legitimacy to their claims. Seizing upon loose or diplomatic language from state agents, the Principality of Hutt River proudly displays evidence on its website of what it regards as implicit de facto recognition of its status as a sovereign state. This includes an Australian Department of Foreign Affairs cablegram issued to international missions and authored in the name of Prime Minister Malcolm Fraser, Foreign Affairs Minister Andrew Peacock and Attorney-General Robert Ellicott referring to legal advice that suggests Casley has not contravened any Australian law. It also includes an undated memorandum from the Department of Territories to the Commonwealth Minister authored by 'B.M.W.' and labelled 'AUSTEO SECRET' that states:

> It is therefore our considered opinion, that subject to the guidelines we have had to adopt, the following points are in fact the situation currently.
>
> 1. The Principality is a legal entity.
> 2. Prince Leonard of Hutt is a person exempt in Australian Law from Taxation under the current guidelines.
> 3. The Passport [sic] as used by the persons claiming to be Principality Citizens are valid, however, the act can be used to isolate them by the requirement of visa's [sic].
> 4. Nothing in any legislation currently would preclude recognition if these facts ever saw the light of day.
>
> It is therefore our suggestion that you at all costs contain this situation.

In diplomatic cables to other states, the Department of Foreign Affairs and Trade has described this document as 'a clumsy forgery'.[115] Nevertheless, the Principality provides other documents to apparently support its claim. They include a notice from the Australian Taxation Office addressed to the 'Principality of Hutt River' that states 'You have

[113] Leiby and Lileks (n 110).

[114] 'Somaliland: Liberland States Mutual Recognition Process with Government in Hargeisa', *Somaliland Sun* (12 October 2017) web.archive.org/web/20180308232441/http://www.somalilandsun.com/2017/10/12/ somaliland-liberland-starts-mutual-recognition-process-with-government-in-hargeisa/.

[115] Commonwealth of Australia Department of Foreign Affairs and Trade 'Diplomatic Documents Relating to the Hutt River Province Released under Freedom of Information Laws' (13 November 1996) 85.

been deemed to be a non-resident of Australia for income tax purposes'[116] and a post-marked envelope from the Office of the Western Australian Governor addressed to:

Prince Leonard
Office of the Sovereign
Principality of Hutt River
Nain
Via Western Australia 6535

In 2016, Prince Leonard received a letter from Queen Elizabeth II. The Palace replied to a letter Casley had written wishing the Queen a happy ninetieth birthday, conveying

> Her Majesty's good wishes to you and all concerned for a most enjoyable and successful celebration on 23rd and 24th April to mark the forty-sixth anniversary of the Principality of Hutt River.[117]

Of course, this form letter does not constitute official recognition. Nonetheless, micronations prize such paraphernalia. The official website of the Principality of Snake Hill in Australia prominently houses a series of post-marked envelopes sent by Australian government departments and officials addressed to 'Princess Paula, The Principality of Snake Hill'.[118] It also displays legal advice concluding that the Australian Constitution 'does not preclude secession',[119] as if that were determinative of the legality of its own actions. Whether or not such advice is correct, it is deployed as a means of providing the micronation with a cloak of legality and authenticity.

Notwithstanding these instances of accidental or uncertain acknowledgement, micronations are not officially recognised by sovereign states. This requires more than incidental recognition such as the addressing of a letter to the micronation. For this reason, most micronational diplomacy is conducted between micronations. Embassies are

[116] Australian Taxation Office, 'Notice of Assessment' (25 June 2008) www.principality-hutt-river.org/Principality%20Downloads/Copy%20of%20HRHPL_ATO.pdf.

[117] Sonia Bonici, 'Letter from Sonia Bonici, Senior Correspondence Officer, Buckingham Palace, to Prince Leonard' (16 April 2016).

[118] Principality of Snake Hill, 'International Recognition of Independence' (15 January 2011) www.snakehillprincipality.blogspot.com/2011/01/blog-post.html.

[119] Letter from Damon Hall to Paula Jensen, 11 October 2010. Available at Principality of Snake Hill, 'Legal Opinion, Australian Secession' (15 January 2011) www.snakehillprincipality.blogspot.com/2011/01/legal-opinion-australian-secession.html.

established, friendship treaties and non-aggression pacts are signed, personal visits are conducted and sometimes even wars are declared. International – or intermicronational – institutions to promote shared aims are also established. The Republic of Molossia has played a considerable role in developing intermicronational diplomacy. President Baugh inaugurated the Intermicronational Olympic Movement in 2000, and established MicroCon, a biennial convention of micronation governments held since 2015.[120] The most recent MicroCon was held in July 2019 in Hamilton, Ontario. In between conventions, over 3,300 people converse, share details about their micronations and offer suggestions to others in the Facebook group 'Micronations and Alternative Polities' run by George Cruickshank, the Emperor of Atlantium.[121] Another 4,100 'nation builders' are members of the micronations page on Reddit.[122] Many other micronational communities exist online.

The creation of intermicronational forums mimics the development of multilateral institutions among independent sovereign states. It also provides unrecognised entities with 'alternative routes to [a] global audience'[123] and confirms the value of ritualised statehood protocols and performative aspects of diplomacy and statecraft.[124] In many ways, micronational diplomacy produces 'stand-alone, parallel international communities'.[125] Micronations may not be officially recognised outside their community, but within their own society they perform and assert their sovereignty in ways that are recognised – and respected – by their peers.

4.2.3 *Challenges*

Performing sovereignty by mimicking state actors can produce complications. Following the establishment of their new country, micronationalists are usually eager to attract citizens. While friends and family may be

120 MicroCon 2015 (Anaheim, CA, 11 April 2015) www.molossia.org/microcon/microcon2015.html.

121 Facebook, 'Micronations and Alternative Polities' www.facebook.com/groups/micronationsandalternativepolities/.

122 Reddit, 'Micronations – Small Nations, New Country Projects, Seasteading' www.reddit.com/r/micronations.

123 Yossi Shain, *The Frontier of Loyalty: Political Exiles in the Age of the Nation-State* (University of Michigan Press, 2005) 128.

124 McConnell, Moreau and Dittmer (n 101) 808.

125 Ibid 805.

cajoled, the ambitions of many founders mean that this is insufficient. Seeking greater recognition, online citizenship forms are often set up. Micronational citizenship can be attractive: the Principality of Sealand notes that it received more than 200 inquiries seeking political asylum after the Brexit referendum and the election of Donald Trump.[126] However, engaging in statehood rituals can confuse ordinary people unaware of the legal status of the entity. In these circumstances, the dance that micronations play between authenticity and illegitimacy can collapse, provoking real tensions.

In the previous chapter we noted that some micronations are founded as means of attention seeking or personal expression. One of these, Ladonia, was established by sculptor Lars Vilks in 1996 in southern Sweden in protest at a decision by the local authority to destroy his illegally situated artwork. Over the years, Ladonia gradually grew into an art project. Initially serving as Chancellor, Vilks transformed Ladonia into a 'remony', a republican monarchy headed by a President. He composed a national anthem – the sound of a stone thrown into water – designed a flag – a green cross on a green background – and drafted a language, consisting of only two words 'waaaaaaaaall for everyday use, and the more solemn ÿp'.[127] Vilks encouraged people to become citizens. In the early years, a steady but small stream of new citizens applied and were registered. In 2002, however, this process became problematic, as migrants and refugees from across the globe, believing Ladonia to be a real country, applied for citizenship with the hope of obtaining a pathway into Sweden and Europe.[128] Vilks described his reaction:

> Suddenly the reality in the world connects in a very direct, very bizarre way. Ladonia is a kind of ridiculous thing. You make a toy country and everyone says, 'well you're just playing around'. But then this comes. Something happens; it has consequences, certain consequences you wouldn't even imagine . . .
>
> They don't know that Ladonia has something to do with an art project. They have no references to such a thing because they say: 'why would you do that?' It happened that some people even thought we played

[126] Taylor-Lehman (n 95) 185.

[127] Lars Vilks, 'Remony of Ladonia' in Tellervo Kalleinen and Oliver Kochta-Kalleinen (eds), *Protocols: Amorph!03Summit of Micronations* (Muu Artists' Association, 2005) 76, 76.

[128] Ibid 77. See also 'Pakistanis Appeal to Net Country', *CNET* (16 August 2002) www.cnet.com/news/pakistanis-appeal-to-net-country/.

> a nasty trick on them, you know. I have collected all the material. I have never thrown away any applications. I still gather them. They still keep coming.[129]

This is not an isolated experience. The Gay and Lesbian Kingdom of the Coral Sea Islands received hundreds of applications for asylum and citizenship from queer people desperate to escape persecution in their home countries and move to remote Cato Island. One of the men involved in establishing the micronation, Willoughby Potter de Grimaldi, recently explained the difficulty on a podcast for WYNC studios (a subsidiary of New York Public Radio):

> I reached back explaining the problem with that and how there isn't a residence there. There – there's nowhere specific to go. But, although you can't necessarily seek asylum *there* on Cato Island, your voice is not lost. We could then connect those people with local organisations, to offer protections for discrimination and things like that.[130]

Belgian Niels Vermeersch, who serves as the Grand Duke of Flandrensis, has also fielded thousands of applications for asylum. He explained to the *Brussels Times*:

> I receive daily requests from people in Syria who beg for a Flandrensis passport. I take the time to answer them that we are not a real country, and we don't give passports, but I can only imagine how desperate they are, which is sad and they should not be used by scammers.[131]

The idea that scammers may target vulnerable people and sell false hope is a real concern. In the midst of the 2015 European refugee crisis, Jedlička, founder of Liberland, offered to provide citizenship to any person willing to pay USD 10,000. In September 2015, he claimed that 378,000 people registered their interest, including 9,647 people from Syria and 1,922 from Libya. Pointing to these figures, Jedlička noted that his country may be 'especially attractive to those from troubled nations'.[132] He even went as far

[129] Interview with Lars Vilks and Martin Schibli (Susan Kelly, 29 August 2003) In Susan Kelly, 'Lobby' in Tellervo Kalleinen and Oliver Kochta-Kalleinen (eds), *Protocols: Amorph! 03Summit of Micronations* (Muu Artists' Association, 2005) 152, 154.

[130] 'Make Australia Gay Again', *Nancy* (WNYC Studios, 21 April 2020) (emphasis in original).

[131] Jason Spinks, 'Springtime of Micronations Spearheaded by Belgian "Grand-Duke" Niels', *Brussels Times* (7 December 2015) www.brusselstimes.com/all-news/magazine/35805/springtime-of-micronations-spearheaded-by-belgian-grand-duke-niels/.

[132] Adam Taylor, 'Almost 10,000 Syrians Have Registered to Live in a Country that Might Not Exist', *The Washington Post* (24 September 2015) www.washingtonpost.com/news/worldviews/wp/2015/09/24/almost-10000-syrians-have-registered-to-live-in-a-country-that-might-not-exist/.

as hosting a Liberland recruitment drive in Istanbul,[133] a key point of transit for many European-bound refugees from Syria and elsewhere.

In another imitation of statehood, Jedlička's action prompted a multilateral response. Olivier Touzeau, Emperor of Angyalistan, drafted an official communiqué on behalf of the Organisation of Microfrancophony condemning his actions:

> The micronations who publish passports are faced with the serious problem of the refugee crisis and the actions needed to give hope to humanity without fooling anyone. Liberland just did exactly the opposite of what can be hoped from a serious micronational project. We strongly condemn the despicable initiative of the leader of the free Republic of Liberland.[134]

The possibility of cloaking illegal actions in the veneer of statehood has proven enticing for other swindlers. One of the more astonishing frauds committed though the guise of micronationalism was organised by convicted American fraudster Mark Pedley. Pedley established the Dominion of Melchizedek (DoM) in the 1990s to facilitate large-scale banking fraud in many parts of the world. Relying on the ignorance of his victims, Pedley purported to create a state that satisfied the Montevideo Convention; it possessed territory, a permanent population, an effective government and a capacity to enter into relations with other nations. Conveniently, the DoM's territory was located in several remote locations where its claims would be difficult to immediately disprove. These included the small island of Malpelo, 500 kilometres off the coast of Colombia; the Karitane Shoal in the South Pacific; the French possession of Clipperton Island lying over 1,000 kilometres south-west of Mexico; and Taongi, an uninhabited Micronesian atoll administered by the Marshall Islands.

Pedley and several collaborators fraudulently obtained considerable sums in 'an astonishing series of worldwide swindles'.[135] In 1991, Branch Vindresser – later found to be a pseudonym used by Pedley – chartered several fake banks in Washington DC. The banks were subsidiaries of a Melchizedekian company that was used to attempt to

[133] 'Liberland Recruits Citizens in Istanbul', *World Bulletin* (17 September 2015) www.worldbulletin.net/balkans/liberland-recruits-citizens-in-istanbul-h164331.html.

[134] Chris Roth, 'Liberland's Empty Promises to Syrian Refugees Scorned by Other Micronations', *The Ladonia Herald* (21 October 2015) www.ladoniaherald.com/2015/liberlands-empty-promises-to-syrian-refugees-scorned-by-other-micronations/.

[135] Bertil Lintner, 'Cyberfraud: The Fictitious "Dominion of Melchizedek"', *The Nation* (Bangkok) (30 May 1999).

secure loans from real banks based on fake DoM securities.[136] In 1995, Austrian Gerhard Bacher was sentenced to six months in prison in Hong Kong for using cheques issued by fake Melchizedek banks to open accounts in legitimate Hong Kong banks.[137] That same year, Bank of England officials raided the London premises of 'Inner Sanctum', a company that offered get-rich-quick investment schemes backed by another Melchizedekian bank. Investors discovered that the bank's assets were not backed by US Treasury Bonds as they had been led to believe, but were worthless instruments issued by the German Weimar republic.[138]

In 1996, Jeffrey Reynolds, the Dominion of Melchizedek's supposed Secretary of Commerce, pleaded guilty to insurance fraud in Texas. Reynolds had sold nearly USD 47 million of bogus policies through a company purportedly domiciled in Melchizedek.[139] In the late 1990s, French citizen Roger Rosemount convinced at least 1,400 people to invest over USD 4 million in the Melchizedek-charted bank Credit Bank International. In what turned out to be a Ponzi scheme, the US Securities Exchange Commission warned potential investors that 'Credit Bank is not a bank, Melchizedek is not a country and Rosemount is not an ambassador'.[140] People connected to the DoM have also sold passports, misrepresenting them as internationally recognised. In 1998, three individuals were arrested in the Philippines, including Australian John Gillespie, having allegedly made USD 1 million from the scam.[141] Gillespie had previously been convicted in the Fine Cotton scandal, in which a syndicate attempted to fix a horse race by painting a horse so that they could pass it off as another. It appears that the Dominion of

[136] Terrence O'Hara, 'D.C. Home to Shadowy Banking Web' (18 February 1991) 9(38) *Washington Business Journal* 1; Terrence O'Hara, 'District Probes Off-Shore Companies for Fraud: U.S. Agencies Also Look into Shell Banking Firms in District' (25 February 1991) 9(39) *Washington Business Journal*; Terrence O'Hara, 'D.C. Office of Banking Probes Shell "Banks": Banking Agency Says Firms Charted without Prior OK' (4 March 1991) 9(40) *Washington Business Journal*.

[137] Manuel Gren, 'Young Pretender Jailed for Princely Fraud', *South China Morning Post* (14 July 1995) 1.

[138] Michael Gillard, 'SFO Enters the Inner Sanctum', *The Guardian* (24 September 1995) 3.

[139] David Pasztor, 'No Man Is an Island', *Dallas Observer* (27 June 1996) www.dallasobserver.com/news/no-man-is-an-island-6403643.

[140] Cited in Robert Tillman, *Global Pirates: Fraud in the Offshore Insurance Industry* (Northeastern University Press, 2002) 114.

[141] Lintner (n 135); Manuel Gren, 'A "Paradise" Struggling for Identity', *South China Morning Post* (21 November 1998) 3.

Melchizedek is based 'more on tax laws than territory' and 'exist[s] mainly so that money can be whisked through shell banks'.[142]

Throughout all of this, Pedley maintained the illusion that the Dominion of Melchizedek was a legitimate state by attempting to engage in the privileges of statehood. In 1995, the DoM faxed a press release to journalists announcing that it had declared war on France in retaliation for nuclear testing in the South Pacific. When answering follow-up questions over the legal status of Melchizedek, Ambassador to the United States, Tzemach Ben David Netzer Korem (another pseudonym of Pedley's) pointed to a copy of the Washington phone book listing the embassy's number.[143] Two years later, in 1997, the DoM announced that it had entered 'official and formal diplomatic relations' with the Kingdom of EnenKio.[144] A product of the imagination of Robert Moore, this Kingdom claimed sovereignty over three uninhabited islands between Hawaii and Guam. Like DoM, Moore established EnenKio as a means to issue fraudulent bonds. In 2000, he reached an agreement with the US SEC restraining him from ruling his Kingdom.[145]

The Dominion of Melchizedek and the Kingdom of EnenKio are outliers. However, the language of statehood can allow dishonest people to defraud unsuspecting individuals by pretending to exercise sovereign prerogatives. All of this is to show that while many, perhaps most, micronations are merely eccentric or bizarre, some have more nefarious goals.

4.3 Conclusion

This chapter has examined how micronations assert their sovereignty. We have outlined how micronations seek to justify their independence and statehood by drawing strained interpretations from foundational legal instruments, principles or eccentric readings of centuries-old agreements. Although these efforts are dismissed by governments, courts and even their fellow citizens, it demonstrates the way in which micronations endeavour to act through the law, rather than in direct contradiction of it.

Micronations also search for legitimacy beyond the moment of secession. They mimic sovereign states by designing and adopting their own

142 Leiby and Lileks (n 110).
143 Ibid.
144 Tillman (n 140) 116.
145 *Securities and Exchange Commission v Robert F. Moore*, Civil No, 00-00651 (26 October 2000).

national symbols and engaging in diplomatic relations. Sometimes imitating independent states proves successful and micronations are unintentionally acknowledged or treated as if they were legitimate nations by state actors or ordinary people. Most of the time, micronations are content with accidental recognition or recognition by other micronations. Unfortunately, some micronations rely on the appearance of statehood to engage in wide-scale fraud and other criminal activity.

5

State Responses

In declaring independence, drafting a constitution, regulating citizenship and issuing passports, micronations position themselves as rival sites of state authority. Internationally recognised states respond in various ways. In some cases, perceiving their existence as a provocation or threat to their own claims of authority and to jurisdiction, states act in swift, decisive and even violent ways to foreclose micronations' scope of action. In other cases, states determine to ignore micronations, considering them to be unserious, unthreatening or simply bizarre. In still other cases, the actions of a wannabe state require concerted attention from the international community, because they either create a diplomatic incident or reveal that no state has formally asserted sovereignty over a parcel of territory. Regardless of the particular response, in all cases states deny the international legal personality of micronations and ensure that any encounter occurs entirely within and according to domestic law.

5.1 Violent Responses

Micronations often appear trivial. For states whose sovereignty is not secure, however, the formation of a new political community can be threatening. This can produce a heavy-handed response that can threaten the viability of the micronational project.[1] Concerned over the consequences for their own sovereignty, recognised states sometimes violently put down micronational challengers. Even if the micronation did not have secessionist goals, the application of force may serve as a warning to future attempts and to others.

Violent responses to micronations were more common in earlier times when new and emerging states were consolidating their power and authority. Consider the ill-fated nineteenth-century Republic of Indian

[1] Erwin S. Strauss, *How to Start Your Own Country* (Paladin Press, 3rd ed, 1999) 5.

Stream in North America.[2] The 1783 Treaty of Paris brought the American Revolutionary War to a close, but it did not always clearly define the boundaries between the new United States and British Canada. For example, in the north-east, the border was agreed to run along 'the northwesternmost head of the Connecticut River',[3] but the difficult geography of the region meant that several interpretations of this line existed. While the British claimed the border lay south along the chain of Connecticut Lakes, the United States maintained the treaty fixed the line further north along Halls Stream. The area that both states claimed comprised around 730 square kilometres. While neither definitively exercised authority over the territory, both sent tax collectors and debt-collecting sheriffs to assert their claims. Frustrated and angry at this situation, the 400 residents of the area repeated the actions of their southern colleagues half a century earlier. On 9 July 1832, they announced the formation of the independent Republic of Indian Stream. Their Constitution stated:

> The people inhabiting the Territory formerly called Indian Stream Territory do hereby solemnly and mutually agree with each other to form themselves into a body politic by the name of Indian Stream and in that capacity to exercise all the powers of a free, sovereign and independent state, so far as it relates to our own internal Government till such time as we can ascertain to what government we properly belong.[4]

The population of the Republic may have been 'ridiculously small', but it nonetheless operated independently for several years.[5] It established institutions of government, collected tax and passed intricate and complex laws. However, the 'success of the unrecognised republic ultimately hastened its demise'.[6] As the population increased, frictions with neighbouring New Hampshire emerged and the state acted decisively to assert its claim over the territory. On 30 July 1835, the Sheriff of Coos County called up the state's militia.[7] Leading two companies of infantry into the territory, he issued an ultimatum to the Republic of Indian Stream's

[2] See Roger H Brown, *The Struggle for the Indian Stream Territory* (Western Reserve University Press, 1955); Daniel Doan, *Indian Stream Republic: Settling a New England Frontier, 1785–1842* (University of New England Press, 1997); Grant Showerman, *The Indian Stream Republic and Luther Parker* (New Hampshire Historical Society, 1905).

[3] *Treaty of Paris 1783*, art 2.

[4] Doan (n 2) 165.

[5] Edwin R Keedy, 'The Constitutions of the State of Franklin, the Indian Stream Republic and the State of Deseret' (1953) 101 *University of Pennsylvania Law Review* 516, 525.

[6] Robert L Tsai, *America's Forgotten Constitutions* (Harvard University Press, 2014) 35.

[7] Doan (n 2) 204.

Assembly. Threatened with forcible military occupation and their protests to the US Secretary of State dismissed, the Assembly capitulated and relented to New Hampshire's annexation. In April 1836, the residents finally accepted that 'New Hampshire has a right to exercise an unconditional control over the territory of Indian Stream',[8] and an uneasy peace between the United States and British Canada endured until the borders were finalised in the 1842 Webster-Ashburton Treaty.[9] That treaty also conclusively ended the pretensions of the Republic of Madawaska, another putative state located in what is now New Brunswick, Canada.[10]

The early years of the American Republic were a perfect opportunity for adventurers and filibusters to attempt to create their own country. In Chapter 3 we noted that Scottish General Gregor McGregor captured Amelia Island in Spanish Florida in June 1817. Following passage of the US 1807 Embargo Act and the 1808 abolition of the American slave trade, Amelia Island off the coast of north-eastern Florida had become a smuggling haven.[11] Although apparently commissioned by South American revolutionaries who desired the island to place further pressure on the Spanish, McGregor was attracted to the potential for profit and wanted the island for himself.[12] Upon scattering the small Spanish garrison, McGregor declared the formation of the Republic of the Floridas.[13] Unable to maintain authority, he abandoned his country and was replaced by French privateer Louis-Michel Aury.[14] After assuming control, Aury built his own institutions of government. He established an administrative body called the 'Supreme Council of the Floridas',[15] directed his secretaries to draw up a constitution and raised

[8] Cited in Showerman (n 2) 110; Tsai (n 6) 44.

[9] *Webster-Ashburton Treaty 1842*, art 1. John PD Dunbabin, '"Red Lines on Maps" Revisited: The Role of Maps in Negotiating and Defending the 1842 Webster-Ashburton Treaty' (2011) 63(1) *Imago Mundi* 39, 40–1.

[10] See Roger Paradis, 'John Baker and the Republic of Madawaska' (1972) 52(1) *The Dalhousie Review* 78.

[11] James Milgram, 'A Florida Cover under American Occupation of Spanish Territory' (1961) 40(1) *The Florida Historical Quarterly* 93, 94.

[12] Richard Lowe, 'American Seizure of Amelia Island' (1966) 45(1) *The Florida Historical Quarterly* 18, 18–20.

[13] Rafe Blaufarb, *Bonapartists in the Borderlands: French Exiles and Refugees on the Gulf Coast, 1815–1835* (University of Alabama Press, 2005) 66.

[14] Judith Ewell, *Venezuela and the United States: From Monroe's Hemisphere to Petroleum's Empire* (University of Georgia Press, 1996) 25–6.

[15] David Head, *Privateers of the Americas: Spanish American Privateering from the United States in the Early Republic* (University of Georgia Press, 2015) 107.

the flag of the revolutionary Republic of Mexico.[16] The United States watched these developments with increasing alarm – particularly the presence of 'an encampment of armed blacks in their neighbourhood'.[17] In December 1817, the US navy invaded and annexed the island.

Even if McGregor and Aury adopted the trappings of statehood to secure profit, each also established governance institutions. Perhaps if the United States had not intervened, a new country could have emerged. This possibility is less clear for several other apparent micronations within the United States that also met violent ends. The Kingdom of Callaway, for instance, emerged out of County Callaway, Missouri during the American Civil War. Missouri did not secede from the Union, but Callaway was a hot-bed of rebel sympathisers. When federal soldiers threatened to invade the county, Colonel Jefferson Jones readied the defences, complete with 'a log painted to look like a cannon'.[18] Aware of their vulnerability, Colonel Jones sought to negotiate a non-aggression pact with Union General John Henderson. Disclaiming any connection to the Confederacy, Jones declared that his men were interested only in defending their home and county and promised to disperse if the Union troops moved on. Henderson refused to recognise Jones' authority and ordered Jones to stand down, but the Union did not invade. Jones and Callaway County perceived this act as constituting formal recognition of the independence of the county. Although this supposed 'independence' did not prevent the Union subsequently engaging the Confederate army in Callaway in the Battle of Moore's Mill, the story of the Kingdom of Callaway is now part of local legend.

United States authorities also put down George Streeter's 'Deestrict of Lake Michigan'. In 1886, while on a trial run testing whether his boat could ferry guns to Honduran rebels, George Streeter ran aground on a sandbar in Lake Michigan some 180 metres from the Chicago shoreline and about 1.5 kilometres from the centre of the city.[19] Instead of repairing his boat and moving on, Streeter had a better idea. He gradually

[16] Lowe (n 12) 21–2.

[17] Rafe Blaufarb, 'The Western Question: The Geopolitics of Latin American Independence' (2007) 112(3) *American Historical Review* 742, 752–3.

[18] Andrew Saeger, 'The Kingdom of Callaway: Callaway County, Missouri During the Civil War' (MA Thesis, Northwest Missouri State University, 2013) 23, 27; Strauss (n 1) 81.

[19] Joseph P. Kearney and Thomas W. Merrill, 'Contested Shore: Property Rights in Reclaimed Land and the Battle for Streeterville' (2013) 107(3) *Northwestern University Law Review* 1057, 1083.

reclaimed land around his boat (charging scavengers to use the site as a dumping ground) and, to the surprise of many Chicago residents, eventually built around 186 acres. Waving around an old 1821 United States government survey that marked the Lake Michigan shoreline considerably farther west than in reality, Streeter claimed that the land did not belong to the city of Chicago, the county of Cook, nor the state of Illinois. Streeter thus asserted his own sovereignty over it on the basis of squatters' rights, his own negotiated 'treaties' with descendants of the original Potawatomi Indians, and a forged land grant purportedly signed by President Grover Cleveland.[20] Using his own pronunciation, Streeter named his territory the 'Deestrict' and began to sell parcels to gullible buyers.[21] The brash, pugilistic and profane Streeter endeared himself to ordinary residents of the city,[22] relying on this image to defend the shantytown from interference for more than 30 years. Nonetheless, after surviving several eviction attempts and gun battles, he was finally evicted by the National Guard.[23] In 1918, his claims to jurisdiction over the area were thrown out in court.[24]

These cases all share a desire on behalf of the state to assert its own authority and quash incipient challengers. While each micronation may have been permitted for many years, the moment that they became too inconvenient or appeared to pose too much of a real threat, the state stepped in. This same pattern recurs in more recent cases. For example, the Italian government tolerated the existence of a platform built off the coast of Rimini and outside their territorial waters until its founders declared it the independent Republic of Rose Island in 1968. From that moment, it took only a few months for the Italians to dynamite the platform, no doubt anxious to avoid the problems that Roy Bates and his Principality of Sealand were causing the United Kingdom.[25] Perhaps

[20] Kenneth Broomell and Harlow Church, 'Streeterville Saga' (1940) 33(2) *Journal of the Illinois State Historical Society* 153; Ron Grossman, 'Captain Streeter's Long Standoff with Chicago', *Chicago Tribune* (14 January 2016) www.chicagotribune.com/opinion/commentary/ct-captain-streeter-chicago-neighborhood-flashback-0117-20160114-story.html.

[21] Kearney and Merrill (n 19) 1088–9.

[22] Wayne Klatt, *King of the Gold Coast: Cap'n Streeter, the Millionaires and the Story of Lake Shore Drive* (Arcadia, 2011).

[23] Byron P White, 'George Streeter's District', *Chicago Tribune* (18 December 2007) www.chicagotribune.com/nation-world/chi-chicagodays-georgestreeter-story-story.html; Strauss (n 1) 149.

[24] 'Court Decision Ousts Streeter from "Deestrict"', *Chicago Tribune* (24 February 1918) 7.

[25] Strauss (n 1) 129.

the United Kingdom realised their mistake. A few months after Bates took control of Roughs Tower, the Royal Marines blew up Sunk Head, another World War II Maunsell fort located just outside the United Kingdom's territorial waters, to prevent an additional political headache. The demolition crew sailed past Roughs Tower and yelled 'You're next'.[26]

The Republic of Liberland has faced similar opposition. Despite laying claim to a small uninhabited portion of land not claimed by any recognised state, Croatia has forcibly impeded its establishment. Concerned over allowing a precedent to develop, Croatian authorities have frequently prevented Vit Jedlička and other supporters from accessing the area.[27] Supporters have been detained, arrested and fined for illegally crossing the Croatian border, and Czech-born Jedlička has even been banned from entering Croatia.[28] The Thai government has adopted a similar confrontational strategy. In 2019, the Royal Thai navy raided a floating cabin anchored 12 nautical miles off the Phuket coast in the Andaman Sea. American Chad Elwartowski and Thai Supranee Thepdetm, who were living on the cabin, avoided capture, but a police complaint alleges that the structure endangered national sovereignty, an offence punishable by death.[29] Rear Admiral Vithanarat Kochaseni explained that 'the couple announced on social media declaring their autonomy beyond the jurisdiction of any courts or law of any countries, including Thailand. We see such action as deteriorating Thailand's independence'.[30]

[26] Dylan Taylor-Lehman, *Sealand: The True Story of the World's Most Stubborn Micronation* (Icon Books, 2020) 44.

[27] Dusan Stojanovic, 'Police in the Balkans Block Inauguration of Europe's New "Mini-State"', *US News* (9 May 2015) www.usnews.com/news/business/articles/2015/05/09/microstate-tax-haven-in-the-balkans-not-that-easy; Sally Hayden, 'Liberland Accuses Croatia of Invasion and Releases Video of "Citizen" Abduction', *Vice News* (20 June 2015) https://news.vice.com/en_us/article/43my8n/liberland-accuses-croatia-of-invasion-and-releases-video-of-citizen-abduction.

[28] Gabriel Rossman, 'Extremely Loud and Incredibly Close (But Still So Far): Assessing Liberland's Claim of Statehood' (2016) 17(1) *Chicago Journal of International Law* 306, 309; Jolyon Jenkins, 'The Man who Created a Tiny Country He Can No Longer Enter', *BBC News* (14 November 2016) www.bbc.com/news/magazine-37941931.

[29] Alan Weedon, 'Bitcoin Couple Could Face Death Penalty in Thailand for "Seastead" Floating Home in International Waters', *ABC News* (19 April 2019) www.abc.net.au/news/2019-04-18/bitcoin-couple-face-death-penalty-in-thailand-for-seastead/11031336.

[30] Oliver Wainwright, 'Seasteading – A Vanity Project for the Rich or the Future of Humanity?', *The Guardian* (24 June 2020) www.theguardian.com/environment/2020/jun/24/seasteading-a-vanity-project-for-the-rich-or-the-future-of-humanity.

Even if this is an extreme reaction, states are wary of the potential for larger geopolitical crises arising from micronationalism. When Travis McHenry announced the formation of the Duchy of Westarctica and claimed sovereignty over Marie Byrd Land in Antarctica he was serving in the US navy. In the immediate aftermath of his declaration, he claims to have been visited by two officials from the Pentagon who interrogated him and threatened to revoke his security clearance. McHenry recused himself from his throne during the remainder of his time in the armed services.[31]

5.2 Non-Violent Responses

Violent responses do occur, but micronations are more commonly seen as simply benign or eccentric entities incapable of doing any real harm. Provided that their founders and supporters follow the ordinary laws of land, including taxation and road rules, states generally ignore the existence of these wannabe states. In some cases, states adopt this approach immediately, choosing to simply ignore the purported declaration of statehood and performative assertions of sovereignty, so long as their domestic laws are obeyed. In other cases, states learn this lesson gradually, as over time confrontation gives way to tacit acceptance and sometimes even a modicum of begrudging respect. In these instances, states can discover that the sort of person who would create their own country, issue their own currency, compose their own national anthem and write to the United Nations outlining the purported legal basis for their action is not scared by bulldozers, threatening letters and court action.

5.2.1 Enforcement of Domestic Laws

The most common response that micronations receive from independent states is no response. Despite their performative assertions of sovereignty and much to their chagrin, micronations are largely ignored by independent states. We have seen, for example, that Leonard Casley's declaration of war between the Principality of Hutt River and Australia – and cessation of hostilities – was simply ignored by Australian government officials. This is hardly unique. Englishman Latham Leslie Moore never

[31] Daisy Alioto, 'Užupis Utopia', *Playboy* (17 December 2019) www.playboy.com/read/uzupis-utopia.

received a reply to the many letters he sent seeking international recognition of his Sultanate of M'Simbati, a 640-acre island off the coast of then-Tanganyika he claimed to have seceded from the mainland on New Year's Day 1959.[32] Much to Moore's disappointment, neither the colonial governors of the colony, the Prime Minister (and later President of Tanzania) Julius Nyerere, nor the United Nations ever responded to the 'Appeal of the M'Simbati islanders'.[33] For some reason, although 'Every country in Africa is now demanding freedom and being granted it', Leslie Moore's assertion that 'there is still a tiny white island that wants to remain loyal to its Queen and country' and his aspiration to 'secede and remain British' were never honoured.[34]

Micronations frequently address themselves to the international community. Although the state they are purportedly seceding from may never engage with their concerns, sovereign states do discuss micronations and the issues that arise from them. Particularly in the pre-Internet age, host states were often forced to explain in formal diplomatic cables or in informal meetings that no newly independent country had emerged within their territory. In the 1970s, for example, Australia pressed Switzerland to discourage one of its national newspapers from publishing stories that 'a new principality' existed in Kangaroo Valley, New South Wales. The Principality of Little Scotland dissolved when its founders, Lindsay and Lilian Munro, were killed in a car crash while travelling in Switzerland seeking investors.[35]

Even where states do not seek to curtail the existence of a micronation, they act to ensure that the micronation cannot avoid the ordinary laws of the land. A key site of contestation between micronations and internationally recognised states is over the enforcement of domestic laws of taxation.

It was an unpaid tax bill that finally struck down one of the most famous micronations, the Principality of Hutt River. Over the years, Leonard Casley and his family appeared in Australian courts numerous times charged with avoiding various tax and other laws. In 1972,

[32] Anatole Broyard, 'Books of the Times', *The New York Times* (29 October 1983) 20.

[33] United Nations Trusteeship Council, 'Petition from Mr. Latham Leslie-Moore Concerning Tanganyika', UN Doc T/PET.2/245/Add.1 (20 June 1961) 2.

[34] United Nations Trusteeship Council, 'Petition from Mr. Latham Leslie-Moore Concerning Tanganyika', UN Doc T/PET.2/245 (16 February 1961) 4. Leslie-Moore hoped that his efforts would 'show the UN that if they grant "freedom" to the Africans all over Africa, they cannot withhold it from the Whites at the same time', p 5.

[35] 'NSW "Royal" Couple Killed in Europe', *Sydney Morning Herald* (9 August 1978) 2.

Leonard's son Wayne Casley was fined AUD 40 for failing to register for national service, while Leonard and another son, Ian Casley, were fined AUD 2 for failing to vote in a federal election. The next year, Leonard defied an order from the Northampton Shire Council to stop building an art gallery, motel, chapel and administration block without a permit,[36] and was fined AUD 125.[37] In 1974, he was convicted of selling wine on his farm, fined AUD 40 and ordered to pay another AUD 60 in costs. Conviction was recorded despite Casley informing the magistrates' court that Hutt River 'did not recognise or submit to its jurisdiction', leaving him to issue a strongly worded 'diplomatic protest'.[38]

A few years later Casley had his first successful court battle. In 1977, he was convicted of failing to provide documents to the Australian Taxation Office, was fined AUD 4 and ordered to pay AUD 50 in costs.[39] Casley refused to pay, and a warrant was issued for his arrest. After attending a police station at Northampton to discuss the matter, he was transferred 50 kilometres south to Geraldton and spent the night of 18 January in jail. His son Ian Casley 'acted without delay and almost immediately set off for Geraldton' in order to pay the fine but arrived thirty minutes after the police station had closed. Leonard was discharged at 8:45 a.m. the following day, 'after having been kept in prison for 16 or 17 hours'.[40] Leonard was apoplectic, declaring to journalists that 'your country has seriously erred' and 'someone in Australia has made a terrible mistake'.[41] The Supreme Court of Western Australia agreed. Casley was successful in an action of false imprisonment against the state of Western Australia and the Superintendent of Geraldton Regional Prison. The court ruled that Leonard should have been released when his son attempted to tender the fine the previous day. He was awarded AUD 200.[42]

In more recent times, Casley had less success. Despite purporting to secede on the basis of a restrictive wheat quota, the Hutt River farm stopped growing wheat and instead focused on tourism. The move was

36 Hugh Schmitt, 'Talk of War: "Prince" and the Council', *Sydney Morning Herald* (25 February 1973) 73.

37 Hugh Schmitt, 'The Stamp of Disapproval', *Sydney Morning Herald* (18 November 1973) 72.

38 'Hutt River Huff Over Fines', *Sydney Morning Herald* (25 May 1974) 3.

39 '"Prince" Is Taxable', *Sydney Morning Herald* (16 February 1977) 3; *Casley v Commonwealth* [1980] WASC 3 (11 January 1980) 3 (Wickham J).

40 *Casley v Commonwealth* [1980] WASC 3 (11 January 1980) 12 (Wickham J).

41 Hugh Schmitt, 'The Prince of Hutt Gets Tough', *Sydney Morning Herald* (22 January 1978).

42 *Casley v Commonwealth* [1980] WASC 3 (11 January 1980); Marilyn Duff, 'The "Prince" Shows a Profit for His Principles', *Sydney Morning Herald* (1 February 1980) 15.

fruitful; by 2010, around 40,000 tourists were visiting each year.[43] However, that success drew the attention of the Australian Taxation Office, which became interested in the income generated from tourism within the Principality. In 2007, the High Court of Australia dismissed an application by Casley for special leave to appeal against a judgment against him for failing to file tax returns. Justice Heydon of the High Court found that arguments that the Principality is 'not part of Australia and not subject to Australian taxation laws' are 'completely unarguable', 'fatuous, frivolous and vexatious'.[44] In 2017, Justice Le Miere of the Western Australian Supreme Court added that they were also 'gobbledygook'.[45] His Honour explained further: 'Anyone can declare themselves a sovereign in their own home but they cannot ignore the laws of Australia or not pay tax'.[46] This decision proved particularly consequential. Leonard Casley was ordered to pay income tax of more AUD 2.7 million, covering several years, while his son, Graeme Casley, was ordered to pay more than AUD 242,600. In August 2020, with tourism drying up as a result of the coronavirus pandemic, Graeme announced that the farm would be sold to pay their tax bill.[47]

The Australian government's relaxed approach to the more extreme dimensions of the Principality of Hutt River's assertion of sovereignty has been combined with a strict approach to the enforcement of domestic law. Other Australian micronations have had similar experiences. In 2005, the Princes of Ponderosa,[48] Virgilio, Philip and Joseph Rigoli, were sentenced to jail and fined AUD 25,000 for failing to declare income from their polystyrene-box manufacturing business,[49] though the conviction was overturned on appeal.[50] The same is true for the Principality of Snake Hill. In a 2012 interview with *The Atlantic*, Princess Paula of

43 Sean Murphy, 'The Mouse that Roared', *ABC Landline* (18 April 2010) www.abc.net.au /landline/the-mouse-that-roared/400444.

44 *Casley v Commissioner of Taxation* [2007] HCATrans 590 (Heydon J).

45 *Deputy Commissioner of Taxation v Casley* [2017] WASC 161, [15] (Le Miere J). See also *Casley v Commonwealth* [2017] WASCA 196.

46 *Deputy Commissioner of Taxation v Casley* [2017] WASC 161, [5].

47 Naaman Zhou and Ben Doherty, 'Hutt River Micronation to Rejoin Australia Due to Coronavirus Pandemic', *The Guardian* (5 August 2020) www.theguardian.com/australia-news/2020/aug/05/hutt-river-micronation-to-rejoin-australia-due-to-coronavirus-pandemic.

48 *Rigoli and Commissioner of Taxation* [2012] AATA 757, [20] (1 November 2012).

49 '"Prince" and Heir Jailed over Tax Fraud', *The Age* (30 July 2005) www.theage .com.au/national/prince-and-heir-jailed-over-tax-fraud-20050730-ge0ltd.html.

50 Peter Gregory, '"Prince" Free as Tax Fraud Overturned', *The Age* (26 January 2006) www .theage.com.au/national/prince-free-as-tax-fraud-overturned-20060126-ge1n0s.html.

Snake Hill explained how the Australian government reacted to their declaration of independence:

> 'We did fully expect the response that most people do get around the world when they try to secede: they usually get a letter or some visits from government employees who try to mediate the situation', Paula says. 'Mum even said that they'll send tanks. I said: "Relax, this is Australia, no one reads anything". And it's true. They just sent a letter saying, "Thank you very much for the letter", and that was it.'[51]

Nonetheless, citizens of the Principality of Snake Hill have been forced to contest actions against a series of banks within Australian courts. In September 2009, the New South Wales Supreme Court held in favour of the Bank of Queensland in a lawsuit to recover over AUD 800,000 from the Royal Family. Princess Paula was unable to bring the case before the International Court of Justice but appeared frequently in New South Wales courts between 2011 and 2014.[52]

One micronation had more luck. In the early 1980s, Tasmanian John Rudge declared the formation of the Duchy of Avram, a 'non-territorial' micronation. Rudge also legally changed his name to incorporate his new title, identifying himself as 'John his Grace the Most Noble the Duke of Avram'. The Australian and Tasmanian governments ignored the Duke, considering him harmless until he opened a 'Royal Bank of Avram' in the small seaside town of Strahan and began issuing his own coins and banknotes. The unlicensed bank and its currency may have been a curiosity, but the Australian Federal Police alleged that the Duke lied to customers telling them that the 'Ducals' could be redeemed for Australian currency in ordinary banks. Although a magistrate disagreed, finding that the purported currency simply constituted 'souvenirs',[53] the Duke maintained that they were legitimate. In 1989, John the Duke was elected to the Tasmanian Parliament as a representative of the centre-right Liberal Party.[54] His Duchy appears to still exist.

[51] Cited in Matt Siegel, 'The Royal Me: What's with Australia's Secession Obsession?' (April 2012) 309(3) *The Atlantic* 21, 22.

[52] See for example *Bank of Queensland v Hoerman* [2011] NSWSC 73 (22 February 2011); *Jensen v Bank of Queensland* [2011] NSWCA 71 (25 March 2011); *Combe v Bank of Queensland* [2011] NSWSC 1347 (11 November 2011); *Bank of Queensland Ltd v Jensen* [2011] NSWSC 1566 (16 December 2011); *Combe v Bank of Queensland (No 3)* [2012] NSWSC 1172 (28 September 2012); *Jensen v Bank of Queensland (No 2)* [2013] NSWSC 1325 (20 September 2013); *Jensen v State of New South Wales* [2014] NSWSC 682 (15 May 2014).

[53] 'Noble Duke Off Hook over Ducals Issue', *Sydney Morning Herald* (19 November 1985).

[54] Andrew Darby, '"Duke" Will Stand as a Liberal in Tasmania', *Sydney Morning Herald* (10 April 1989).

That a 'Duke' could win election to Parliament is representative of Australia's relaxed attitude to micronations. Indeed, although the simplicity with which a person can found a micronation means it is challenging to identify with precision the total number operating across the globe, our estimate suggests that at least 135 micronations that claim physical territory (as opposed to merely simulationist micronations) have existed in some form or another.[55] These entities have not been spread evenly around the world. Australia has a disproportionately high representation of secessionist micronations relative to its population. It is unclear why Australia is 'over represented',[56] but the state's non-violent approach towards micronations is likely key. Three reasons for this attitude can be proffered.

First, the act of seceding from the state and declaring one's own country is consistent with an Australian culture that celebrates larrikinism and mocking authority. The 'Aussie larrikin' emerged in the second half of the nineteenth century as respectable society was increasingly preoccupied with attempting to shed the 'stigma of convict origins'.[57] Initially an object of alarm and derision, around the turn of the century writers began to 'humanis[e] the larrikin as an interesting urban type or depict[] larrikinism as symptomatic of colonial culture in a wider sense'.[58] Today, the larrikin stands for 'the rejection of received opinion and defiance towards insensible authority'.[59] A larrikin is, Clem Gorman explains,

> almost archly self-conscious, too smart for his or her own good, witty rather than humorous, exceeding limits, bending rules and sailing close to the wind, avoiding rather than evading responsibility, playing up to an audience, mocking pomposity and smugness.[60]

Even if Australians are in fact 'very obedient' towards impersonal authority, they remain, John Hirst has argued, 'suspicious of persons in

[55] As noted in the Introduction, this number does not include those rural townships and villages that claimed independence in Japan in the 1980s. Little information exists on this phenomenon.

[56] Judy Lattas, 'DIY Sovereignty and the Popular Right in Australia' (Paper presented at the Conference of the Centre for Research on Social Inclusion, Macquarie University, 2004) 3.

[57] John Rickard, 'Lovable Larrikins and Awful Ockers' (1998) 22 *Journal of Australian Studies* 78; Melissa Bellanta, *Larrikins: A History* (University of Queensland Press, 2012).

[58] Rickard (n 57) 79.

[59] Manning Clark, 'Larrikins – The Context' in Clem Gordon (ed), *The Larrikin Streak: Australian Writers Look at the Legend* (Pan Macmillan, 1990) 37, 39.

[60] Clem Gordon (ed), *The Larrikin Streak: Australian Writers Look at the Legend* (Pan Macmillan, 1990) ix, xiii.

authority'.[61] These qualities have been confirmed by social scientists. In the most influential study of cross-cultural differences in workplaces, Geert Hofstede has found that Australians are highly individualistic and suspicious of hierarchy.[62] More recently, in reviewing and synthesising almost two decades of empirical research on Australian national identity, Catherine Austin and Farida Fozdar concluded that national symbols like bushranger Ned Kelly, the 'historical embodiment of Australian larrikinism', 'remain significant to a large majority' of Australians.[63] Kelly himself denotes 'a romantic and rebellious aspect of national identity in contemporary Australia'.[64] In this way, the '*idea* of larrikinism is celebrated and recognised as an Australian cultural stereotype'.[65] What better way to exemplify these traits than by 'thumbing your nose' at the nation and founding your own country? As His Imperial Majesty George II of Atlantium identifies, micronationalism in Australia stems 'from our convict heritage and disrespect for authority. American groups like the Davidian Branch tend to be more violently whacko, whereas Australians are just quaintly eccentric'.[66]

A second key reason for the remarkable number of micronations in Australia draws on notions of security and stability. Because Australia is secure in its own sovereignty, occupying an entire continent and otherwise unthreatened, it sees wannabe states as irrelevant or at worst a nuisance, rather than a genuine threat. As we have seen, Australia does not entirely ignore its micronations. The state ensures that they pay their taxes and comply with all road and other rules. Nonetheless, Australia's general approach contrasts markedly with other states that may view the formation of micronations as a dangerous, incipient call for separatism that could provoke or catalyse further threats. The different approach in Australia is a product of legal factors and the nation's history and culture.

[61] John Hirst, *Sense and Nonsense in Australian History* (Black Inc, 2009) 306.

[62] Geert Hofstede, *Culture's Consequences: Comparing Values, Behaviors, Institutions, and Organizations across Nations* (Sage, 2nd ed, 2001) 500.

[63] Catherine Austin and Farida Fozdar, 'Australian National Identity: Empirical Research since 1998' (2018) 20(3) *National Identities* 277, 281 and 288

[64] Bruce Tranter and Jed Donoghue, 'Bushrangers: Ned Kelly and Australian Identity' (2008) 44(4) *Journal of Sociology* 373, 386.

[65] Lili Pâquet, 'Cleaver Greene: The Legal Larrikin on Australian Screens' in Kim Weinert et al (eds), *Law, Lawyers and Justice through Australian Lenses* (Routledge 2020) 202, 208.

[66] Justin Norrie, 'The Boy from Hurstville Who Now Rules a Big Flat' *Sydney Morning Herald* (7 May 2004) www.smh.com.au/national/the-boy-from-hurstville-who-now-rules-a-big-flat-20040507-gdivms.html.

Although there is no federal law concerning secession, it is clear that it is prohibited by the Australian Constitution. In the most comprehensive examination of this issue, Gregory Craven has convincingly demonstrated the Australian states 'do not possess an inherent right of unilateral secession',[67] and nor does the Constitution incorporate an implied right to secede.[68] The only reference to secession in the Constitution itself is limited to its preamble, which speaks of an 'indissoluble Federal Commonwealth'. The effect is that micronations that purport to secede are not granted any legal status and are therefore invisible to the law. Even if their nomenclature mirrors state actors, they remain subject to Australian law and are obligated to follow that law.

Secession may be illegal, but threats of secessionism have a long history in Australia, contributing to a broader political and cultural climate that views such threats as unserious. This was not always the case. In the 1930s, the prospect of Western Australia seceding was treated with alarm in Canberra. In 1933, in the midst of an economic crisis caused by the Great Depression, Western Australians voted overwhelmingly in a referendum to secede from the Commonwealth. A delegation was sent to London to petition the United Kingdom Parliament to allow Western Australia to become a self-governing Dominion within the British Empire. Wary of intervening, Westminster formed a Joint Select Committee to determine whether it could legally receive the petition. In 1935, after hearing arguments for and against from both Western Australia and the Commonwealth, the Committee concluded that it would not entertain the petition. As economic conditions improved and the Commonwealth began making special financial assistance grants to the state, support for secessionism dissipated.[69]

Secessionist threats continue, however. In the 1980s Tasmanian Premiers from both major parties suggested secession as a response to clashes with the federal government over environmental regulation, and Queensland and Western Australian Premiers often invoked the notion. More recently, in 2017, the centre-right Western Australian Liberal Party passed a resolution at its State Conference calling on the establishment of a committee to 'examine the option of Western Australia becoming a financially independent state'.[70]

[67] Gregory Craven, *Secession: The Ultimate States' Right* (Melbourne University Press, 1986) 81.

[68] Ibid 107.

[69] Ibid; Thomas Musgrave, 'The Western Australian Secessionist Movement' (2003) 3 *Macquarie Law Journal* 95.

[70] Eliza Laschon, 'WA Liberal Party Votes for Watered-Down Secession Motion' *ABC News* (3 September 2017) www.abc.net.au/news/2017-09-03/wa-liberal-party-to-form-wa-exit-committee/8867918.

In the midst of the coronavirus pandemic, secessionism appears to be on the rise; according to a recent survey, 28 per cent of Western Australians want to secede.[71] Nonetheless, perhaps because secession has never occurred, or because of the 'ritual' nature of its invocation, the idea of secession in Australia is today largely regarded as 'an essentially ceremonial challenge, rarely meant seriously by the State from which it issues, and never received seriously by those whom it is intended to impress'.[72] Rather, it is meant to indicate displeasure with policies or actions undertaken and adopted by the federal government as well as a healthy disrespect for their claim to authority.

This relaxed approach is also manifested in response to Indigenous assertions of sovereignty. Consider the Murrawarri Republic's declaration of independence. The Murrawarri people are an Indigenous nation whose traditional lands stretch across northern New South Wales and south-western Queensland. On 30 March 2013, the newly formed People's Council of the Murrawarri Republic issued letters to Queen Elizabeth II, Prime Minister Julia Gillard and State Premiers Barry O'Farrell and Campbell Newman asking them to provide documents by 8 May demonstrating that the Murrawarri Nation had ceded their sovereignty and land to the British Crown. No response was received. For the Council, this constituted 'affirmation by the Crown of the Murrawarri Republic to be a continued Free and Independent State, in line with International law and covenants'.[73] The Murrawarri Republic's declaration received attention internationally, but not domestically. The first official response was made in response to an inquiry from an American journalist. A spokesperson for the Attorney-General's Department noted that the government had not replied to the Council's assertion of sovereignty

> because 'there are no constitutional means available for the establishment of separate political communities in Australia', adding that the Australian Commonwealth's sovereignty over the continent is recognised in international law.[74]

[71] Alexis Carey, 'WAxit: Western Australia Premier Mark McGowan Says Secession Referendum "Won't be Happening"', *News.com.au* (8 October 2020).

[72] Craven (n 67) 9.

[73] Murrawarri Republic, 'Queen Recognises Murrawarri Republic' (Media Release, 10 May 2013) http://nationalunitygovernment.org/pdf/2013/MurrawarriRepublic MediaRelease10May13.pdf.

[74] Ian Lloyd Neubauer, 'Australia's Aborigines Launch a Bold Legal Push for Independence', *TIME* (30 May 2013) world.time.com/2013/05/30/australias-aborigines-launch-a-bold-legal-push-for-independence/.

A final, related reason for the prevalence of micronationalism within Australia is spatial. Australia is a large country with a relatively small population. With 25 million people occupying over 7.6 million square kilometres, Australia has a population density of three people per square kilometre. This ranks Australia 192 out of 194 countries in the world for population density, ahead only of Namibia and Mongolia. Population density figures are complicated by the spatial dimension of Australia's population centres. Australia is one of the most urbanised countries in the world, with approximately 89 per cent of the population living in urban centres,[75] and 85 per cent living within 50 kilometres of the coast.[76] In practice, this means that vast areas of the continent are sparsely populated. For instance, approximately 79 per cent of the Western Australian population lives within the Greater Perth area,[77] leaving around 550,000 people spread over the remainder of the state's 2.6 million square kilometres. Population geography may not account for all micronations – the Principality of Wy is situated in the northern Sydney suburb of Mosman – but it does help explain why the Principality of Hutt River survived for fifty years.

Australia's carefree attitude is followed by others. Indeed, sometimes sovereign states even overlook failure to pay certain taxation, perhaps because the micronation is so insignificant, the value of enforcement so marginal or the person behind the sovereign claim is considered odd rather than dangerous. It is only when the founder or proponent acts in a manner that may injure or negatively affect other citizens that the state feels compelled to intervene. Consider the Sovereign State of Forvik.

After declaring the formation of his new country, Stuart Hill wrote to 'everyone from the Queen down' demanding that they demonstrate the legal basis for the United Kingdom's authority in Shetland.[78] Hill never received a reply to his letters, so he determined to prove the issue in court. For that, he needed to be arrested. Hill built a house without planning permission, informed the Crown Estates that he was carrying out work on the seabed illegally and stopped paying value-added tax or council

[75] Australian Bureau of Statistics, 'Estimated Resident Population by Remoteness Structure, 2014–2015' (30 March 2016).

[76] Australian Bureau of Statistics, 'How Many People Live in Australia's Coastal Areas?' (27 February 2004).

[77] Australian Bureau of Statistics (n 75).

[78] George Nelson, 'Meet "Captain Calamity", the Man Who Wants to Free Shetland from the UK's "Imperial Ruling Class"', *Vice* (29 April 2015) www.vice.com/en/article/nn9w88/captain-calamity-and-the-quest-for-shetlands-independence-930.

rates. None of these actions led to his arrest; a situation Hill regarded as amounting to de facto recognition of his legitimacy. In 2011, Hill was finally arrested for driving around Shetland without insurance and state-approved number plates; his van 'was decorated with "The Sovereign State of Forvik; consular vehicle No 2" and the island's state flag'.[79] The arrest presented an opportunity for Hill to present his case. It did not go well. Hill was declared bankrupt due to monies owed to the Royal Bank of Scotland.[80] Sheriff Philip Mann considered Hill's position:

> If you're correct I might as well just close up my computer, fold up my papers and walk out now, because all these people [in the court] would potentially have the same argument you would have. The people of Shetland have accepted the jurisdiction of this court for hundreds of years. This is the first time someone has come to challenge the jurisdiction of the court in the way you have done. As a matter of international law, Scottish courts and Scottish lawmakers have undisputed jurisdiction, and I don't see how I can competently make a ruling that I'm sitting here incompetently.[81]

Finding that independent states are careful to strictly enforce their domestic laws, micronations often attempt to resolve disputes with their larger neighbours through creative means. Many examples exist. The Republic of Molossia, for instance, continues to pay property taxes to the relevant Nevadan local government, but characterises it as foreign aid.[82] Similarly, despite the Principality of Hutt River's longstanding clashes over taxation with the Australian government, it paid local shire rates for many years. Rather than accept this as tax, however, it reported this action variously as 'an annual gift, a goodwill gesture to the local community, international courtesy, or a donation'.[83] Although it is unlikely that the local shire paid much attention to the terminology, it ensured that the Principality could continue to assert and exercise its sovereignty without further attention from the Australian state.

Another interesting case comes from the United Kingdom via the West Indies. The Kingdom of Redonda claims sovereignty over the tiny

[79] Ibid.

[80] *The Royal Bank of Scotland Plc v Stuart Hill* [2012] CSOH 110.

[81] Cited in Adam Grydehøj, 'Captain Calamity's Sovereign State of Forvik: Micronations and the Failure of Cultural Nationalism' (2014) 8(1) *Shima: The International Journal of Research into Island Cultures* 34, 43.

[82] John Ryan, George Dunford and Simon Sellars (eds), *Micronations: The Lonely Planet Guide to Home-Made Nations* (Lonely Planet, 2006) 63.

[83] Vicente Bicudo de Castro and Ralph Kober, 'The Principality of Hutt River: A Territory Marooned in the Western Australian Outback' (2018) 12(1) *Shima: The International Journal of Research into Island Cultures* 143, 154.

uninhabited Caribbean island of Redonda. Lying between the islands of Nevis and Montserrat, within the inner arc of the Leeward Islands chain, the island of Redonda is a mere 1,500 metres long and 500 metres wide. Formally, Redonda is a dependency of Antigua and Barbuda. The Kingdom first emerged in the writings of English author M.P. Shiel. In a 1929 pamphlet, Shiel claimed that his father had established the Kingdom in 1865 on the basis of *terra nullius*, and he himself had been crowned the second King of Redonda in July 1880. Shortly thereafter, however, the British annexed the island to exploit the significant guano deposits,[84] sending the Kingdom into exile. Upon his death in 1947, Shiel appointed his literary executor, John Gasworth, heir to the Kingdom, though 'after that it gets messy'.[85] Gasworth – also known as King Juan I – bestowed countless titles 'emblazoned on the back of a beer-coaster' in exchange for a drink, leading today to several competing claims for the throne.[86]

Whether the Kingdom of Redonda ever actually existed, it is clear that it ceased upon the acquisition by the British. Nevertheless, as Russel McDougall notes, the Kingdom was 'real enough at one stage' to include an enterprising Ambassador to California. The Ambassador must have been particularly effective; the Kingdom appears in several American guidebooks published in the second half of the twentieth century, including *Fodor's Caribbean Guide to the Bahamas and Bermudas* (1974), *The Caribbean & the Bahamas* (Cadogan Guide, 1994) and the *Caribbean Islands Handbook (with the Bahamas)* in the Footprint series, USA Passport Books (1996).[87] Some people have drawn on its indeterminate and ambiguous existence and contested title in an effort to avoid state laws. In 2007, for example, the Wellington Arms pub in Southampton England, declared itself an embassy of Redonda in an effort to gain diplomatic immunity from a nationwide ban on smoking in enclosed workplaces. Bob Beech, the owner of the pub, explained:

> We came up with the idea that this pub could become the British consulate for the Kingdom of Redonda – and the king thought it was a good idea. We had a ceremony for that and I was made a knight. Subsequent to that it was decided that we wanted to become an embassy. Our legal team are

[84] Russell McDougall, 'Micronations of the Caribbean' in Maria Cristina Fumagalli et al (eds), *Surveying the American Tropics: A Literary Geography from New York to Rio* (Liverpool University Press, 2013) 231, 252.
[85] Ibid 252–3.
[86] Ibid 253.
[87] Ibid.

> waiting to hear if that's possible. We intend to go ahead with the full benefits of an embassy.[88]

Unfortunately for Beech and his regulars, the UK Foreign Office did not grant formal accreditation and the embassy bid failed. In the United Kingdom's eyes at least, Redonda is part of Antigua and Barbuda.[89]

5.2.2 *Pretend to Entertain Their Existence*

Many people, including state actors, find micronations weird and wacky rather than threatening. So long as these wannabe states are not any actual risk to a recognised state's capacity to exercise authority and jurisdiction over territory, state actors may choose to entertain their eccentricities. While any engagement does not extend to formal recognition, by 'playing along' states may appear to offer de facto or tacit acceptance of the existence of a micronation. The French post office, for example, issued a postal stamp commemorating the Republic of Saugeais – a micronation in eastern France – in 1987. Many other examples exist.

In the nineteenth and twentieth centuries, a family on tiny Tavolara Island off the coast of Sardinia purported to run their own kingdom. The island had been abandoned in the 1730s because of North-African piracy, and by the 1830s, shepherd Giuseppe Bertoleoni was the island's only inhabitant – Bertoleoni had apparently married two sisters in Sardinia and was escaping bigamy charges. In 1836, Bertoleoni claimed that during a hunting trip to the island Charles Albert, King of Sardinia, appointed him King of Tavolara. Despite newspaper reports suggesting that Italy recognised the kingdom in 1887,[90] and a tale that Queen Victoria commissioned a photograph of the 'royal family',[91] Tavolara's statehood has never been recognised. In 1962, Italy allowed NATO to build a base on the island, thereby foreclosing any claim to independence.

The Empire of Austenasia was founded on 20 September 2008 by the father and son team of Terry and Jonathan Austen.[92] Claiming sovereignty

[88] 'Pub "Embassy" Dodges Smoking Ban', *BBC News* (27 June 2007) news.bbc.co.uk/2/hi/uk_news/england/hampshire/6246006.stm.

[89] Ibid.

[90] 'Smallest State in the World', *The New York Times* (19 June 1896) 6.

[91] Eliot Stein, 'The World's Smallest Kingdom', *BBC Travel* (8 March 2016) www.bbc.com/travel/story/20160304-the-worlds-smallest-kingdom.

[92] Kevin Barnes, 'Carshalton Home Declares Itself Independent State', *Sutton and Croydon Guardian* (22 January 2009) www.yourlocalguardian.co.uk/news/4064529.carshalton-home-declares-itself-independent-state/.

over their house in Carshalton, South London, the Austens have frequently sought to engage with UK authorities. Letters informing their (former) local MP, Prime Minister and Home Office of the reasons for their declaration of independence were initially ignored, but in 2011 Jonathan met with Tom Brake MP. Entertaining Jonathan's questions, Brake agreed, on Jonathan's behalf, to ask Foreign Secretary William Hague about the criteria by which the United Kingdom recognises new states. Brake later noted to a journalist: 'I wish Mr Austen every luck with his campaign but wonder where the border controls would be set up'.[93] Fortunately, the Empire has never had any trouble with the British authorities. Prince Jonathan explained: 'We haven't encountered any difficulties with taxes because, while our subjects don't pay British taxes under Austenasian law, in practice, all of them do to keep their British citizenships, which they are allowed as well as Austenasian subjectships'.[94]

A more complex case – for several reasons – comes from Northern Israel. In 1952, an Iranian-born sailor and former member of the Palmach – the elite fighting force of the Haganah, the underground army of the Jewish community during the period of the British Mandate for Palestine – moved into the deserted village of Az Zeeb on the Israeli west coast. The village had been abandoned in 1948 when Israeli forces evicted the Palestinian community. At first, Eli Avivi worked as a fisherman before later moving into a house owned by a Palestinian family.[95] Initially, he claims to have led an idyllic life, fishing in the Mediterranean and selling his catch to a nearby kibbutz. At some point, confrontation with Israeli authorities commenced.

In the late 1950s, the Israeli army sought to develop the land to construct an army base.[96] Avivi protested to Prime Minister David Ben-Gurion, who apparently replied expressing his support. The army agreed to let Avivi stay in the derelict village on the condition that he join Shin Bet, the state's domestic intelligence agency.[97] Around the same time,

[93] 'Carshalton "Micronation" Pushes for Independence from Sutton', *Sutton and Croydon Guardian* (23 September 2011) www.yourlocalguardian.co.uk/news/9263842.carshalton-micronation-pushes-for-independence-from-sutton/.

[94] Barnes (n 92).

[95] Peter Lagerquist, 'Vacation from History: Ethnic Cleansing as the Club Med Experience' (2006) 36(1) *Journal of Palestinian Studies* 43, 48–9. We thank Asaf Lubin for comments on this section.

[96] Raffi Berg, 'One-Man Rule in Israel's Hippy Micro-State', *BBC News* (10 March 2015) www.bbc.com/news/magazine-31800580.

[97] The extent of Avivi's collaboration with Israeli intelligence services is unknown. The Shin Bet has never officially acknowledged any involvement.

Avivi began renting houses in the village, attracting hippies and celebrities like Sophia Loren, and becoming a national sensation. Musicians, comedians and other artists also flocked to the bohemian village; leading Israeli musician Naomi Shemer visited and wrote 'A Night on Achziv Beach'.[98] This did not prevent confrontation with the state, however. In 1963, the Israeli government decided to transform the area into a national park. Bulldozers levelled a number of houses, and Avivi suffered several broken bones while attempting to stop the destruction. In 1971, officials wanted to enlarge the park and erected a fence, blocking his access to the beach. Avivi had had enough. Ripping up his passport, he declared the formation of Akhzivland. He designed a flag, composed a national anthem and created a new passport for his new country.

There are several stories concerning what happened next. One says that Avivi was taken to court and charged with 'establishing a country without permission'. Another says that he marched to the capital and convinced Prime Minister Golda Meir to lease him the land for ninety-nine years.[99] On either account, the state dropped its plans to enlarge the park and decided to leave Avivi alone. Perhaps it is because he used media attention to his advantage. In 1972, he put on the Israeli Woodstock, causing traffic jams for up to 100 kilometres – unsurprisingly, court action subsequently prevented Avivi from holding future music festivals. Nonetheless, Israel largely decided to give up on forcing Avivi from his home. The two sides reached a compromise. Avivi paid the government for access to the beach through the fence, while 'on the main road outside, an official tourist sign points the way to "Eli Avivi" (not "Achzivland", which might perhaps be taken as signalling recognition)'.[100] Avivi passed away in 2018.[101]

One curious case of recognition comes from Portugal. In 2007, Renato Barros, an art teacher from Madeira, Portugal, established the Principality of Pontinha. The Principality claims jurisdiction over a fortified islet that Barros had bought in 2000 on the basis of a royal charter from 1903. That year, King Carlos I of Portugal sold the islet to a private family. Barros asserted that the royal charter transferred both

[98] A documentary film drawing on considerable archival footage and interviews with many of these artists was released in 2009: *Achziv, A Place for Love* (Etty Wieseltier, 2009).

[99] Ryan, Dunford and Sellars (n 82) 48–51.

[100] Berg (n 96).

[101] Roy Arad, 'President of Fancied Hippie Micro-State Achzivland in Northern Israel Dies at 88', *Hareetz* (17 May 2018) www.haaretz.com/israel-news/.premium-eli-avivi-president-of-fancied-state-of-achzivland-dies-at-88-1.6095276.

ownership of the territory and dominion, or sovereignty, over the land. The Portuguese government maintains that this is not the case, but has also unsuccessfully tried to buy the island off Barros several times. That has not stopped the state from attempting to force the issue. Barros recounts a meeting with the Governor of Madeira:

> He said that unless I sold it back to the state, he wouldn't let me connect to any electricity. So now, as long as I don't cause any trouble (for instance, trying to charge cruise ships that dock here) they will leave me alone.[102]

Not all state actors are so confrontational. In February 2017, Madeiran politician José Manuel Coelho sought political asylum in the principality in a bid to avoid a prison sentence. Perhaps the bid was tongue-in-cheek. Coelho explained to waiting journalists in an arrival staged for the cameras:

> I came away from the Portuguese Republic because they want to arrest me at weekends. The Portuguese Republic can steal my salary and everything I have, but it cannot rob me of my sense of humour and desire for freedom.[103]

Perhaps the strangest example of state entanglement involves the Kingdom of Wallachia. Founded in 1997 by Czech photographer Tomáš Harabiš as part 'elaborate practical joke' part tourism venture, the Kingdom is located in the south-east corner of the Czech Republic and claims to have around 80,000 citizens.[104] While the Kingdom is fictitious, it draws much of its imagery and symbolism from the real region of Wallachia, now part of Romania. Perhaps this is part of the reason for the Kingdom's success; local businesses recognised the Kingdom's potential to encourage visitors into the region, and Harabiš' enterprise grew into 'one of the most successful tourist ventures in the country'.[105]

[102] Renato Barros, 'Experience: I Founded My Own Country', *The Guardian* (15 November 2014) www.theguardian.com/lifeandstyle/2014/nov/14/experience-i-founded-my-own-country.

[103] 'José Manuel Coelho pede asilo ao Principado da Pontinha', *CM Journal* (6 February 2017) www.cmjornal.pt/politica/detalhe/jose-manuel-coelho-pede-asilo-ao-principado-da-pontinha; Lusa, '"Príncipe do ilhéu da Pontinha' detido pela GNR na Madeira', *CM Journal* (25 September 2017) www.cmjornal.pt/portugal/detalhe/principe-do-ilheu-da-pontinha-detido-pela-gnr-na-madeira.

[104] 'Court to Hear Appeal in "Wallachian Kingdom" Dispute', *Radio Prague International* (2 September 2008) https://english.radio.cz/court-hear-appeal-wallachian-kingdom-dispute-8592511; Rob Cameron, 'Wallachian Kingdom: Reporting from a Land that Doesn't Exist', *Radio Prague International* (15 October 2008) https://english.radio.cz/wallachian-kingdom-reporting-a-land-doesnt-exist-8591109.

[105] Rob Cameron, 'Czech Court to Rule on Fairy-Tale Kingdom', *BBC News* (6 October 2008) http://news.bbc.co.uk/2/hi/europe/7654513.stm.

Following its creation, Harabiš cast around for a suitable king to lead the nation, eventually settling on Czech comic actor Bolek Polívka. Polívka was the obvious choice; in 1993, he had himself crowned as 'Wallachian King, Boleslav I the Gracious, Forever' on his own TV show. At first, the partnership prospered. Polívka travelled around the Kingdom in his royal limousine (a bright yellow, Communist-era Trabant, with a plastic body and two-stroke engine), presided over national events and allowed his signature to grace Wallachian passports. In 2000, a formal coronation was even held in the small town of Vsetin. The event was televised nationally and attended by 5,000 guests. Journalists report that '[s]oldiers in traditional pointy shepherd hats fired cannons as the king inspected his subjects from atop a horse'.[106] However, a problem soon emerged. Harabiš explains:

> Unfortunately, the king soon started confusing fiction with reality, and tried to rule the kingdom's economy. But the kingdom is run by my company, and we couldn't let him interfere with our contracts, business partners, and money.[107]

King Boleslav allegedly demanded 1 million Czech korunas for services, a price that would bankrupt the business. In 2001, the Wallachian government conducted a palace coup, deposing the King and accusing him of having behaved unconstitutionally. Unperturbed, Polívka travelled the realm gathering support for his restoration. Asserting that his 1993 coronation gave him the right to use the Kingdom of Wallachia trademark, he maintained that '23 of 28 municipalities across the kingdom still regarded him as the rightful king', claiming further that there 'is an air force loyal to me, a royal guard; we even have a Trabant tank division'.[108] Unable to resolve the issue internally, the dispute was heard in a real Czech court. The court sided with Harabiš. Polívka appealed unsuccessfully to the Czech High Court and maintains a government-in-exile. As a representative noted, 'the court case was only about the trademark, no court has forbidden Mr Polívka from playing the King of Wallachia'.[109]

By their very definition, micronations do not have a lawful basis for their existence. However, because recognition is a political act, micronations

[106] Dan Bilefsky, 'Battle Royal Over Chief for a Czech State of Mind', *The New York Times* (1 February 2009) A7 www.nytimes.com/2009/02/02/world/europe/02iht-02czech.19858341.html.

[107] Daniel McLoughlin, 'Coup in Fantasy Kingdom Inside Czech Republic', *The Independent* (13 October 2008) www.independent.co.uk/news/world/europe/coup-in-fantasy-kingdom-inside-czech-republic-959310.html.

[108] Bilefsky (n 106).

[109] McLoughlin (n 107).

established with a clear ideological position may hope that fellow travellers in other countries might put pressure on their own state to formally open diplomatic ties to help ground the micronation's claim for sovereignty and statehood. The libertarian-inspired Liberland on the Danube River has perhaps gone furthest in this regard. Although no state has formally recognised Liberland's existence, right-wing politicians in several states have pressured their own governments to do so. So far at least, no government has moved.

In most cases, calls for recognition have come from small, fringe libertarian political parties without elected representatives at the national level. For example, in April 2015, the libertarian Swiss Independence Party up! (now named the Libertarian Party) called for Switzerland to recognise Liberland.[110] The next month, Petr Mach, the leader of the classical liberal right-libertarian Czech Free Citizens Party expressed support for the creation of Liberland and called upon the Czech Republic to follow its lead.[111] In May, these calls were joined by the Norwegian Capitalist Party[112] and the Spanish Libertarian Party.[113] In 2018, the Libertarian Party of Canada and the US Libertarian Party also expressed their support and desire that Liberland be recognised.[114] As noted, none of these parties was represented in the national parliament. However, in 2016, seven members of the anti-establishment, right-wing Kukiz'15 movement serving in the Polish Parliament asked the Polish Minister of Foreign Affairs when Poland would recognise Liberland as an independent state.[115] The Minister demurred, explaining that Liberland does not meet the criteria for statehood.[116]

[110] 'up! fordert die Anerkennung der Freien Republik Liberland', *Up!Schweiz* (16 April 2015) www.up-schweiz.ch/blog/2015/04/16/wir-fordern-die-anerkennung-der-freien-republik-liberland/.

[111] Petr Mach, 'Liberland', *PaliamentiniListy* (20 May 2015) www.parlamentnilisty.cz/profily/Petr-Mach-47661/otazka/Liberland-84886.

[112] 'Presidenten av verdens yngste land kommer til Norge', *Liberalistene: Ditt Liv. Ditt Valg!* (28 May 2015) www.liberalistene.org/presidenten-av-verdens-yngste-land-kommer-til-norge/.

[113] P-Lib, 'El Partido libertario insta a exteriors a reconconcer el nuevo microestado' (31 May 2015) www.p-lib.es/politica-exterior/el-p-lib-con-la-republica-libre-de-liberland.

[114] @moen_tim (Tim Moen) (Twitter, 20 February 2018, 7:35am AEST) https://twitter.com/moen_tim/ status/965686321871114240; 'Libertarians Resolve to Support Development of Liberland', *Libertarian* (12 December 2018) www.lp.org/libertarians-resolve-to-support-development-of-liberland/.

[115] Interpelacja nr 4903 do ministra spraw zagranicznych w sprawie notyfikowania uznania niepodległości Wolnej Republiki Liberlandu (22 August 2016).

[116] Odpowiedź na interpelację ponowną nr 4903 w sprawie notyfikowania uznania niepodległości Wolnej Republiki Liberlandu (26 September 2016).

5.3 International Responses

Micronations are usually considered a nuisance for the state they purport to secede from. In some cases, micronations can become a larger concern for two or more states, or even the international community at large. We have already seen that imaginary nations can serve as vehicles for financial crimes, and that persons have entered states bearing unrecognised passports. In this section we explore more significant instances where micronational assertions of statehood and claims to sovereignty have merited an international response. Once again, although these micronations have achieved a key goal of international attention, states are quick to foreclose their ability to act on the international plane. These, and indeed all, micronations remain unrecognised and illegitimate.

5.3.1 Diplomatic Incidents

One of the most famous micronations also caused the largest international incident. As we noted in the introduction, the United Kingdom eventually reached an uneasy but pragmatic position with respect to the Principality of Sealand. So long as Roy Bates and his family and supporters did not bother or harm anyone, the UK government would allow him to stay on Roughs Tower, the abandoned World War II-era naval fort. The United Kingdom remained committed to this approach, though Bates' actions often provoked consternation.

The first challenge emerged in the early 1970s as Sealand sought to engineer international recognition.[117] In 1969, Bates and a group of Frenchmen and Belgians approached the Belgian government. Hoping to establish diplomatic and commercial ties, the group pressed the British government to confirm the sovereign status of Sealand. Unfortunately for the group, British officials assured their Belgian counterparts that Sealand was not a sovereign nation. Roy and his son Michael Bates may have avoided conviction on firearms charges in 1968, but that was only because the 1937 Firearms Act did not operate with extraterritorial effect;[118] the decision of the Essex Assizes was certainly not a formal or informal act of recognition. As if to emphasise this point, the same officials ignored the inquiries from Sealand's representatives. Following

[117] James Grimmelmann, 'Sealand, Havenco, and the Rule of Law' (2012) 2 *University of Illinois Law Review* 405, 423; Taylor-Lehman (n 26) 66–7.

[118] *R v Bates*, The Shire Hall, Chelmsford (25 October 1968) 8 (Chapman J). See further discussion in the Introduction.

this disappointment, Sealand began to focus their attention on a group of interested Germans who approached the Bateses after seeing an advertisement in a newspaper.

Among the group was a former diamond dealer named Alexander Achenbach and a World War II secret agent called Walter Scheffel who collected big cats and claimed to have received a landed title from Queen Elizabeth II. The group quickly set about conducing a 'diplomatic offensive'[119] by sending letters to 150 countries. In 1973 and 1974 they contacted the British Embassy in Bonn, and made direct entreaties to Scotland, Morocco and the Federal Republic of Germany. The Second Secretary in Bonn sent a memorandum to the German government, 'No one knows why various European businessmen should take such an interest in it . . . It is possible that they wish to encourage the creation of a tax haven or even to be able to claim oil discoveries in the area'.[120]

In 1976 they stepped up their efforts. They

> asked the Australian Embassy for visas in their Sealand passports, went to the Sri Lankan Embassy with a briefcase containing 100,000 Deutsche Marks to request a visa to set up a five-million dollar gem exhibition, and approached the Indonesian, Senegalese, Irish, and Nigerian embassies with similar requests.[121]

At the same time, Sealand also contacted several international agencies. Armed with a legal opinion claiming that Sealand was a state under international law, they contacted the International Frequency Registration Board to reserve radio frequencies.[122] None of these efforts succeeded. States and international agencies that received attention from Sealand and its supporters generally contacted the United Kingdom for advice on how they should proceed. The Foreign and Commonwealth Office was adamant that the Principality was not a state.[123] The United Nations were also not interested; one spokesperson explained, 'the United Nations is an organisation of governments, not gun platforms. The secretary-general has a nut file for such applications'.[124]

[119] Taylor-Lehman (n 26) 70.

[120] Grant Hibberd, 'The Last Great Adventure of the Twentieth Century: The Sealand Affair in British Diplomacy' (2011) 4(2) *Britain and the World* 269, 272.

[121] Grimmelmann (n 117) 425.

[122] Ibid.

[123] Hibberd (n 120) 271.

[124] Taylor-Lehman (n 26) 70.

Towards the middle of the decade, Sealand's potential for harm increased, provoking some consternation in the United Kingdom and its neighbours. The Germans had earlier established a business in Luxembourg called 'Sealand Information Gathering and Messaging Agency' through which they sought to sell Sealand stamps and coins. In 1976, Achenbach and several others were arrested in Luxembourg and charged with 'engaging in fraudulent business based in an imaginary country'.[125] Achenbach tried to raise Sealand's sovereignty as a defence by attempting to file a motion in the International Court of Justice at the Hague, hopeful that it would conclude the charges to be an act of aggression. Not worried by this ploy but nonetheless concerned that 'Luxembourg's financial name should not be sullied in any way', officials consulted the British government before reducing the charges. A court found the men guilty of selling stamps and coins without a licence and fined each around £400. At this stage, Achenbach adopted a different strategy. On 2 August 1976, he petitioned the Cologne Administrative Court to revoke his German citizenship on the grounds that he was a citizen of the Principality of Sealand. The court ultimately rejected his petition, finding that Sealand was not a state. It satisfied neither the territory nor the population requirements of the Montevideo Convention.[126]

The decision did not diminish Achenbach's interest in Sealand. In 1977, he and his supporters fixed upon the idea of using the Principality as a tax haven.[127] Their plan relied on Sealand's ambiguous legal position. Germany considered Sealand to be part of the United Kingdom for the purposes of the tax treaty between the two states, but the United Kingdom did not levy taxes for activities that took place on Roughs Tower. Consequently, German citizens might be able to avoid paying taxes on income generated in Sealand. Unfortunately, their ingenious plan was scuppered. Although the United Kingdom's Inland Revenue were concerned, German authorities resolved the matter. Because Roughs Tower sat outside the United Kingdom's territorial waters, German taxes applied. Despite the ruling, the potential that Sealand would spark conflict between Germany and the United Kingdom would only increase.

One week after the judgment of the Cologne Administrative Court, Achenbach invited Roy and Joan Bates to Austria to discuss his proposal

[125] Ibid; Grimmelmann (n 117) 426.
[126] *In re Duchy of Sealand* (1978) 80 ILR 683.
[127] Grimmelmann (n 117) 426.

to buy the fort.[128] The bid was a ruse. While Roy and Joan travelled to the continent, they left their son, Michael Bates, alone on the platform. A group of Germans led by Gernot Pütz, Achenbach's lawyer, arrived at Sealand by helicopter, brandishing a forged document purportedly declaring that Roy had sold the Principality. Imprisoning Michael for a few days, they then put him in a boat and sent him to the Netherlands, from where he eventually made his way home. Becoming suspicious when the meeting was postponed, Roy and Joan returned to England where they reconnected with Michael. Once there, they launched their own assault from a helicopter flown by the stunt pilot in the 1969 James Bond film, *On Her Majesty's Secret Service*. In a pre-dawn raid, they successfully recaptured the fort. The commotion attracted several journalists who sailed out to the fort to interview Roy.

Unsurprisingly, the action also drew the attention of the Netherlands and Germany. Dutch officials asked the United Kingdom to help secure the release of their citizen – Dutchman Hans Lavoo had sailed to the fort to help negotiate the release of the German prisoners but had himself been taken hostage by Bates – and wondered whether the fort could be destroyed. At the same time, Germany 'encouraged the British government to classify the Bateses' effrontery as piracy'.[129] Relying on its ambiguous legal status, the British demurred, replying flatly that any false imprisonment was taking place 'outside British jurisdiction'.[130] The British did not respond to further German correspondence. In any event, within a few days all but one of the hostages were released.

Only Pütz remained. As a Sealand citizen, Roy considered that he had committed treason. Although Joan noted that the United Kingdom executed people for treason, Sealand did not. Roy later explained: 'I've killed a lot of Germans in my time. Another one wouldn't have made much difference, but I didn't want to kill anything else, really'.[131] Pütz was fined 75,000 Deutsche Marks and ordered to remain on the fort until he could discharge the penalty. Growing frustrated with the United Kingdom's failure to resolve the issue, Germany dispatched a diplomatic official to Sealand to negotiate the release of their

128 Ibid 427–9; Taylor-Lehman (n 26) 75–9.

129 Taylor-Lehman (n 26) 79.

130 Grimmelmann (n 117) 429; Taylor-Lehman (n 26) 79; Hibberd (n 120) 281; 'Secret Government Sealand Revelations', *Ipswich Star* (9 March 2010) www.ipswichstar.co.uk/news/secret-government-sealand-revelations-1-169303.

131 Grimmelmann (n 117) 428 n 191; Taylor-Lehman (n 26) 80.

citizen.[132] Dr Christoph Neimoller was unable to secure Pütz's release but was baffled by the situation and wondered whether the entire event was an elaborate publicity stunt. If so, it appears to have worked. Sealand had hosted an official from an independent, recognised state, who negotiated with them as they would a peer. With that success achieved, Bates finally released Pütz a few days later; the pair shook hands, smiled and posed for the cameras.

The situation may have resolved itself, but it provoked further questions within the UK government. In December 1978, Lord Kennet asked the Minister of State, Foreign and Commonwealth Office: '[I]s it not the case that what this time may be a harmless and colourful escapade could next time, in law, be a moderately dangerous act by an unfriendly foreign Power?'[133] Others questioned whether the fort might be a navigational hazard and should be destroyed,[134] or towed within the United Kingdom's territorial waters.[135] The government acknowledged the Lords' concerns but did not definitively respond. It was not until 1987 that the United Kingdom extended its territorial sea in line with the international standard of 12 nautical miles, encompassing Roughs Tower and putting away doubt over its authority over the fort.[136] Sealand maintains that as it was already a sovereign nation the United Kingdom's actions do not affect the Principality.

5.3.2 *Sovereign Claims*

Micronations like the Principality of Sealand prioritise the development of a functional state. For this reason, recognised states generally act with more concern when engaging with and responding to these types of micronations, for they correctly identify that they are genuinely interested in statehood, international legal personality, and potentially disputing the state's own ability to exercise jurisdiction and authority. In some cases, the sudden emergence of a micronation on unclaimed or contested territory prompts recognised states to formally claim or assert their own jurisdiction over that land. The most prominent of these cases involves

[132] Taylor-Lehman (n 26) 82–4; Grimmelmann (n 117) 429–30.
[133] United Kingdom, *Parliamentary Debates*, House of Lords, vol 397, cols 4–7 (Lord Kennet) (5 December 1978).
[134] Ibid (Lord Hailsham).
[135] Ibid (Lord Segal).
[136] *Territorial Sea Act 1987* c 49.

the Republic of Minerva, a micronation founded by a wealthy Nevadan real estate mogul that we explored in Chapter 3.

The Republic of Minerva claimed sovereignty over the Minerva Reefs. Known as Ongo Teleki in the Tongan language, the reefs are a group of two submerged atolls in the Pacific Ocean. Located around 500 kilometres south-west of the southernmost group of Tongan islands and about 700 kilometres south-east of Fiji's main islands, the atolls are a considerable distance from inhabited territory. Although Tongan and Fijian fishermen visited the reefs occasionally over many generations,[137] neither state initially included the reefs within their territorial claim.[138] Interestingly, Hans Bucholz suggests that the Minerva Reefs could have potentially been included within the Tongan border, which was first set in 1887. However, perhaps because the two atolls could not sustain human life or because international law at the time would not permit the reefs to ground a claim to a territorial sea, they were 'regarded as useless' and so were excluded.[139] They were also seldom visited. Olaf Ruhen notes that 'not much sea traffic was likely to encounter them' because they were far from sea routes.[140] It was only 'in storms that ships, especially small wind ships, were blown far off their accustomed sea routes and hit the Minerva Reefs'.[141]

In July 1962, the *Tuaikaepau* ('Slow But Sure'), a Tongan vessel en route to New Zealand, was caught in such a storm and struck the South Minerva Reef.[142] The captain, Tevita Fitita, his son Sateki Fifita and another crew member, Tevita Uaisele, constructed a raft and sailed to Fiji to seek help. Sateki Fifita drowned after eight days at sea without food or water, but the two remaining men arrived on Fiji's Kadavu Island and were able to raise the alarm. After 102 days, the *Tuaikaepau* crew and passengers trapped on the reef were finally rescued by the Royal New Zealand Air Force, save four people who had passed away in the meantime. Upon the return of the

137 Lili Song, 'The Curious History of the Minerva Reefs: Tracing the Origin of Tongan and Fijian Claims Over the Minerva Reefs' (2019) 54(3) *The Journal of Pacific History* 417, 419.

138 For Tonga see: Royal Proclamation, 24 August 1887; Tonga *Government Gazette*, vol II-No. 55 (24 August 1887).

139 Hans Jürgen Buchholz, *Law of the Sea Zones in the Pacific Ocean* (Institute of Southeast Asian Studies, 1987) 2.

140 Olaf Ruhen, *Minerva Reef* (Minerva Bookshop Limited, 1963) 7–8; Sherry Broder and Jon van Dyke, 'Ocean Boundaries in the South Pacific' (1982) 4 *University of Hawaii Law Review* 1, 27.

141 Song (n 137) 419; Lawrence Horn, 'To Be or Not to Be: The Republic of Minerva: Nation Founding by Individuals' (1973) 12 *Columbia Journal of Transnational Law* 520, 549.

142 Song (n 137) 420; Horn (n 141) 527.

shipwreck survivors, Tonga held a national celebration in the capital Nuku'alofa. Four years later, Tevita Fifita returned to the South Minerva Reef with a group of Tongans. They reburied the remains of two people who had died during the shipwreck, placed a copy of Olaf Ruhen's book *Minerva Reefs*, coconuts and watermelons on each grave, and raised the Tongan flag.

Lili Song observes that the '*Tuaikaepau* incident undoubtedly sealed the Tongans' emotive connection' to the Minerva Reefs,[143] but formally at least the atolls had not been claimed by any state. Into this void stepped Michael Oliver and the Ocean Life Research Foundation. After traversing the globe seeking a suitable location for their libertarian paradise, Oliver and his supporters arrived at the reefs in August 1971. After six months of land reclamation and rudimentary construction, the group proclaimed the establishment of the Republic of Minerva on 19 January 1972.

The sudden emergence of the up-start republic prompted alarm from their neighbours. In late January 1972, Fijian Prime Minister Ratu Sir Kamisese Mara noted that the purported declaration of independence could create a 'dangerous precedent', asking, 'If these people can claim Minerva, what would stop them from doing it here?'[144] The next month, a Tongan government spokesperson acknowledged that Tonga had never formally asserted sovereignty over the reefs. He explained that the raising of a Tongan flag in 1966 was believed to be in memory of fallen crew rather than a declaration of sovereignty. Nonetheless, he noted that as a result of the *Tuaikaepau* shipwreck, 'Tonga would always look upon the reefs with special concern and had strong feelings about any claim'.[145] Larger powers were less interested. The United States maintained a position of 'no position', while New Zealand 'seemed generally too busy to care'.[146] A British diplomat joked to a journalist:

> Heaven forbid for this kind of thing to happen. We'll have every crackpot with an ounce of imagination claiming sovereignty over every last scrap of unclaimed land. The next thing you know, they'll be demanding loans from the World Bank.[147]

143 Song (n 137) 420.

144 Editorial, 'Minerva Reefs "Republic" Fails to Impress PM', *The Fiji Times* (28 January 1972) 1; Robert Trumbull, 'Pacific Islanders Fight Reef Plan', *The New York Times* (27 February 1972) 5.

145 Editorial, 'Tonga Opposes Reef "Republic"', *The Tonga Chronicle*, 3 February 1972, 1. Cited in Song (n 137) 421.

146 Horn (n 141) 526.

147 'South Seas: The Minerva Ploy', *Newsweek* (23 October 1972) 52. Cited in Samuel Pyeatt Menefee, '"Republics of the Reefs": Nation-Building on the Continental Shelf and in the World's Oceans' (1994) 25 *Case Western International Law Journal* 81, 101.

Tonga determined to take stronger action. In February, the Tongan boat *Ekiaki* sailed to the South Minerva Reef to establish a refuge station. Tonga's Marine Department subsequently issued a notice to mariners announcing the newly built station and advised Fiji, New Zealand, Australia and the United Kingdom of its location. A government spokesperson explained that the refuge station was intended to substantiate Tonga's 'longstanding connection with the reefs'.[148] Two days later, the issue was considered further at the South Pacific Forum. At this meeting, representatives from Fiji, Tonga, Nauru, Western Samoa, the Cook Islands, Australia and New Zealand resolved to support 'the stand of Tonga in relation to Minerva Reef'. The leaders also agreed to investigate the precise legal status of the reefs and ask the United States to pressure Ocean Life Research Foundation to halt their venture.[149] Prince Tuiplehake, the Tongan Prime Minister, was adamant: 'We can't have people setting up empires on our doorstep'.[150]

Tongan interest intensified. In May, King Tupou IV of Tonga visited the reefs. The King dismissed rumours that he intended to claim the reefs on behalf of Tonga, instead noting that he was simply there to investigate the situation. Nonetheless, he explained to *The Tonga Chronicle* that 'it was in the best interest of Tonga not to allow a group of people, whose objects were to make money and whose activities could be harmful, to become established on the reefs'.[151]

Throughout this period, Tonga refrained from formally asserting sovereignty over the atolls. Their hesitation may have stemmed from ambiguity over the proper legal status of the reefs; that uncertainty, however, eventually gave way to such a claim. Article 11(2) of the 1958 Convention on the Territorial Sea and the Contiguous Zone provides that naturally formed areas of land above water at low tide but submerged at high tide and in the high seas do not possess a territorial sea. However, it does not clarify whether low-tide elevations are appropriable themselves. Indeed, no treaty or custom on this point existed. For this reason, Tonga's legal adviser, Professor Daniel O'Connell, advised that 'to claim the reef under

148 Tongan Ministry of Information and Communications, '1972: Mission to Minerva' (22 March 2010). www.mic.gov.to/index.php?option=com_content&view=article&id=1221:1972-mission-to-minerva.

149 South Pacific Forum, *Leaders' Communique* (Canberra, 23–25 February 1972); Trumbull (n 144); Horn (n 141) 526.

150 Trumbull (n 144).

151 Editorial, 'King Goes to Minerva Reefs to Investigate', *The Tonga Chronicle* (1 June 1972) 1. Cited in Song (n 137) 422.

international law [. . .] it would be necessary to build a permanent structure above high water – "a sort of island"'.[152] In early June, Tonga followed that advice, sending ninety prisoners to construct two artificial islands.[153] On 15 June 1972, Tonga formally declared sovereignty over the two artificial islands on the reefs in a royal proclamation:

> WHEREAS the Reefs known as North Minerva Reef and South Minerva Reef have long served as fishing grounds for the Tongan people and have long been regarded as belonging to the Kingdom of Tonga; AND WHEREAS the Kingdom of Tonga has now created on these Reefs islands known as Teleki Tokelau and Teleki Tonga; AND WHEREAS it is expedient that we should now confirm the rights of the Kingdom of Tonga to these islands; THEREFORE we do hereby AFFIRM and PROCLAIM that the islands, rocks, reefs, foreshores and waters lying within a radius of twelve miles [19.31 km] thereof are part of our Kingdom of Tonga.[154]

Several days later on 26 June, King Tupou IV held a formal ceremony on the North Minerva Reef. The Tongan Defence Force tore down the Minervan flag and raised the Tongan flag. The King read the royal proclamation, and his royal yacht *Olovaha* fired a salute. Morris Davis, the President of Minerva, flew to Nuku'alofa seeking an audience with the King but was snubbed. He spoke to *The New York Times*: 'We can't for the life of us understand why the King should suddenly decide he wants the reefs. He never had any use for them before'.[155] Other supporters offered inducements to the King to recognise the Minervan claim, including 'an airline, low-voltage television station, a shipyard and other considerations'.[156] Unfortunately for Oliver and his supporters, even if Tonga's neighbours did not accept King Tupou IV's claim, they would not recognise the Republic of Minerva. In September, the South Pacific Forum issued a communiqué noting:

> Members of the Forum recognised Tonga's historical association with the Minerva Reefs, welcomed the Tongan Government's continuing interest in the area and agreed that there could be no question of recognising other

152 Song (n 137) 423; Menefee (n 147) 100.

153 Editorial, 'King to Lead Flag Raising on Teleki on Monday', *The Tonga Chronicle*, 22 June 1972. Cited in Song (n 137) 424; 'Republic of Minerva' (1 July 1972) 43(2) *Pacific Islands Monthly* 121–3.

154 Tonga Royal Proclamation, 15 June 1972.

155 Song (n 137) 426; Roy Bongartz, 'Nations Off the Beaten Track', *The New York Times* (28 March 1976) 292.

156 Anthony van Fossen, *Tax Havens and Sovereignty in the Pacific Islands* (University of Queensland ePress, 2012) 114.

claims, and specifically that of the Ocean Life Research Foundation, to sovereignty over the reefs.[157]

The South Pacific Forum leaders' communiqué is careful not to recognise Tonga's sovereign claims. Although it makes clear that no other claims would be accepted, it merely recognises Tonga's 'historical association' to the atolls. This distinction is important because, in 2005, Fiji lodged a complaint with the International Seabed Authority, claiming the Minerva Reefs as part of their exclusive economic zone (EEZ). Tonga lodged a counterclaim, but the dispute has not yet been resolved. In the absence of a conclusive resolution, the Fijian navy has reportedly destroyed navigational equipment on the atolls several times.[158]

Developments in international law since 1972 suggest the following. First, it is unlikely that the atolls themselves can be claimed as territory by any state. In the 2001 decision of *Qatar v Bahrain*, the International Court of Justice held that low-tide elevations 'cannot be equated with islands' for the purposes of rules concerning the acquisition of sovereignty.[159] The Court noted further that 'a coastal State has sovereignty over low-tide elevations which are situated within its territorial sea, since it has sovereignty over the territorial sea itself', but that low-tide elevations outside a territorial sea cannot be appropriated.[160] This position was confirmed in *Nicaragua v Colombia*.[161] Second, the artificial islands constructed by Tonga also do not possess a territorial sea for the purpose of international law. This is clearly stated in Article 60(8) of the 1982 Convention on the Law of the Sea. Third, because the artificial islands are constructed within Tonga's EEZ, they may constitute territory and be capable of appropriation.[162] However, this view relies on a finding that construction was not illegal, given that the Minerva Reefs are also located within Fiji's EEZ. Tonga may succeed here because Teleki Tokelau and Teleki Tonga were built before entry into force of the EEZ

[157] South Pacific Forum, *Leaders' Communique* (Suva, 12–14 September 1972).

[158] See for example Michael Field, 'Fiji, Tonga War Over Minerva Reef', *Stuff* (16 May 2011) www.stuff.co.nz/world/south-pacific/5008060/Fiji-Tonga-war-over-Minerva-Reef.

[159] *Case Concerning Maritime Delimitation and Territorial Questions between Qatar and Bahrain (Qatar v Bahrain) (Merits)* [2001] ICJ Rep 40, 101–2 [205]–[209].

[160] Ibid 101 [204].

[161] *Territorial and Maritime Dispute (Nicaragua v Colombia) (Merits)* [2012] ICJ Rep 624, 21 [26].

[162] Imogen Saunders, 'Artificial Islands and Territory in International Law' (2019) 52 *Vanderbilt Journal of International Law* 643, 680.

regime. These are ultimately questions for Tonga and Fiji to resolve; the libertarian prompt no longer exists.

The Republic of Minerva is not the only micronation whose sudden emergence has catalysed a claim to territorial authority by a recognised state. That said, it may be one of the only micronations that has had a realistic, albeit small, opportunity to perfect its assertion of sovereignty. Other micronations may have made a loud and vocal claim to jurisdiction, but there was little chance that they would ever be recognised. Even so, that did not calm states abruptly confronted by a potential challenger. Consider the Principality of Trinidad.

In 1893, American James Harden-Hickey claimed the small uninhabited island of Trindade in the South Atlantic about 1,100 kilometres off the coast of Brazil.[163] Declaring himself James I, Prince of Trinidad, Harden-Hickey intended to establish a military dictatorship. It appears that James I made substantial progress. He designed postage stamps, a national flag, a coat of arms, and established a chivalric order, the Cross of Trinidad. He apparently convinced the *New-York Tribune* that he had also bought a schooner to transport colonists.[164] James I engaged in considerable diplomatic activity to press his claim. He opened a consular office in New York City, appointed a Secretary of State and issued government bonds purportedly to finance the construction of infrastructure on the island. These actions provoked a response.

In July 1895, the British attempted to take possession of the island on the basis of a 1700 visit by English astronomer Edmund Halley. At this stage, Brazil pressed its own claim, arguing that the island was discovered and occupied by Portuguese navigators in 1502. Ejected from the island, Trinidad's Secretary of State requested the United States intervene to 'accord its powerful assistance to the cause of right and justice, misunderstood by England and Brazil [and] put an end to a situation which threatens to disturb the peace'.[165] The United States demurred. In November 1895, Brazilian claims were accepted,[166] and the British

163 'Principality of Trinidad: John H. Flagler's Son-in-Law Is Its Sovereign, Self-Proclaimed as James I', *The New York Times* (10 June 1894).

164 William Bryk, 'News and Columns' (10 December 2002) 15(50) *New York Press* https://web.archive.org/web/20060430105931/http://www.nypress.com/15/50/news%26columns/oldsmoke.cfm.

165 'Trinidad's Prince Awake: An Appeal to Washington Against Brazil and Great Britain', *The New York Times* (1 August 1895) 1; 'Trinidad's Case in Washington', *The New York Times* (7 August 1895) 1; 'Trinidad and England', *The New York Times* (8 October 1895) 4; 'Trinidad's Diplomat in Action', *The New York Times* (9 August 1895).

166 'Brazil Will Have Trinidad', *The New York Times* (15 November 1895) 1.

evacuated. In 1897, Harden-Hickey designed plans to invade England and sought to finance the operation by selling lands in Mexico. These efforts fell through, and the once King committed suicide in a Texas hotel in February 1898; 'In his trunk was the crown of Trinidad'.[167]

Another case comes from the Spratly Islands in the South China Sea. In 1956, Filipino fishermen Tomás Cloma and Filemon Cloma, and around forty crew, landed on an uninhabited island outside the jurisdiction of the Philippines and issued a 'Notice to the Whole World' announcing the formation of the 'Free Territory of Freedomland'. The Cloma brothers predicated their claim to the 168,000-square-kilometre territory on 'the rights of discovery and/or occupation', arguing that Japan had abandoned the land after World War II as part of the Treaty of San Francisco.[168] The group then sought to perfect their title by erecting obelisks and plaques and raising flags. The declaration was not made on behalf of the Philippines government,[169] though evidence suggests they were encouraged in their actions by the Philippines Vice President.[170]

Almost immediately, the claim was challenged. The Peoples Republic of China, Vietnam, France and the Netherlands lodged various claims and counterclaims to the Spratly Islands, while the Taiwanese navy detained Tomás Cloma and forced him to sign a document stating that Freedomland belonged to Taiwan. Cloma sought assistance from the United Nations, but the Philippines ran interference. The legal basis of the claim was weak, but in a significant instance of de facto recognition, for many years the Philippines grounded their own claims to sovereignty in the region on the Cloma claim.[171] In 1974, Philippines dictator Ferdinand Marcos imprisoned Tomás Cloma and compelled him to sign an agreement waiving whatever rights and interests he may have had in the land in favour of the Philippines for one peso.[172] Marcos renamed the area Kalayaan and incorporated it within the Philippines state. It was not until 2014, when the Philippines sought adjudication of

[167] Bryk (n 164).

[168] *Treaty of Peace with Japan ('Treaty of San Francisco')*, 136 UNTS 45 (8 September 1951), entered into force 28 April 1952, art 2(f).

[169] Rodolfo Severino, *Where in the World Is the Philippines? Debating Its National Territory* (Institute of Southeast Asian Studies, 2010) 67.

[170] Stein Tønnesson, 'The History of the Dispute' in Timo Kivimäki (ed), *War or Peace in the South China Sea?* (Nordic Institute of Asian Studies, 2002) 6, 13.

[171] Brantly Womack, *China and Vietnam: The Politics of Asymmetry* (Cambridge University Press, 2006) 218.

[172] Ma Ceres P. Doyo, 'The Old Man and the Sea', *Inquirer* (25 June 2015) https://opinion.inquirer.net/86123/the-old-man-and-the-sea.

its territorial dispute with China in the International Court of Arbitration, that it abandoned the Cloma claim, instead asserting a 200-mile territorial claim as part of its EEZ.[173] Freedomland (now known as Colonia), argues that the Philippines relinquishment of the claim leaves it as the only successor claimant to the Cloma territory. Other states disagree.

One final example is considered. In the previous chapter we discussed the purported Kingdom of EnenKio, established by Robert Moore as a means to engage in financial fraud. The Kingdom, as well as the related Dominion of Melchizedek claimed authority over Wake Island in the western Pacific Ocean. Wake Island is one of the most isolated coral atolls in the world. Located over 2,400 kilometres east of Guam and almost 3,700 kilometres west of Honolulu, its nearest inhabited neighbour is the Marshall Islands' Utirik Atoll, some 953 kilometres away. Formally, Wake Island is an unorganised and unincorporated territory of the United States. It is also claimed by the Republic of the Marshall Islands (itself an associated state of the United States), which it calls Enen-kio. The Marshall Islands have vigorously protested United States authority on Enen-kio, but so far to no avail.[174] When Moore began advertising the Kingdom of EnenKio, the Marshall Islands acted promptly. On 23 April 1998, it issued a Circular Note denying the claims of the Kingdom of EnenKio and the Dominion of Melchizedek:

> The Government of the Republic of the Marshall Islands condemns the claims and activities asserted by representatives of the 'Kingdom of EnenKio' and the 'Dominion of Melchizedek'. The representatives making claims of separate sovereignty are not citizens of the Republic of the Marshall Islands and have no right to make claims on behalf of Marshallese landowners. Furthermore, these representatives are making fraudulent assertions that violate the Republic of the Marshall Islands' constitution. The area of land and ocean which the 'Kingdom of EnenKio' asserts as a sovereign nation separate from the Marshall Islands and the area of land and ocean which the 'Dominion of Melchizedek' is asserting control over are areas within the geographical and political boundaries of the Republic of the Marshall Islands. The Government of the Republic of the Marshall Islands discourages all independent sovereign nations having diplomatic relations with the Republic from acknowledging any

173 'Memorial Submitted by the Philippines', *The South China Sea Arbitration (Philippines v China)* (Permanent Court of Arbitration, Case No. 2013–19, 30 March 2014) 33 [2.37], 34 [2.40]. For more micronational claims in the Spratly Islands see Chapter 3.

174 See for example, Jon Anderson, 'Wake Island Claimed by Marshall Islanders', *The Cameron Herald* (8 February 1973) 2.

> fraudulent claims made by representatives of the 'Kingdom of EnenKio' and the 'Dominion of Melchizedek'.[175]

The Marshall Islands may have dismissed these two pretenders, but they have had more trouble overcoming the United States.

5.4 Conclusion

This chapter has explored the various ways that states respond to micronations. As we have demonstrated, responses stretch from forcible and violent suppression, to ignoring their declarations of independence and performative assertions of sovereignty, to playing along with their bizarre or eccentric claims. Despite sending letters to hundreds of countries and international agencies, micronations are usually considered the problem of the state from which they purported to secede. In some cases, however, because of their potential to provoke diplomatic incidents, cause transnational harm or even reveal a lacuna in de jure control over territory, a larger collection of states engages with and responds to these wannabe countries.

What accounts for the difference in responses? Generally speaking, the survival of a micronation is 'completely dependent upon the attitude and actions of its ... neighbour'.[176] So long as a micronation does not seriously inconvenience the governance or jurisdiction of a recognised state, it will likely be permitted to engage in whatever aspects of pretend sovereignty it chooses.[177] While some states may put up with greater or lesser levels of 'mild embarrassment',[178] none will allow their security to be threatened or serious criminality to take place. It appears that most micronations are well aware of this unstated arrangement. Consider the Principality of Sealand again.

Over the years, the Principality has been contacted by various groups interested in leveraging its ambiguous legal status for different ends. In the late 1970s, representatives of the Spanish government sought to purchase the Principality in a bid to regain sovereignty over Gibraltar.[179] Similarly, during the Falklands War a group of Argentinians apparently asked to buy the fort and set up 'their own Malvinas' right on Britain's doorstep'.[180] At

[175] Republic of the Marshall Islands, Ministry of Foreign Affairs, 'Circular Note 01-98' (23 April 1998).
[176] Hibberd (n 120) 273.
[177] Strauss (n 1) 28.
[178] Hibberd (n 120) 278.
[179] Taylor-Lehman (n 26) 88.
[180] Ibid.

another point Muammar Gaddafi 'offered Roy a "pot of gold" to use the tower'.[181] Roy dismissed each offer, explaining: 'Of course I sent them away. I'd never do anything that would pose a threat to the UK'.[182] After all, doing otherwise would pose a threat to Sealand.

In 2000, the Principality reached agreement with HavenCo, a US data hosting company. For an initial payment of USD 250,000 and a share of the company, the Bateses would allow HavenCo to operate from Roughs Tower. HavenCo was interested in operating a 'data haven'. Similar to a tax haven, data havens offer 'no-questions-asked data storage web hosting and encrypted communication'.[183] HavenCo's anarcho-libertarian directors promised their customers 'a combination of first-world infrastructure and third-world regulation'.[184] As they explained:

> HavenCo will allow for gambling, pyramid schemes, adult porn, sub-poena-proof email, and untraceable bank accounts. But not everything will fly. In addition to the spam and child-porn ban, corporate cybersaboteurs are forbidden.[185]

The directors fixed upon Sealand because of its uncertain status. Even if the law was and is clear – Sealand is part of the United Kingdom – the directors reasoned that in practice, the United Kingdom has tolerated and would continue to tolerate some level of criminality.[186] Perhaps they were correct, a US State Department official monitoring the situation explained: '[R]ight now, we aren't even concerned with something like Sealand because they are not representing any kind of a threat ... It would not be an issue for us unless, for example, they are hooking up with Osama bin Laden'.[187] Ultimately, however, the arrangement collapsed after only a few years. Concerned that HavenCo 'was bad for Sealand's image and quest for sovereignty', the Bateses ejected the original US directors and adopted a new acceptable use policy consistent with international and European Union laws.[188] To do otherwise would invite a state response that could threaten the viability of Sealand.

[181] Ibid 67.
[182] Ibid 88.
[183] Ibid 109; Grimmelmann, (n 117); See further Nate Anderson, *Internet Police: How Crime Went Online, and the Cops Followed* (W.W. Norton & Co, 2014).
[184] Grimmelmann (n 117) 451.
[185] Simson Garfinkel, 'Welcome to Sealand. Now Bugger Off' (July 2000) 8(7) *Wired* www.wired.com/2000/07/haven-2/.
[186] Ibid.
[187] Taylor-Lehman (n 26) 116.
[188] Grimmelmann (n 117) 455–6.

6

The Future of Micronationalism

In this concluding chapter we consider the future of micronationalism. We begin by outlining five major themes gleaned from our exploration of micronations. We examine the relationship between micronations and recognised states, the creativity needed to identify supposed fissures in international and domestic law to build a (doomed) case for independence, the diversity of this phenomenon, the transitory nature of micronations and the gendered quality of micronationalism.

Recognising the varied motivations that underpin the decision to establish one's own country, we then consider in detail the value gained by claiming statehood. As we have documented throughout this book, countless differences exist between individual micronations, yet all share a common connection: despite little or no chance of success, they make a claim for statehood and speak in the language of sovereignty. Finally, we conclude by asking whether micronations succeed or fail. Even though no micronation has ever become a recognised sovereign state, we argue that the future of micronationalism is anything but gloomy.

6.1 Five Major Themes

The first major theme that emerges from our study is the dependent relationship between micronations and recognised states. Micronations are an extension of the contemporary concept of the state, even if they are defined in negative terms by their inability to attain that status. Before the state became the dominant form of political community across the globe, hundreds if not thousands of very small, more or less independent, territorial units existed. Even after the rise of the Westphalian system in Europe, many city-states like the Free and Hanseatic City of Hamburg and the Free City of Kraków continued to enjoy considerable powers of autonomy and self-governance. Of course, not every territorially small principality or city-state was eventually swallowed up into a larger state.

In Europe, the existence of Monaco, Vatican City, Andorra and Liechtenstein offer (false) hope to micronationalists.

Prior to the emergence of the state and the development of international law regulating the creation of the state, micronations did not exist. Micronations are defined by their relationship to the state. Without the state there are no micronations. Rather, there is a wide spectrum of political communities exercising or seeking varied degrees of independence and control. Micronations dress in the language of sovereignty and mimic statehood protocols; they experiment with governance systems, develop national symbols and seek to engage recognised nations in diplomatic relations. However, despite all this effort they are not states. In fact, the central feature of micronationalism is that they express a claim of sovereignty despite the absence of any basis in domestic and international law for that claim or for their existence. In this sense, it is not so much that micronations exist in the shadow of the law as in complete contradiction to it.

A second, related, theme is the creativity and ingenuity of those that found micronations. Micronations may have no legal basis for statehood but in searching for a foothold in the law with which they can scale the lofty heights necessary to join the international plane, they develop imaginative and often clever – albeit ineffective – legal theories. Many micronationalists trace detailed alternative histories, where marriage contracts, peace treaties, private land sales and the like were either misplaced, misattributed or made ineffective in some manner. Positioning themselves as truth tellers, these founders argue that, as a result, vast swathes of territory are today under illegal occupation. In their eyes, micronations are not secessionist at all. They are captive nations governed by illegitimate rule that are yearning to be free.

Other micronations scan international covenants and agreements looking for loopholes or a crack in the law. The Antarctic Treaty System may preclude sovereign claims to the icy continent,[1] but does it say anything about the claims of individuals? If the 1958 Geneva Convention on the High Seas declared that the high seas were open to all nations,[2] does that mean that an individual can build their own nation outside the jurisdiction of the nearest coastal state? What about land that has never been formally claimed? If the British could assert lawful

[1] *The Antarctic Treaty* 402 UNTS 71 (opened for signature 1 December 1959 and entered into force 23 June 1961) art IV.

[2] *Convention on the High Seas* 450 UNTS 11 (opened for signature 29 April 1958 and entered into force 30 September 1962) art 2.

authority over the entire continent of Australia – in spite of the existence of hundreds of Aboriginal and Torres Strait Islander nations who had possessed the land for over 60,000 years – why is an individual not permitted to establish their own nation on land that is neither occupied nor claimed? While the legal skills of micronationalists are generally more playful than analytical, some do pose difficult questions for the legitimacy of recognised sovereign states.

One challenge in separating micronations that provoke real questions over sovereignty, statehood and international legal personality, and those that do not, is their sheer multiplicity. This is the third major theme that emerges from this book. As we have established, micronationalism is an astonishingly diverse phenomenon. Even if we put simulationist or virtual micronations to one side, the (at least) 135 territorial micronations that have operated at one time or another vary widely in form and function. Some are established in frustration with state authority and government policy, while others combine anger at bureaucracy with a strong sense of personal and political injustice. Others are established to poke fun at national symbols or challenge and critique statehood. Others still are primarily designed to make money, either as scams for personal enrichment or as attempts to boost tourism in small communities.

This diversity is amplified when one considers the thousands of micronations that exist wholly online. On social media, message boards and online forums, people from all over the world build their own simulationist micronations. Founders draft rich and detailed national histories, complex governance institutions and creative cultural traditions for fun and as a way to connect with others across the Internet and at regular face-to-face meetings. Simulationist micronations are intricate and involved. On MicroWiki,[3] one can find democratic, socialist, monarchical, republican, theocratic, autocratic and oligarchic micronations. There are pages that rank micronations according to a Micronational Democracy Index, a Micronational Human Development Index – and even GDP. Other pages compare micronations according to size, official religions, major ethnicities, political parties, armed forces, motion picture content rating systems, LGBT rights and whether alcohol is permitted. Those developing their own micronation can also gain inspiration from curated lists of official symbols, such as coats of arms, flags, national mottos, national animals and national sports cars.

[3] See MicroWiki, 'Lists of Micronations' https://micronations.wiki/wiki/Lists_of_micronations.

Simulationist micronations are extraordinarily diverse, but they do not give rise to the same questions as micronations that actually claim real territory. Territorial micronations that assert jurisdiction over specific land, sea or space can give rise to more difficult questions relating to the creation of states in international law as well as the enforcement of domestic laws. When is secession legal? The International Court of Justice is yet to clearly grapple with this fundamental question.[4] Can a state be built on reclaimed land in the high seas? What about on artificial structures outside national jurisdiction? Answers to these questions have not yet been firmly resolved. Even if and when they are, it is likely that devoted individuals dedicated to their project will find cracks in the law that may be prised open.

Fourth, micronations tend to be ephemeral. As we have seen, it takes considerable energy and effort over a sustained period to 'play' a nation – particularly in circumstances where no one else plays along. Founders get bored. President Baugh of the Republic of Molossia explains, '[t]he average lifespan of a micronation is about 90 days, because that's the average attention span of a teenage boy'.[5] Even the largest and loudest do not survive for long. Despite the global prominence and arguable success of the Principalities of Sealand and Hutt River for instance, the outlook for both of these micronations is far from rosy. Roy Bates passed away in 2012 and was succeeded by his son Michael Bates. Desiring an education for his children, Michael and his family had left the decommissioned fort many years earlier, preferring to settle in an Essex seaside town where he built a shellfish business to support his family – and to pay for necessary upkeep on the installation.[6] Michael has now retired from the business, and although there are several heirs to the throne, it is possible that his children and grandchildren will lose interest in the 4,100-tonne abandoned naval fort sitting off the UK coast.

Hutt River's situation is clearer. In 2020, the Principality of Hutt River marked its fiftieth anniversary; the date was a moment to celebrate Prince Leonard and his tenacity to 'bring about the survival of the

[4] *Accordance with International Law of the Unilateral Declaration of Independence in Respect of Kosovo (Advisory Opinion)* [2010] ICJ Rep 403 ('*Kosovo Advisory Opinion*'); Marko Milanović and Michael Wood (eds), *The Law and Politics of the Kosovo Advisory Opinion* (Oxford University Press, 2015).

[5] Robin Reid, 'Micronations of the World', *Smithsonian Magazine* (23 August 2009) www.smithsonianmag.com/travel/micronations-of-the-world-43181804/.

[6] Dylan Taylor-Lehman, *Sealand: The True Story of the World's Most Stubborn Micronation* (Icon Books, 2020) ch 19.

Casley farm',[7] but it was also tinged with sadness and uncertainty. Prince Leonard had passed away the previous year, and his youngest son Prince Graeme had acceded to the throne in 2017. The Principality's finances were in a precarious state, with AUD 3 million owed to the Australian Taxation Office. In January 2020, the Principality closed its borders and public offices so that it could reassess its future, citing declining agricultural revenue, reduced numbers of tourists 'passing by and dropping in for a chat' and the increasing costs involved in running 'a small country'.[8] In August 2020, Prince Graeme announced his decision. The farm would be sold to pay debts, and the Principality would be dissolved.[9] The demise of Hutt River and the potential passing of Sealand is not unexpected.

Reflecting the moral and political strength of their claims and legal foundations, micronations are often short-lived, surviving only as long as their charismatic or eccentric founder. Those rare entities that persist beyond their creator, like Sealand, largely do so because they become a symbol for something much larger. Others may appear more akin to a social club than a state. The Republic of Parva Domus Magna Quies, which has operated in Montevideo, Uruguay since 1878, limits citizenship to 250 people; a number that permits its members to enjoy social, cultural and recreational activities. The Kingdom of Elleore on the small Danish island of the same name is also more a social club than a nation. Although it has existed since 1944, the Kingdom traces its ancestry to an Irish monastic society that supposedly set up camp in 944. The island so reminded them of their homeland that upon landing 'one monk declared "Hic est elie ore!" (Here is the golden island)'.[10] The Kingdom of Elleore developed several peculiar traditions, including banning the novel *Robinson Crusoe* and operating on 'Elleore Standard Time' – 12 minutes

[7] Laura Meachim and Glenn Barndon, 'Hutt River Province Celebrates Its 50th Anniversary as Western Australia's Micronation', *ABC News* (21 April 2020) www.abc.net.au/news/2020-04-21/hutt-river-marks-fifty-years-but-is-the-micronation-dream-over/12166302 'The Second Largest Country in Australia', *National Geographic* (5 September 2017) www.nationalgeographic.com.au/history/the-second-largest-country-in-australia.aspx.

[8] HRH Prince Graeme, Sovereign, Principality of Hutt River. 'Principality of Hutt River to Close Its Borders' (Media Release, 27 December 2019) www.principality-hutt-river.com/Media_Release/PHR_MEDIA_RELEASE_27_Dec_2019.htm.

[9] Naaman Zhou and Ben Doherty, 'Hutt River Micronation to Rejoin Australia Due to Coronavirus Pandemic', *Guardian Australia* (5 August 2020) www.theguardian.com/australia-news/2020/aug/05/hutt-river-micronation-to-rejoin-australia-due-to-coronavirus-pandemic.

[10] John Ryan, George Dunford and Simon Sellars, *Micronations: The Lonely Planet Guide to Home-Made Nations* (Lonely Planet, 2006) 43.

behind Danish time. However, as its proponents grew older and lost energy the nature of their nation shifted. Now deserted for much of the year, Elleore is only occupied for a one-week celebration.[11]

The fifth theme is that the founders of micronations are almost universally male. So too are the masculine accoutrements that often accompany micronational assertions of statehood: think brash military medals, faux royal titles, dictatorships as well as bombastic declarations of war against both recognised and other wannabe states. Simon Sellars, co-author of the *Lonely Planet Guide to Home-Made Nations*, has remarked on this point, noting:

> It does appear to be an especially male enterprise, starting up your own micronation. It's like piecing together a model train set, I think – that common little-boy fantasy of building, managing and controlling every single aspect of a miniature world. But then again, little girls have dollhouses and tea sets, and that's a virtual world as well, with its own rules for social interaction.[12]

Others are less forgiving. Daisy Alioto wonders whether the gendered nature of micronationalism is 'a testament to the male desire to conquer even a thimble's worth of territory'.[13]

Micronations may be overwhelmingly male but not all are geared towards authority and control. Nonetheless, even if some micronations are explicitly non-territorial or pacifistic, few are founded or led by women. The Ambulatory Free States of Obsidia is an exception. Established by American artist Carolyn Yagjian on 8 March 2015 (International Women's Day), Obsidia is 'the world's only feminist micronation'.[14] Located at the 'confluence of feminism and geography', Obsidia is 'a tiny, matriarchal micronation', whose 'humble' territory comprises a two-pound chunk of obsidian rock.[15] The micronation is 'easily transported in its official state briefcase', but is currently situated in Oakland, California. The Grand Marshal describes the governance structure and ethos of the state:

> Obsidia has an egalitarian structure and our officials hold no real power. In Obsidia We strive to find alternatives to capitalism and promote self-expression through creative nation building projects. The objectives of the

11 Ibid 42–7.

12 Interview with Simon Sellars (Geoff Manaugh, BLDGBLOG, 23 November 2006) www.bldgblog.com/2006/11/the-lonely-planet-guide-to-micronations-an-interview-with-simon-sellars/.

13 Daisy Alioto, 'Užupis Utopia', *Playboy* (17 December 2019) www.playboy.com/read/uzupis-utopia.

14 Ambulatory Free States of Obsidia www.obsidiagov.org/.

15 Ibid.

> government of Obsidia are to institutionalize leadership for those traditionally excluded, increase visibility for femme/feminist/LGBTQ people and explore concepts for an ideal governance.[16]

Obsidia supports these values in practice. At the 2017 MicroCon, Yagjian explained how the micronation is working with Women on Waves, a Dutch organisation that travels the world providing safe abortions in international waters off the coast of countries where the procedure is illegal. Yagjian explained further to a journalist covering the event:

> 'Borders are the enemy of mutual aid, of autonomy, of feminism, and, indeed, freedom,' she says. Obsidia wants an international sisterhood, where the only boundaries for women are the ones they mandate over their own bodies.[17]

Yagjian sees the Ambulatory Free States of Obsidia as a means to draw attention to and support her political ideals: the abolition of the patriarchy and the empowerment of women across the globe. How does the creation of a micronation assist this goal? What value is there in claiming to be a state? It is to this question that we turn next.

6.2 Why Claim Statehood?

Micronations have no legitimate basis in domestic or international law and yet nevertheless make an earnest or eccentric claim for sovereignty and international legal personality. Why? The existence and persistence of micronations is a challenge to conventional understandings of statehood. Why do micronations assert sovereignty and dress in the language of statehood? What value do they see in the status of a state, as opposed to adopting corporate personhood, organising as an autonomous community or even simply starting a book club?

Developments in international law have affected notions of statehood and international legal personality. As we explored in Chapter 2, while states were historically considered the sole subjects of international law, today a variety of non-state entities, including 'international organisations, individuals, minorities, corporations and even animals and rivers',[18] enjoy

[16] Ibid.

[17] Heather Buckner, 'You Probably Didn't Know, But Leaders from 26 Micronations Just Gathered in Atlanta', *Atlanta* (30 June 2017) www.atlantamagazine.com/news-culture-articles/probably-didnt-know-leaders-26-micronations-just-gathered-atlanta/.

[18] Matthew Craven and Rose Parfitt, 'Statehood, Self-Determination and Recognition' in Malcolm Evans (ed), *International Law* (Oxford University Press, 5th ed, 2018) 177, 181.

some form of international personality. Even so, in the creation of international law and popular consciousness, the perception that states are 'paramount'[19] remains. It is still true, James Crawford has noted, that international forums 'are created and ultimately controlled by States or by intergovernmental organizations, and it is these entities that remain the gatekeepers and legislators of the international system';[20] 'the "international plane" is a construct, not a place – but it remains an arena to which, in most circumstances, one still needs a ticket'.[21] A claim of statehood is that ticket; for micronations it is the device that distinguishes 'between those social entities relevant to the international legal system and those excluded from it'.[22]

In this light, micronational assertions of statehood may be genuinely understood as claims to international legal personality and the associated privileges and immunities. It is clear, for example, that irrespective of the viability of their project, Michael Oliver and the Ocean Life Research Foundation were desirous of establishing an internationally recognised and effective state on the Minerva Reefs. Though many consider Vit Jedlička's Free Republic of Liberland a publicity stunt, he too may sincerely be interested in building a nation to trial and propagate his political views. Such a goal may be one only for dreamers and the deluded, but statehood carries considerable advantages. If the Republic of Minerva had successfully perfected its claim, it would have enjoyed exclusive competence with respect to its internal affairs; Oliver may well have been able to see his libertarian paradise take flight. Perhaps more significant, the Republic of Minerva would have been protected from the sort of external interference from Tonga that eventually doomed the Land of the Rising Atoll.[23] It may also have masked some of his more questionable activities with the cloak of state immunity.

It is for this reason that already existing states often act swiftly to deny the capacity of micronations to assert their sovereignty. Understanding such claims as geared towards secession and independence, states

19 James Crawford, *Brownlie's Principles of International Law* (Oxford University Press, 9th ed, 2018) 432.

20 James Crawford, *The Creation of States in International Law* (Oxford University Press, 2nd ed, 2007) 29.

21 Crawford (n 19) 116.

22 Roland Portman, *International Legal Personality in International Law* (Cambridge University Press, 2010) 1.

23 United Nations General Assembly, *Declaration on Principles of International Law Concerning Friendly Relations*, UN Doc GA Res 2625 (24 October 1970); Crawford (n 19) 116.

jealously guard their exclusive authority and jurisdiction. As we examined in Chapter 5, states can respond forcibly, peaceably or in coalition with others to decisively quell incipient challengers. These responses are supported by international law, which does not generally recognise unilateral secession outside the colonial context as lawful.[24] However, not all micronations are interested in wielding power, challenging existing states or even achieving statehood.

A micronation may be created to parrot the workings of a state simply because this offers a path to material advancement. In Chapters 3 and 4 we examined how con artists have fabricated intricate (and remote) micronations as a means to engage in large-scale financial fraud. This is not a novel endeavour; the Internet has only increased the range of potential marks. Gregor McGregor – the supposed Cazique of Poyais – profited handsomely from his brazen confidence trick in the 1820s. Even if a person is not interested in scams or swindles, however, one can still turn a tidy profit by attracting tourists or designing and selling statehood symbols, such as stamps, coins and passports. So long as it is clear that such paraphernalia has no legal value but is merely a collectible it is likely that recognised states will permit their design and sale. In this regard, these micronations are no different from states that 'profit by selling or renting out their sovereign prerogatives'.[25] Many states, even larger ones, sell citizenship, diplomatic recognition and votes on international organisations.[26] Founders and proponents of micronations may be interested in profiting likewise.

Other reasons exist. A claim for statehood does not necessarily need to be politically or financially motivated. Micronations may not be established to access the range of entitlements, duties and liabilities imposed by international law on states, but for something more intangible – relevance. In the words of Fleur Johns, to lay claim to international legal personality is an argument that 'the subjectivity of the entity in question merits international legal notice and respect',[27] that it deserves 'to be taken seriously'.[28] By asserting their status as states, even though in

[24] Crawford (n 20) 415. Cf. *Kosovo Advisory Opinion* (n 4).

[25] JC Sharman, 'Sovereignty at the Extremes: Micro-States in World Polities' (2017) 65(3) *Political Studies* 559, 561.

[26] Natalie J Lockwood, 'International Vote Buying' (2013) 54(1) *Harvard International Law Journal* 97.

[27] Fleur Johns, 'Introduction' in Fleur Johns (ed), *International Legal Personality* (Ashgate, 2010) xi, xxv.

[28] Jan Klabbers, 'The Concept of International Legal Personality' in Fleur Johns (ed), *International Legal Personality* (Ashgate, 2010) 3, 30–1.

fact they lack any legal claim to such status, micronations 'come into sight' and are made 'visible' to the domestic and international legal community.[29] Recognising this, micronations should not always be conceived as initiating a challenge over jurisdiction, but perhaps as a means to draw attention and engage with particular issues and claims. In this sense, an interest in statehood goes well beyond the statehood spectrum. It has meaning even as an unattainable goal. There is a power in attracting attention and gaining relevance such that aspiring to statehood can be attractive even to those who can never attain it. As Prince Leonard Casley's son, Prince Graeme, explained in the aftermath of Leonard's death in February 2019:

> Hopefully, the Australian Government will sit around the table and talk to us about things, which is what Prince Leonard had been asking for the 47 years he was sovereign of the principality.[30]

As Prince Graeme intimates, assertions of statehood should not necessarily be taken literally, but as an avenue to promote dialogue, either with a state or with fellow citizens. Statehood as dialogue can be effective. Residents of the Florida Keys found the US government far more amenable to their concerns over traffic jams when they styled themselves as citizens of the breakaway Conch Republic.

Connected to ideas of relevance is the notion of belonging. Some micronations – particularly simulationist micronations – are more akin to a social club than a secessionist project; they do not want statehood and would not take actual power even if it was offered to them.[31] The Republic of Talossa, founded in 1979 by 14-year-old Robert Madison, falls within this category. Although most micronations flounder over the years, Talossa flourished thanks to the growth of the Internet. New citizens from all over the world are encouraged to spend time in Talossa by posting on the state's discussion boards and as a community they have developed an incredibly intricate history and culture. There is a Talossan language (el glheþ Talossan) consisting of over 121,000 words,[32] and a faux etymology tracing its origins 'to a 5th-century sect

[29] Janne Nijman, *The Concept of International Legal Personality, An Inquiry into the History and Theory of International Law* (TMC Asser Press, 2004) 455–6.

[30] Laura Meachim, 'Hutt River Province at $3m Stalemate with ATO after Death of Prince Leonard', *ABC News* (6 March 2019) www.abc.net.au/news/2019-03-06/what-happens-to-prince-leonard-ato-debt-now-he-is-dead/10850968.

[31] Alex Blumberg, 'It's Good to Be King' (March 2000) 8(3) *Wired* 132.

[32] Kingdom of Talossa, 'El Glheþ Talossan' (2020) http://talossan.com/history/modern-history/.

of Latin-speaking North African Berbers'.[33] There is also an active legislative programme.[34] One citizen, Chris Gruber, explains what the community means to him:

> 'The great thing about Talossa', he says, 'is that all these people are doing stuff that would otherwise be very solitary, but they're together. Like, I design and play my own games, I write and play music, I'm interested in writing sketch comedy and parody, and for years I've designed my own religions. So I'm sitting here doing all this stuff, but it's all solitary – I'm alone. And I think everyone in Talossa feels that way. We all have our selfish indulgences we do by ourselves. But Talossa is a place where we can do them together, rather than as isolated geeks all over the country, which is essentially what we are'.[35]

The Queen of Ruritania also enjoys the sense of belonging generated by micronationalism. Located in Stone Mountain in Georgia, USA, the Kingdom of Ruritania – named for the fictional central European country in the novels of Anthony Hope – is somewhere in-between a new country project and a hobby. The Kingdom styles itself as 'an actual nation under the Montevideo Convention with the right of self-determination'; it is 'not a game, model, or secessionist state',[36] but it is also particularly active in the micronational community, having co-hosted the 2017 MicroCon gathering. In a documentary for *Vice News*, Queen Anastasia hinted at the reasons for the Kingdom's endurance, noting that when her husband, King Wilhelm-Rudolph, passed away she received 'about 100 condolence letters from other micronations'.[37]

People looking for a sense of community have many options. They may start a book club, volunteer in a local organisation or join a sporting club. Those that found micronations may do so because they are drawn to the pageantry of statehood and diplomacy. They enjoy designing flags, wearing medals and dressing up as a king or queen. Once again, these types of micronation are not interested in genuine authority, but the satisfaction that comes from 'a big fantasy role-playing game'.[38] As the

33 Blumberg (n 31).
34 Kingdom of Talossa, '55th Cosa – Clark #1' (November 2020) www.talossa.ca/files/clark.php?cosa= 55&clark=1.
35 Blumberg (n 31).
36 Kingdom of Ruritania, 'Government and Information' (2019) www.ruritania.net/government-info.
37 Vice News, *The People Who Rule the World's Smallest Countries* (YouTube, 3 August 2017) www.youtube.com/watch?v=BpvNg-wrTkk.
38 Steven Scharff cited in Jennifer Parker, 'The Weird, Wild World of Micro-Nations Where Anyone Can Be King', *Bloomberg* (30 April 2015) www.bloomberg.com/news/articles/2015-04-30/the-weird-wild-world-of-micronations-where-anybody-can-be-king.

Queen of Ruritania has explained, 'when I am not being the Queen, I am being what other people want me to be. When I am being the Queen, I'm who I want to be'.[39]

Micronations also draw on a rich cultural tradition that celebrates the underdog and the improbability of tiny nations holding their own against larger states. Many founders and proponents cite the 1949 British comedy, *Passport to Pimlico* and/or Leonard Wibley's 1955 Cold War satirical novel, *The Mouse that Roared*, as an influence on their own claim to statehood.[40] In *Passport to Pimlico*, an unexploded World War II bomb detonates in the London suburb of Pimlico, unearthing a buried cellar that contains a royal charter of Edward IV. The charter ceded a house and its estates to Charles VII, the last Duke of Burgundy, in 1477. Deemed authentic and found to have never been revoked, the area of Pimlico is declared to be legally Burgundy – and therefore exempt from post-war rationing and other bureaucratic restrictions imposed by the British government.

The Mouse that Roared centres on the Duchy of Grand Fenwick, a made-up European microstate supposedly located between Switzerland and France, and whose entire economy is based on exporting Pinot Grand Fenwick wine. When a Californian winery begins making a knock-off version, the Duchy is put on the verge of bankruptcy. Their only option is to declare war on the United States, suffer a quick and total defeat, and then rebuild their economy through the considerable financial support the United States offers all vanquished enemies, such as Germany and via the Marshall Plan. The Duchy's declaration of war is misplaced by the US State Department, forcing the Duchy to reluctantly go through with their plans. Hiring a boat, twenty men sail across the Atlantic and land in a deserted New York City undergoing a citywide disaster drill. The Grand Fenwick army wander across the city and into a secret government lab and unintentionally capture a prototype 'Quadium Bomb', which is more powerful than all of the nuclear weapons in existence. Upon discovering that they have been at war for over two months – and that the Duchy of Grand Fenwick possess the deadliest weapon in the world – the United States is sheepishly forced to surrender and agree to the Duchy's terms.

[39] Ibid.

[40] Simon Sellars, '"Zones of Transition": Micronationalism in the Work of J.G. Ballard' in Jeanette Baxter and Roland Wymer (eds), *J.G. Ballard: Visions and Revisions* (Palgrave Macmillan, 2012) 230.

Despite their improbability, many micronations adopt these or similar strategies. As we noted earlier, the Conch Republic in the Florida Keys immediately declared war on the United States with the aim of obtaining USD 1 billion in foreign aid to restore the local economy.[41] The Principality of Hutt River also declared war on Australia, not to gain financial assistance but in an ill-fated attempt to gain recognition.

Such cultural traditions are not limited to Anglophone countries; popular fiction launched a micronation boom in Japan in the 1980s.[42] Drawing on reports of Leicester Hemingway's 'New Atlantis', novelist Hisashi Inoue authored *Kirikirijin*, a satirical tale that centred on a secluded village in rural northern Japan that seceded, made their regional dialect an official language and fought a war of independence. The success of the book sparked much excitement; within a few years, more than 200 communities had declared their own independence. Most of these efforts were primarily concerned with attracting tourists to promote revenue and counter the effects of out-migration of young adults, rather than genuinely engaging in micronational rituals. However, some did engage in performative assertions of statehood. The Nikoniko Republic established Nikoniko Standard Time (set at one hour behind Tokyo), constructed welcome signs at their border, minted their own currency and renamed the local tofu shop the National Protein Research Institute. The Japanese Minister of Internal Trade and Industry even signed a parodic treaty of friendship between the nation of Japan and the Kingdom of Inobhutan. Several of these nations also established their own Olympic Games, which received primetime television coverage, and micro-United Nations, which held summit talks between 1983 and 1985. However, when the Japanese asset price bubble burst in 1991, many villages were forced to merge with neighbouring larger cities and the micronations they had established dissolved.

6.3 Success and Failure

At one level, it might appear that this book has told a story about failure. No entity has transitioned from a micronation to a recognised state.

[41] 'Key West, in Protest on Aliens, "Secedes"', *The New York Times* (25 April 1982) 12.

[42] See Jennifer Robertson, 'Empire of Nostalgia: Rethinking "Internationalization" in Japan' (1997) 14(4) *Theory, Culture & Society* 97, 108–10; Adam Pasion, 'The Will to Secede: Japan's Micro-Nation Boom', *Japan Daily* (9 February 2016) https://japandaily.jp/will-secede-japans-micro-nation-boom-2573/. We thank Nobumichi Teramura for comments on this material.

Despite the countless hours and money that individuals have poured into their projects, their assertions of sovereignty remain merely performative. It is likely to be this way into the future as existing states act decisively to ensure that founders and proponents of micronations follow the ordinary laws of the land.

This is a jaundiced view. While the likelihood that a micronation will achieve real sovereignty is remote, success should be judged in light of each individual micronation's motivations and intentions, not in respect of the impossible dream of statehood. While some micronations with ambitious plans, like the Republic of Minerva, did not succeed, many others have met their goals, which may be as simple as drawing public attention to themselves or an issue of concern. Artistic micronations that provoke challenging questions on sovereignty and statehood often succeed. So too have many of those established for personal amusement, attention seeking and tourism. As the small township of Whangamōmona, New Zealand, welcomed another thousand visitors to its Republic Day in January 2021,[43] who is to say that micronationalism has not more than met its goals?

Micronations have had mixed success, but one thing is clear: the future of micronationalism is bright. The success and prominence of many micronations, will, by itself, encourage further activity. It is likely that community events like MicroCon and social media such as MicroWiki, Facebook and Reddit will lead to further developments that foster even more micronational activity in the future. Some people will always enjoy the theatrical and communal aspects of state-building, designing flags, drafting constitutions and composing national anthems. Others will continue to be interested in testing the boundaries of statehood through art and critique. Others still will look around the world as it is and know in their heart that they can do a better job of running a country. So long as the state remains the primary forum for political activity, micronations will persist. There are nonetheless important differences between micronations with a semi-serious claim for statehood, those practised almost entirely online and those with more nefarious aims. In this final part, we explore the future of these three models of micronationalism.

Few micronations have a genuine desire for statehood. Notwithstanding the adventurous claims of extra-terrestrial sovereignty offered by groups like the Space Kingdom of Asgardia, the possibility that a micronation's claims

[43] Ilona Hanne, 'Incumbent Republic of Whangamōmona President Keeps Top Job after Tight Election Race', *Stratford Press* (24 January 2021) www.nzherald.co.nz/stratford-press/news/incumbent-republic-of-whangamomona-president-keeps-top-job-after-tight-election-race/TUBCLPY52IRTFSLUFY65C4OO44/.

may be recognised and accepted appear dim. Reflecting on the history of micronationalism reveals a pattern in statehood claims and legal responses and suggests why Asgardia and others are unlikely to succeed.

Territory is an integral component of any state. Although international law may not require that a state possess any specific amount of territory, it does demand that it hold some territory upon which it exercises governing authority. In earlier years, micronationalists intending to build a new country could attempt to establish claims on unclaimed parcels of land purportedly on the basis of terra nullius and discovery. As the capacity of existing states to project their own authority has increased, however, the number of unclaimed and uninhabited areas has fallen. Today, there are precious few opportunities for those desiring to create their own Island of Refreshments, Kingdom of Trinidad or even Free Republic of Liberland. For this reason, many micronationalists began to look further afield.

In the 1960s, several prominent micronations emerged on reclaimed coral atolls and abandoned or rebuilt artificial structures in the sea. This shift was not coincidental. Rather, it was a response to the absence of unclaimed territory on land and the undeveloped state of the law of the sea. Before the conclusion of the 1982 United Nations Convention on the Law of the Sea (UNCLOS), many coastal states claimed jurisdiction only over their territorial sea, which in some cases extended a mere three miles offshore. The limited geographic claims by these coastal states allowed enterprising micronationalists to lay their own claim to reefs, banks and structures located near a state but just outside its authority.[44] It is no surprise that following the entry into force of the UNCLOS and its extensive 200-nautical-mile Exclusive Economic Zone, sea steading projects have either been proposed on the high seas, well beyond the horizon of coastal states – as Joe Quirk notes, 'Nearly half of the world's surface is unclaimed'[45] – or pitched as economic partnerships with sovereign states.

The point here is not that states have developed law and legal regimes to respond to the claims of micronations. Rather, it is that technological developments that have made certain previously inaccessible areas of the

[44] Samuel Pyeatt Menefee, '"Republics of the Reefs": Nation-Building on the Continental Shelf and in the World's Oceans' (1994) 25 *California Western International Law Journal* 81, 111.

[45] Cited in Oliver Wainwright, 'Seasteading – A Vanity Project for the Rich or the Future of Humanity?', *The Guardian* (24 June 2020) www.theguardian.com/environment/2020/jun/24/seasteading-a-vanity-project-for-the-rich-or-the-future-of-humanity. See further Tom Bell, *Your Next Government? From Nation State to Stateless Nation* (Cambridge University Press, 2018) 59.

globe accessible, have necessitated a change in the law. Micronations have simply been caught up in this change. This point was noted by Jean Gottman over half a century ago:

> Accessibility is the determining factor: areas to which men have no access do not have any political standing or problems. The sovereignty of the moon has no importance whatsoever today, because men cannot reach it nor obtain anything from it. The Antarctic had no political standing before navigators began going there, but since it was made accessible by its discoverers, the icy continent has been divided into portions like an apple pie.[46]

It is likely that if the moon ever does become accessible, micronational claims will not be far behind. The fact that such a claim would be contrary to the Outer Space Treaty[47] is immaterial. Just as the UNCLOS has produced gaps, so too there may well be gaps for enterprising and eccentric individuals to discover as humans expand on that frontier. Another potential frontier lies beneath the waters. In 1975 two Americans 'sent a letter to Henry Kissinger laying claim to the floor of the Pacific Ocean, "completely excluding therefrom, all Sea Water extending above the Ocean Floor"'.[48] It is not clear whether they received a response. However, while the technology to create underwater cities did not exist in 1975, it does exist today.[49] And yet, though there may be more territory on the planet left to claim, the likelihood that a micronation will ever become a state is remote. There will always be those dissatisfied with the status quo, but micronationalism is not the hope that these founders desire.

Many of those dissatisfied will be content to build virtual nations. The Internet has 'accelerated interest in micro-nations . . . [and] divorced the movement from physical territories'.[50] It has also made the creation of simulationist micronations far simpler. On social media sites like Facebook, Reddit and MicroWiki, individuals can share lessons and ideas as well as gain inspiration to establish their own country. Micronations built entirely on the internet often have incredibly elaborate histories. The State of Sandus, for instance, established in 2009, has

46 Jean Gottman, *The Significance of Territory* (University of Virginia Press, 1973) 11.

47 *Treaty on Principles Governing the Activities of States in the Exploration and Use of Outer Space, including the Moon and Other Celestial Bodies*, 610 UNTS 205 (opened for signature 27 January 1967, entered into force 10 October 1967) art II.

48 David Owen, 'Ephemeral States: At the Frontiers of Geography', *The Atlantic Monthly* (January 1988) 15, 16.

49 Rachel Nuwer, 'Will We Ever . . . Live in Underwater Cities?', *BBC Future* (30 September 2013) www.bbc.com/future/article/20130930-can-we-build-underwater-cities.

50 Alioto (n 13).

undergone considerable shifts in its culture and governance framework over the years – from French Barony to Socialist People's Republic to a period of no government to direct democracy based on Roman beliefs and ethics – all meticulously detailed on its website.[51] Almost half of the micronations established by attendees at biannual MicroCons 'exist solely on the Internet and are difficult to differentiate from other social networks or message boards'.[52] As long as individuals continue to find enjoyment in building a virtual society, it is likely that this trend will continue. For these forms of micronationalism, 'success' – measured in terms of friends gained and satisfaction had – is achievable.

Less pleasant to consider is the future of micronational scams. As we have noted throughout this book, micronations are largely created for affirmative or constructive reasons: to boost tourism, for personal enjoyment, as part of an artistic practice or even to experiment with political philosophies. Nonetheless, a small group of micronations are designed for more nefarious reasons. Unscrupulous individuals will of course always look for any way to swindle money from unsuspecting victims. Some such schemes can involve fake countries. Phony universities supposedly incorporated or chartered in micronations have sold college diplomas and transcripts; fraudulent banks have been employed in complex securities fraud. Perhaps most alarming are individuals who prey on the most vulnerable. In Chapter 4, we noted that at the height of the 2015 European refugee crisis, Vit Jedlička offered to grant Liberland citizenship to any person able to pay USD 10,000. Proudly boasting that almost 10,000 people from Syria and around 2,000 people from Libya had registered their interest, Jedlička preached the virtues of his Libertarian paradise.[53] Adam Taylor of *The Washington Post* notes that his plan was not supported by all members of the micronation:

> On the forum on Liberland's Web site, some hopeful Liberland citizens discussed whether the country should open its borders to Syrians and others fleeing persecution. 'The answer is no, because Liberland is for Libertarians. Not some random ass migrants,' one user wrote. 'Don't

[51] Sandus, 'Our History' https://sandus.org/about-sandus/about-the-history-of-sandus/.

[52] Jennifer Parker, 'The Weird, Wild World of Micro-Nations Where Anybody Can Be King: Passport Not Required', *Bloomberg* (30 April 2015) www.bloomberg.com/news/articles/2015-04-30/the-weird-wild-world-of-micronations-where-anybody-can-be-king.

[53] Adam Taylor, 'Almost 10,000 Syrians Have Registered to Live in a Country that Might Not Exist', *The Washington Post* (24 September 2015) www.washingtonpost.com/news/worldviews/wp/2015/09/24/almost-10000-syrians-have-registered-to-live-in-a-country-that-might-not-exist/.

> mistake libertarian with anarchy,' wrote another. 'Anarchy currently is in Syria.'[54]

Jedlička's actions were also not supported across the micronational community. Many micronations signed an opening letter censuring Liberland:

> The free Republic of Liberland is a media smokescreen that throws ridiculous and vain shadows at the expense of human distress on the ideals of most serious micronations and shows thus the full extent of the intellectual swindle it stands for.[55]

George II, Emperor of Atlantium expanded:

> Liberland is a financial scam dressed up in the language of 'freedom' that is used by libertarians and other conservatives to deliver the exact opposite: the entrenchment of power and privilege and the denial of opportunity.[56]

Intermicronational activity may have sought to draw critical attention to Jedlička's plans, but it remains true that some bad actors will use micronations for dishonest purposes. After all, how many people escaping Syria or Libya would have seen that open letter – published by Ladonia's online newspaper – and discovered that Liberland was not a real state? In mimicking recognised nations, micronations create opportunities for criminal exploitation. In this activity, success may be measured in the scale of fraud.

* * * * *

Micronations are frequently dismissed as trivial or mere oddities. However, as we have demonstrated, in dressing in the garb of statehood and purporting to claim sovereignty these non-state entities provoke important questions. Whatever their character or form, micronations catalyse enquiries over the nature of statehood, international legal personality and legitimate authority. Their existence and persistence forces renewed consideration as to why some political communities are accepted as states, and others are not.

Even if micronations are defined by their relationship to states, not all micronations are genuinely interested in statehood. In this book we have

[54] Ibid.

[55] Chris Roth, 'Liberland's Empty Promises to Syrian Refugees Scorned by Other Micronations', *The Ladonia Herald* (21 October 2015) www.ladoniaherald.com/2015/liberlands-empty-promises-to-syrian-refugees-scorned-by-other-micronations/.

[56] Ibid.

explored the way in which micronations have succeeded as a vehicle for realising many other motivations. Micronations have helped to build and bind communities together, drawn public attention to issues that people are passionate about, shone a light on the absurdities of statehood itself and sometimes been used to turn a profit.

Exploring the phenomenon of micronationalism also sheds light on the manner in which the politics of recognition plays out. Micronations can identify themselves as competing sites of authority, capable of exercising, or legitimately entitled to exercise, jurisdiction over place and people. On this account, disputes between recognised and unrecognised authorities are part of a larger story that concerns 'encounters between rival jurisdictions'.[57] States do not accept this framing. Under international and domestic law, micronations are not sovereign. Micronations resist this. As we have traced in this book, micronations continue to assert their sovereignty in myriad ways, even if there is no prospect this will lead to their recognition as states. After all, as the Principality of Hutt River's motto recorded, 'While I Breathe, I Hope'.[58]

57 Sundhya Pahuja, 'Laws of Encounter: A Jurisdictional Account of International Law' (2013) 1 *London Review of International Law* 63, 65.

58 Mark McGinness, '"Prince" Leonard of Hutt River Province', *Sydney Morning Herald* (27 February 2019) www.smh.com.au/national/prince-leonard-of-hutt-river-province-20190227-p510iq.html.

Appendix

List of Micronations Discussed

The following table sets out the micronations that we have explored or examined in this book. As we have noted, the nature of micronationalism and the ease with which they can be founded (and abandoned) means that our list and our study are necessarily incomplete. We have nonetheless endeavoured to note some of the more prominent micronations. In doing so, our list focuses on those that claim physical territory rather than virtual entities.

Name	Affected State	Years Active	Description
Abalonia	United States	1966–1966	A libertarian-inspired micronation that would have been built on a shallow ridge 110 miles west of San Diego, California. US authorities prevented its creation.
Aeterna Lucina	Australia	1978–1996	An Australian micronation founded by a self-proclaimed baron, who claimed properties he owned in New South Wales as its territory. Charged with fraud, the case was eventually discontinued.
Aigues-Mortes	France	2011	A micronation built around the small medieval town of the same name. It seeks to promote tourism.
Akhzivland	Israel	1971–	Founded by Iranian-born Israeli ex-soldier Eli Avivi in response to the Israeli government demolishing his illegally inhabited house.
Angyalistan	Great Pacific Garbage Patch	1999–	A micronation that claims garbage patches in the open oceans to draw attention to environmental harm. The Angyalistan Empire is the only micronation that seeks its own destruction.
Aramoana	New Zealand	1980–1981	A small New Zealand community that declared itself independent to protest the building of an aluminium smelter on nearby land.
Asgardia	Space	2016–	Founded by Russian scientist and businessman Igor Ashurbeyli, Asgardia aims to build habitable structures in space and become a recognised state.
Atlantis, Isle of Gold	United States	1966	A micronation that was to be built on several reefs off the coast of Florida. It had competition from the Grand Capri Republic, as well as the United States.

(*cont.*)

Name	Affected State	Years Active	Description
Atlantium	Australia	1981–	A long running micronation based in Australia, the Empire of Atlantium describes itself as a 'secular, pluralistic, liberal, social democratic republican monarchy'. Emperor George II is particularly active in the micronational community and as a spokesperson for micronationalism in mainstream media.
Austenasia	United Kingdom	2008–	A father and son micronation based out of their home in London.
Avram	Australia	1980s	A non-territorial micronation founded by an eccentric self-proclaimed duke, who was later elected to the Tasmanian state parliament.
Bible Based Christians of the Call	Australia	2014–	Founded in response to court orders compelling the property owner to destroy structures built on his land that were not approved by the local council.
British West Florida	United States	2005–	A micronation that aims to revive the former British colony of the same name.
Bumbunga	Australia	1976–1999	Monarchist Alec Brackstone declared his small South Australian property an independent province loyal to the British Crown in protest at the growth of republicanism in Australia.
Callaway	United States	1861–	A pro-rebel Missouri county whose independence was purportedly recognised by the Union army.

Capri Republic	United States	1966	A competing micronation that was to be built on the same set of reefs off the coast of Florida as Atlantis, Isle of Gold.
Celestia	Space	1949–	A micronation that claims the entirety of the universe excepting Earth. Founded on 1 January 1949 by James Mangan to stop other countries from claiming outer space.
Conch Republic	United States	1982–	Founded by the mayor of Key West, Florida, Dennis Wardlow, it seceded from the United States in protest at a checkpoint established by the US Border Patrol.
Dubeldeka	Australia	2001–	Established following a dispute over council construction of a sewerage system that damaged the founders' business.
Elgaland-Vargaland	N/A	1992–	A conceptual art project by two Swedish artists, Carl Michael von Hausswolff and Leif Elggren. Elgaland-Vargaland claims the borders of all nations as its territory.
Elleore	Denmark	1944–	A micronation that parodies the governance and traditions of Denmark. It was founded by a group of schoolteachers as a summer camp on the island of Elleore, Denmark. The micronation is now populated for only one week each year.
EnenKio	United States	1994–	A micronation established to further financial crimes. The Kingdom of EnenKio purports to claim Wake Atoll, a US territory north of the Marshall Islands.

(*cont.*)

Name	Affected State	Years Active	Description
Filettino	Italy	2011–	Created by the mayor of Filettino in protest at the Italian government's austerity measure that reorganised the local government of towns with fewer than 1,000 residents.
Finismund	Antarctica	2008–2009	A micronation that claimed a portion of Antarctica and was active in the Antarctic micronational community.
Flandrensis	Antarctica	2008–	A prominent Antarctic micronation that seeks to draw attention to environmental concerns.
Floridas	Spain/United States	1817	The Republic of the Floridas was established and run by General Gregor McGregor following his capture of Amelia Island in Spanish Florida in 1817. Conquered by United States troops in December 1817.
Forvik	United Kingdom	2008–	An islet in Shetland, Scotland, declared a Crown dependency by Stuart Hill as part of a secessionist agenda.
Freedomland	Spratly Islands, disputed	1956–1974	Micronation established by Filipino fisherman Tomás Cloma claiming the Spratly Islands in the South China Sea. At one stage, the Philippines government sought to rely on Cloma's claim to ground its own claim to the territory.
Freedonia	United States	1997–2004	Established in a college dorm room, the Principality of Freedonia was based on libertarian principles.
Frestonia	United Kingdom	1977–1980s	Residents of Freston Road in West London purported to secede from the United Kingdom in protest against a plan to evict them.

Gay and Lesbian Kingdom of the Coral Sea Islands	Australia	2004–2017	Established as a symbolic political protest by a group of gay rights activists, the Gay and Lesbian Kingdom of the Coral Sea Islands was a micronation based on an island in the Coral Sea near the Australian state of Queensland. The Kingdom was dissolved after Australia legalised same-sex marriage.
Glacier Republic	Chile	2014–	Founded by Greenpeace activists in Chile for the purpose of drawing attention to Chile's lack of environmental protection for glaciers.
Global Country of World Peace	United States	2000–	'A country without borders for peace loving people everywhere' created by Maharishi Mahesh Yogi, that sought to buy territory and become a real state.
Hajdučka Republika	Bosnia and Herzegovina	2002	A micronation based in Blidinje Nature Park that emerged because of problems with the local electricity supply.
Hay-on-Wye	United Kingdom	1977–2005	Founded in 1977 by Richard Booth in an attempt to revitalise his decaying market town in Wales.
Humanity	Spratly Islands, disputed	1878–1963	A micronation that occupied the Spratly Islands and merged into the Republic of Morac-Songhrati-Meads in 1963.
Hutt River	Australia	1970–2020	A large farm in the Australian state of Western Australia that unilaterally seceded from the Commonwealth and declared itself to be a sovereign nation in protest at the introduction of wheat quotas. In 2020, after fifty years of existence, the micronation

(*cont.*)

Name	Affected State	Years Active	Description
			announced it would be dissolved and its land sold to pay back taxes to the Australian Tax Office.
Indian Stream	United States	1832–1836	A dispute over the Canada–United States border meant that this small community in New England was taxed by both authorities. Unhappy, they declared the formation of an independent republic.
Inobhutan	Japan	1980s	A village that declared itself to be a micronation in response to increasing out-migration of young adults and to increase tourism revenue.
Jamtland	Sweden	1963–	The region of Jamtland was self-governing from the tenth to the twelfth century. The micronation was founded to preserve and promote Jamtlandic culture, language and way of life.
Kugelmugel	Austria	1984–2015	A ball-shaped house, located in the Vienna Prater, and formed after a dispute with authorities over building permits.
Ladonia	Sweden	1980–	A micronation created by Swedish artist Lars Vilks as the home to sculptures created by him in the Kullaberg nature reserve in north-west Skåne.
Lagoan Isles	United Kingdom	2005	Founded by a schoolteacher who claims that three tiny islands in a Portsmouth pond are not owned by the local council, and so has declared them an independent state.

Lake Michigan	United States	1886–1921	The Deestrict of Lake Michigan was built on around 186 acres of reclaimed land a mere 180 metres from the Chicago shoreline. American George Streeter claimed he owned the land and sold land titles to many people, thereby complicating US efforts to evict him.
L'Anse-Saint-Jean	Canada	1997	A micronation aimed at promoting tourism to the region.
Liberland	Croatia (though not claimed by Croatia)	2015–	A micronation created by Czech politician Vít Jedlička, which claims an uninhabited parcel of disputed land on the western bank of the Danube River, between Croatia and Serbia.
Little Scotland	Australia	1970s	A micronation created by a husband and wife following a dispute with the local council. The Principality dissolved when the couple were killed in a car accident while seeking investors in Europe.
Llanrwst	United Kingdom	1947–	The Free Borough of Llanrwst was a special privilege granted to the Welsh town of Llanrwst by Llywelyn ap Gruffudd, the last sovereign Prince of Wales. Now a small town and community on the River Conwy, it has its own coat of arms, flag and motto: 'Cymru, Lloegr a Llanrwst' (Wales, England and Llanrwst).
Lovely	United Kingdom	2004–	A nation created by comedian Danny Wallace as part of his BBC series, *How to Start Your Own Country*.

(cont.)

Name	Affected State	Years Active	Description
Madawaska	Canada	1827–1842	Like the Republic of Indian Stream, this micronation relied on the uncertain border between the United States and Canada in the 1830s.
Marie State	Antarctica	2000s	Another Antarctica-based micronation active in that community.
Marlborough	Australia	1993	A short-lived micronation in Australia whose creator declared his farm an independent country to avoid eviction after bankruptcy. Despite rallying a group of supporters to his cause, he was evicted less than a week later by police.
Melchizedek	Colombia; Cook Islands; France; Marshall Islands; Antarctica	1986–	A micronation known principally for facilitating large-scale banking fraud in many parts of the world.
Minerva	Tonga	1973–1982	An attempt to build an artificial island and create a new libertarian country. The new land was located on Minerva Reef, a coral atoll in the South Pacific. The island was seized and annexed by Tonga shortly afterward.
Molossia	United States	1999–	A micronation founded by Kevin Baugh, occupying his semi-rural residential acreage in Nevada. It is styled as a dictatorial banana republic.

Morac-Songhrati-Meads	Spratly Islands, disputed	1959–1985	A micronation that claims to occupy the Spratly Islands. The territory is under de facto military control by China, Malaysia, the Philippines, Taiwan and Vietnam.
M'Simbati	Tanganyika (formerly)	1959–1980	An eccentric Englishman attempted to declare independent 1.6km^2 of territory he inhabited on the coast of Tanganyika which he had purchased in 1924.
Naminara	South Korea	2006–	A tourism company operating on a privately owned island in South Korea that has declared its independence.
Neue Slowenische Kunst	N/A	1991–	The NSK is a political art collective that claims to be a stateless state. Its members' work is performed under the guise of an embassy or territory of NSK.
New Atlantis	Off the coast of Jamaica	1964–1966	A floating barge created by Leicester Hemingway and claimed as a sovereign republic. It was destroyed by storms shortly after establishment.
New Oceania	Australia	2003	A micronation established in response to a council dispute.
New Utopia	Caribbean Sea (unclaimed)	1990s–	A micronation based on libertarian principles that would have been built on platforms in the Caribbean Sea. Its founder, American entrepreneur Lazarus Long, ran into trouble with the US Securities and Exchange Commission.
Nikoniko Republic	Japan	1980s	One of several villages that declared themselves a micronation as part of the micronational boom in Japan in the 1980s.

(cont.)

Name	Affected State	Years Active	Description
North Dumpling	United States	1986–	An island in Fishers Island Sound, New York, declared independent after its owner Dean Kamen was denied permission to build a wind turbine on the island.
North Sudan	Bir Tawil (formally claimed neither by Egypt nor Sudan)	2014–	A micronation formed in an uninhabited and unclaimed area along the Egyptian and Sudanese border that has been claimed by an American, purportedly to fulfil a promise to make his daughter a princess.
Nutopia	N/A	1973	A conceptual nation founded by John Lennon and Yoko Ono to draw attention to Lennon's immigration troubles.
Obsidia	United States	2015–	The world's only feminist micronation, the Ambulatory Free States of Obsidia comprises a two-pound chunk of obsidian rock that is transported in the official state briefcase.
Ocussi-Ambeno	East Timor	1968–	A micronation designed to parody statehood. Its founder has relied on the good faith of others to sell fake stamps and exchange letters.
Outer Baldonia	Canada	1950s–1973	A micronation on Outer Bald Tusket Island, Nova Scotia, used for seasonal fishing. Its constitution and national symbols revolved around fishing. Women were banned from the island. It briefly attracted attention from the Soviet Union.

Papaala and Me'ekamui	Papua New Guinea, Solomon Islands	2004–	A micronation designed to facilitate financial fraud that relies on the state's incapacity to exercise political authority throughout its territory.
Parva Domus	Uruguay	1878–	Located in Montevideo, Uruguay, this micronation has operated since 1878 as a social and recreational association that mimics the functioning of a real country. It is the oldest micronation still functioning.
Ponderosa	Australia	1990s–2000s	A micronation formed in protest at public servants bulldozing an infected fruit crop. The nation was ringed by a moat and guarded by a border patrol.
Pontinha	Portugal	2007–	A micronation on an islet physically joined to Madeira Island, Portugal. The owner of the property claims the islet has been independent since 1903.
Poyais	Honduras	1822–1837	Invented by Scottish adventurer and South American independence hero Gregor MacGregor in the early nineteenth century. MacGregor claimed that the land was granted to him by a king of the Mosquito people in present-day Honduras. Weaving one of history's most elaborate hoaxes, he convinced hundreds of people in the UK to buy land and settle in Poyais.
Rainbow Creek	Australia	1979–1980s	Founded by a farmer who purported to secede from the Australian state of Victoria over damage to farmlands caused by flooding, which he claimed was exacerbated by the incompetence of the state government water management agency.

(*cont.*)

Name	Affected State	Years Active	Description
Rathnelly	Canada	1967–	A Toronto neighbourhood declared itself an independent republic during the celebration of Canada's centennial on 1 July 1967 in response to the proposed construction of an expressway.
Redonda	Antigua and Barbuda (formerly unclaimed)	1865–	A small uninhabited island in the Caribbean Sea, now legally part of Antigua and Barbuda. In 1865, a citizen of Montserrat was supposedly permitted by Queen Victoria to claim the title of King of Redonda so long as he did not incite revolt against colonial authority.
Refreshment, Islands of	Tristan da Cunha (formerly unclaimed)	1811–1816	A micronation created by the first permanent inhabitants of Tristan da Cunha, including Jonathan Lambert, who established himself as monarch. Tristan da Cunha was officially annexed by the United Kingdom on 14 August 1816.
Romanov Empire	Attempted to buy land in: Montenegro, Macedonia, Albania, Gambia, and Antigua and Barbuda	2011–	The Imperial Throne was founded by Russian businessman Anton Bakov as a successor to the Russian Empire. It has sought to buy land and develop a new state.
Rose Island	Italy	1968–1969	An attempt to create a sovereign state on an offshore platform in international waters near the Italian city of Rimini. It was completed, but shortly afterward seized by the Italian government and destroyed with explosives.

Ruritania	Eastern Europe (though its embassy is in the United States)	1967	A long-running micronation claiming territory somewhere between Dresden and Prague that operates out of its American embassy in the state of Georgia. Rare among micronations, it is led by a woman, Queen Anastasia.
Sabotage	Australia	2003–	The State of Sabotage began as an art project aimed at critiquing statehood. Its founder subsequently bought land near Tenterfield on the New South Wales/Queensland border in Australia because it was here that in 1889 Henry Parkes delivered the Tenterfield Oration advocating the federation of the Australian colonies.
Sandus	N/A	2009–	A virtual micronation with a complex and detailed history.
Saugeais	France	1947–	A tongue-in-cheek micronation located in eastern France in the département of Doubs.
Sealand	United Kingdom	1967–	A World War II military facility consisting of a man-made structure located off the English coast. Pirate radio operator Roy Bates declared the structure to be an independent state. It continues to be run by Bates' heirs.
Seborga	Italy	1963–	A town in the Italian region of Liguria that claims never to have been a part of the modern Italian state.
Snake Hill	Australia	2003–	Members of an Australian family struggling to pay their mortgage were inspired by the Principality of Hutt River to form their own country.
Talossa	United States	1979/2005–	A micronation founded in the bedroom of Milwaukee, Wisconsin resident Robert Madison.

(cont.)

Name	Affected State	Years Active	Description
Taluga	United States	1966	Similar to Abalonia, Taluga was an attempt to build a micronation on the coast of San Diego, California. It too was abandoned after pressure from US authorities.
Tavolara	Italy	1836	A tiny kingdom claiming independence in the nineteenth and twentieth centuries in Tavolara Island, off the north-east coast of Sardinia. Set up by the Bertoleoni family and allegedly sanctioned by the King of Sardinia, it claimed to be one of the smallest kingdoms in the world.
Trinidad, Principality of	Brazil	1893–1895	American James Harden-Hickey landed and subsequently claimed the uninhabited island of Trindade in the South Atlantic, declaring himself as James I, Prince of Trinidad. His claim prompted attempts by the UK to assert jurisdiction, but a Brazilian claim was eventually successfully pressed.
Užupis	Lithuania	1997–	Užupis is a neighbourhood largely located in the Old Town of Vilnius, Lithuania. In 1997, the residents of the area declared the Republic of Užupis.
Veyshnoria	Belarus	2017	A micronation that emerged as a political riposte to the autocratic Belarusian state conducting joint military exercises with Russia in Western Belarus.

Vikesland	Canada	2005–2018	A former micronation located in Manitoba, Canada founded for the purposes of a TV documentary about micronations.
Wallachia	Czech Republic	1997–	A tongue-in-cheek micronation founded in 1997 as an 'elaborate practical joke' and located in the north-east corner of the Czech Republic. A dispute over the kingdom was heard in Czech courts.
Waveland	United Kingdom	1997	In 1997, Greenpeace occupied the tiny granite outcrop of Rockall for a short time, calling it Waveland, to protest against overfishing. Greenpeace declared the island to be a 'new Global State' and offered citizenship to anyone willing to take their pledge of allegiance.
Wendland	Germany	1980	A German anti-nuclear protest in Wendland. It was reoccupied by thousands of policemen after a few weeks.
Westarctica	Antarctica	2001–	The Grand Duchy of Westarctica is an Antarctic micronation established in 2001 that claims the territory known as Marie Byrd Land.
Whangamōmona	New Zealand	1989–	A tongue-in-cheek micronation created as a tourism booster for the local town. Past elected presidents have included a goat.
Wy	Australia	2004–	Established by Paul Delprat during a dispute with a local council in Sydney over the construction of a driveway to his property.
Zaqistan	United States	2005–	A small tract of land in Box Elder County, a remote part of Utah, on which its owner has built monuments.

INDEX

Printed in the USA
CPSIA information can be obtained
at www.ICGtesting.com
CBHW061835101024
15550CB00029B/36